Political Pioneer of the Press

Women in American Political History

Series Editors: Pam Parry and David R. Davies

Advisory Board: Maurine Beasley, Barbara G. Friedman, Karla K. Gower, Janice Hume, Margot Opdycke Lamme, and Jane Marcellus

Women in American Political History focuses on influential women throughout the history of American politics. From the Colonial period through the founding up to the present, women often have played significant and meaningful roles in politics, both directly and indirectly. Many of their contributions have been overlooked. This interdisciplinary series seeks to advance the dialogue concerning the role of women in politics in America and highlight their various contributions, including women who were elected and appointed to office and those who have wielded political power behind the scenes, such as first ladies, journalists, activists, and public relations practitioners. The series welcomes contributions from all methodologies and disciplines across the social sciences and humanities.

Recent Titles

Press Portrayals of Women Politicians, 1870s–2000s: From "Lunatic" Woodhull to "Polarizing" Palin
Teri Finneman, 2015

Gendered Politics: Campaign Strategies of California Women Candidates, 1912–1970
Linda Van Ingen, 2017

Ruby A. Black: Eleanor Roosevelt, Puerto Rico, and Political Journalism in Washington
Maurine H. Beasley, 2017

Women Politicking Politely: Advancing Feminism in the 1960s and 1970s
Kimberly Wilmot Voss, 2017

Political Pioneer of the Press: Ida B. Wells-Barnett and Her Transnational Crusade for Social Justice
Edited by Lori Amber Roessner and Jodi L. Rightler-McDaniels, 2018

Political Pioneer of the Press

Ida B. Wells-Barnett
and Her Transnational Crusade
for Social Justice

Edited by
Lori Amber Roessner and
Jodi L. Rightler-McDaniels

LEXINGTON BOOKS
Lanham • Boulder • New York • London

Published by Lexington Books
An imprint of The Rowman & Littlefield Publishing Group, Inc.
4501 Forbes Boulevard, Suite 200, Lanham, Maryland 20706
www.rowman.com

Unit A, Whitacre Mews, 26-34 Stannary Street, London SE11 4AB

Copyright © 2018 The Rowman & Littlefield Publishing Group, Inc.

British Library Cataloguing in Publication Information Available

The hardback edition of this book was previously catalogued by the Library of Congress as follows:

Library of Congress Cataloging-in-Publication Data Available

ISBN: 978-1-4985-3032-3 (cloth)
ISBN: 978-1-4985-3033-0 (electronic)
ISBN: 978-1-4985-3034-7 (pbk.)

To the fearless social justice crusaders, who are dedicated to righting wrongs by following the example of Ida B. Wells-Barnett and shining "the light of truth upon them."

Contents

Acknowledgments

When School of Journalism & Electronic Media Director Peter Gross walked into my office in spring 2012, Jimmy Carter, the peanut farmer from Plains who told the world that "the time for racial discrimination was over," peered out from the files scattered on my desk. Gross understood that Carter, the subject of my next book project, was the focus of much of my attention, but nevertheless, he asked for my assistance. Ida B. Wells-Barnett's great-granddaughter Michelle Duster had been in contact with him about an effort to construct a monument to the memory of Wells-Barnett in Bronzeville, the South Side Chicago neighborhood where the social justice crusader had lived and worked after 1895. Gross was not able to offer much by way of financial support, but he promised to do what he could to raise awareness about the project. On that day, without fully realizing it, Gross set the wheels of this project into motion; thank you, sir, for your prompt to reexamine the life and legacy of this extraordinary social justice crusader. As one of the contributors to this volume notes, Ida and idea are only "one letter, one step removed from something significant."[1]

Thank you, Peter, for making that step real to me.

That conversation prompted me to temporarily cast my Carter files aside to make way for my pen and steno pad; in the notebook, I sketched an outline for what would become the Ida Initiative, an interdisciplinary project to foster research about the life, work, and legacy of Ida B. Wells-Barnett and other likeminded social justice crusaders, and I enlisted the help of an interested doctoral student, Jodi L. Rightler-McDaniels, to assist me in constructing a living monument to the life and legacy of Wells-Barnett. In the ensuing years, participants in the Ida Initiative have constructed a permanent website dedicated to raising awareness about the life, work, and legacy of Wells-Barnett, facilitated several scholarly panels on Wells-Barnett, and organized the inaugural Ida B. & Beyond conference, a one-day symposium hosted in spring 2015 at the University of Tennessee, which featured keynote speaker Mia Bay and scholarship about the life, work, and legacy of Wells-Barnett and other likeminded social justice crusaders.

The conference papers presented at the inaugural Ida B. & Beyond conference inspired this edited volume, and without the tireless efforts of participants in the Ida Initiative and the Ida B. & Beyond conference, this volume would not exist. A special thanks is deserved for the early participants in the Ida Initiative—the University of Tennessee's (UT) Ready for the World Program; UT undergraduate students enrolled in the history of mass communications; then-UT graduate students Jodi L. Rightler-McDaniels and Shiela Hawkins; and UT College Scholar R.J. Vogt, who inspired by the initiative wrote his undergraduate senior thesis on the advocacy journalism of Wells-Barnett—and for those who answered Ida's call and participated in the inaugural Ida B. & Beyond conference, especially to keynote speaker Mia Bay and the scholars, such as Jinx Coleman Broussard and Chandra Clark, who contributed conference papers to the symposium. The conference inspired other contributors to answer Ida's call; some, such as historians Patricia A. Schechter and Kris DuRocher, had spent years researching the life of Wells-Barnett for books and monographs; others, such as Kathy Roberts Forde, were casting fresh eyes upon Wells-Barnett to consider her early contributions to the African-American freedom struggle and to place her work against the backdrop of a white supremacist New South. Together, in this volume, we have constructed what *Chicago Defender* columnist Rebecca Stiles Taylor referred to as a "spiritual monument" to the life and legacy of Wells-Barnett.

Monuments, as Taylor acknowledged, are not constructed without the toiling of a community, and I would be remiss not to reserve my greatest words of appreciation for coeditor Jodi L. Rightler-McDaniels and UT graduate assistant Monique Freemon for their amazing contributions to this volume. Next in line, a special thanks must go to series co-editor Pam Parry, who attended an Ida Initiative panel at the American Journalism Historians Association, answered Ida's call, and found us. Parry suggested that Wells-Barnett would be the perfect subject for Lexington Books' "Women in American Political History" series and became a tireless champion of this project. She, alongside series coeditor Dave Davies, offered invaluable feedback on the manuscript; likewise, the staff at Lexington Books, in particular Emily Roderick, have made this journey seamless. Thank you.

Our journeys also were made more manageable by those closest to us—our families. A special thanks to my parents; my son, Joseph Roessner; and our respective partners, David Roessner and Will McDaniels.

Our final words of thanks, however, are reserved for those social justice crusaders, who like Wells-Barnett, encountered great adversity, yet nevertheless, persisted. You have our eternal gratitude.

NOTE

1. Lori Amber Roessner and Jodi L. Rightler-McDaniels, eds., *Political Pioneer of the Press: Ida B. Wells-Barnett and Her Transnational Crusade for Social Justice* (New York: Lexington Books, 2018), xviii.

Ida Timeline

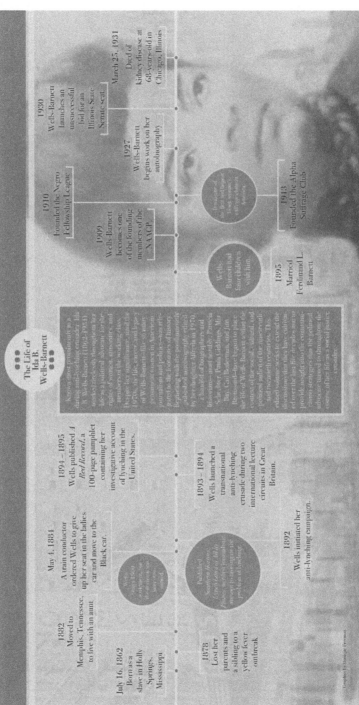

The Life of Ida B. Wells-Barnett

July 16, 1862
Born as a slave in Holly Springs, Mississippi

1878
Lost her parents and a sibling to a yellow fever outbreak

1882
Moved to Memphis, Tennessee, to live with an aunt

May 4, 1884
A train conductor ordered Wells to give up her seat in the ladies car and move to the Black car.

1892
Wells initiated her anti-lynching campaign.

1893 - 1894
Wells launched a transnational anti-lynching crusade during two international lecture circuits in Great Britain.

1894 - 1895
Wells published *A Red Record*, a 100-page pamphlet containing her investigative account of lynching in the United States.

1895
Married Ferdinand L. Barnett

1909
Wells-Barnett becomes one of the founding members of the NAACP

1910
Founded the Negro Fellowship League

1913
Founded the Alpha Suffrage Club

1927
Wells-Barnett begins work on her autobiography

1930
Wells-Barnett launches an unsuccessful bid for an Illinois State Senate seat.

March 25, 1931
Died of kidney disease at 68-years-old in Chicago, Illinois

Illustration by Monique Freemon

Foreword

Ida & Me: A Call to Performance

Chandra D. Snell Clark

Imagine.
It's well past midnight.
After a long, hard day at work
You're sound asleep.
Your spouse at your side.
The children are also asleep.
Suddenly, you hear a sound
That jolts you upright.[1]

***

It begins with Alice Walker.

I was in high school the first time I read Walker's short story, "Advancing Luna—and Ida B. Wells."[2] I have only a vague idea of Ida, but, because of this hazy knowledge, and also due to both Walker and Ida's stark subject matter—rape and its role in the lynching of Black[3] men—the latter both fascinates and repels me. But, safely encased in the comfortable cocoon of ignorance from the bulk of US history's unsavory underbelly, I naively, tentatively, and hopefully set off for the world after graduation, eagerly believing in the myth of an egalitarian, racism-free America. This is the experience of many African-American children who are the products of public schools. Watts writes, "I am the product of institutions such as the [B]lack church, which provided me an avenue to study African American 'greatness.' However, this study was not forwarded or carried forth meaningfully in school. Schools could have fostered the idea that I come from people such as Ida B. Wells."[4]

***

Then—
It's unmistakable.
You smell smoke.
And you shake your spouse.
Just then
You both hear a shout—
'Nigga, we gotcha now!'[5]

***

Sure, I had glimpsed the horrible photos in Black history books—namely, Johnson Publishing Company's *Ebony Pictorial History of Black America*.[6] As a young child, volumes I and II of the three-volume set particularly horrified me with their graphic depictions of Black men hanging lifelessly from trees, while white spectators, including children about my age, happily mugged for the cameras, as though at the county fair. And my ignorance did not extend to not knowing what Billie Holiday meant by "strange fruit."[7] But, as a teen, I was just too frightened to delve too deeply into this particular aspect of my history. So, with Ida neatly filed away into the far crevices of my mind, I was OK for a long time.

But Ida was patient.

Fast forward more than ten years. By the mid-1990s, I was at least attempting to reconcile myself with the knowledge of America's long, bloody history of hypocrisy, spouting democracy, liberty, and justice, on the one hand, while simultaneously systematically subjugating entire peoples on the other. By then, I'd read (no thanks to secondary school, or even college) *The Autobiography of Malcolm X*;[8] even H. Rap Brown's *Die Nigger Die*.[9] I'd thought more deeply about the pictures in family albums of my Baby Boomer father, then a young man, with his fist raised in the Black Power salute, taken some time during the late 1960s or early 1970s. Indeed, ignorance was a luxury I knew I could ill afford, but having earned one degree—in journalism, with failed romantic notions of changing the world—I was cynically working on another, yet I still hadn't completely divested myself of my faith in what America said she stood for, even if her actions frequently belied those claims. As a young adult, I skeptically peeked out from my rapidly disintegrating comfort zone, trying to accurately size up what lay beyond.

Ida watched.

Then one day, I saw it in Barnes & Noble—an elegant, sepia-toned, cellophane-wrapped tome. I recognized the authoritative stance of the elegant, confident matron who peered at me from its cover. Without hesitation, I scooped it up—*Crusade for Justice: The Autobiography of Ida B. Wells*.[10]

Ida smiled.

I bought it, I believe, temporarily forgetting my earlier squeamishness concerning its subject, because by this time, I knew that Ida, like me, had once been a journalist. Perhaps I felt that, having something in common, I could relate to her better—I'm not sure.

But I didn't engage with her right away.

Instead, I placed Ida in my overcrowded bookcase. Applauding myself for at least having bought the book (for surely, this is a sign of my progress), I admired her quiet sophistication, cellophane safely still intact.

So, yet again, Ida waited.

***

Frantically,
As your spouse begins to cry
You jump out of bed,
And grab your shotgun,
As the children run into the room
Crying and holding on to you
Then you hear,
"Come on out, nigga!"[11]

***

Several years later, master's degree proudly in hand, I still felt restless. Although I had sworn off any more formal schooling at this point, I found, incredulously, that my mind still yearned for—even demanded—sustained intellectual stimulation. It looked into dark corners and under rocks. It enquired into alternate (to newspaper journalism) career tracks, but came up wanting. Not knowing what else to do, I depended even more heavily on my old standby, books. So I faithfully patronized my local public library, walking to and fro along the dusty aisles, seeking what my mind might take a fancy to and subsequently devour.

Then, I spotted it.

Linda McMurry's *To Keep the Waters Troubled: The Life of Ida B. Wells* tempted me with its attractive cover and by my own questionable reasoning that, as a biography, it's probably less raw than Ida's own words about her life, which were still languishing, unread, on my bookshelf.[12] But who can really explain human motivations? Anyway, I checked out the biography and barely came up for air, to eat, or bathe until I finished it. Go figure.

Ida smiled.

In McMurry's account, I read about Ida being orphaned as a teen. About her pluck, resourcefulness, and intelligence. About her career as a teacher. About her determination to take care of her younger siblings. About her bravery as a young, outspoken, enterprising Black woman in the post-Reconstruction South. And yes, about her anti-lynching campaign and resultant fame (or infamy). And I learned that I am indeed hardy enough to read about the atrocities done to my people without being consumed by the horror, rage, and grief that they provoke.

Ida laughed.

***

"Careful, honey," your spouse whimpers,
As flames begin to lick the doorway.
Ignoring the thumping of your heart,
You rush outside,
Ready to defend yourself and your family.
And you're grabbed by the arm.

Then
There is much wailing
Shots ring out
And the next thing you know
A noose is around your neck
And you're swinging from a tree.[13]

***

Shortly after finishing the biography, my life took it up a notch. I had a child, which, I was dismayed to discover, was a time-consuming endeavor, not for the faint of heart. I found that my mental prowess was temporarily reduced, any extraneous abilities now being rerouted away from selfish intellectual pursuits toward the care of my son. But, once I got the hang of caring for my newly expanded family, I was eager to resume working professionally full-time. I found a job in public affairs, utilizing my journalistic training, and for a while, I was satisfied.

Ida watched.

But it was only a matter of time before the old restlessness returned, yet this time, it was somehow worse. The sinking feeling I got when I asked myself, "Is this it?" The shame of, once again, being somehow still dissatisfied with my life's many blessings.

Ida perked up.

I questioned. I sought. I read. I meditated.

Then, I questioned some more.

And finally, I dreamed.

The dreams were vivid.

I was lucid, appraising.

And I thought I had found my calling.

***

Had you been a Black American
Particularly a Black man—
In the late nineteenth
And early twentieth centuries
The threat of mob lynching
Especially in the American South
For offences real or imagined
Would have cast a pall over your life.[14]

***

I came to believe that my calling concerned speaking. Talking. Communication. Voice. I pursued this long-unacknowledged gift like a new love. I *was* in love. And I avidly began to look for places, spaces, from which I could share the fullness of my passion with the world. The world responded, beckoning me forward. And I followed.

***

And just who am I?
You might be asking yourself.
Well, I'm going to tell you.
I'm going to tell you about how I exercised my freedom of speech
To help expose and expunge that terrible crime against humanity—
Lynching!
I'll tell you how,
Despite the consequences—
Through voice and pen
I persevered.[15]

***

A year or so later, my interest in public speaking morphed into a fascination with theater. I voraciously soaked up all things dramatic—including a weekend community theater workshop that my friend G. tells me about. Academics, students, aspiring thespians, and other assorted artsy types were all present.

It is here that I was introduced to B., an English professor. In the middle of getting acquainted, with minimal warning, she declared, "You should do something on Ida B. Wells."

Dumfounded, yet intrigued, I replied, "You know, it's funny you should say that, because I've been kind of interested in her for a long time."

"Well, you'd be good," B. authoritatively proclaimed, on the strength of our five-minute relationship. "Decide on your project and finish it—you may even be able to get a grant—people do it all the time."

I wrote down her suggestions, and we exchanged contact information.

Ida's autobiography beckoned yet again, but this time with a definite purpose. So, finally, I unwrapped the cellophane.

Ida smiled.

Physically, it's a beautiful book. On the cover, Ida, at the apex of her fame and influence, stands proudly before an ornate, Gilded Age-looking chair, dignified and sure. Her thick, white/silver hair is elegantly swept in its signature up-do. During the early years of the last century, it is apparent that Ida hasn't lost faith in her ability to affect change, to leave the world better than she found it. I, too, if belatedly, believed.

So I read.

Slowly, bits and pieces of a shadowy idea begin to take shape. I highlighted and underlined passages I found especially illuminating and made notes in the margins. On the inside front cover, I wrote:

Scenes/monologues from early life,
Call to ministry,
Example of speech (or excerpt),
England trip,
p. 247 and all of chapter 30,
How she managed career/family,
Examples of how she dealt with/
Experienced racism/sexism.
Read p. 225—entire chapter on Susan B. Anthony.[16]

***

Could I do something with this? With Ida? Ida—idea—one letter, one step removed from something significant. But what? What will it be? A play? A poem? I don't have an answer, but, hungrily, I read on.

Sadly, though, the book came to an end, as all books must. But I didn't forget Ida/idea. I tucked her away like a precious trinket, taking her out every now and then when I wanted to admire her, and then putting her away again, carefully.

A few months later, G. called me again. At this time, she served on the national board of the Association for Women in Communications. The group was sponsoring a national public speaking contest on First Amendment issues. G. knew I was a burgeoning public speaker. Will I enter the contest on behalf of AWC's local chapter, she asked.

Of course, I said. Then immediately panicked.

Sure, I knew about freedom of the press and all that—I was a former journalist, after all. Vaguely, I recalled my undergraduate mass media law class. Other than that, as far as a specific topic for my speech, I came up empty.

Wait a minute—Ida? Ida/idea? Yes, of course! She certainly used her freedom of speech to get her point across. Finally, a chance to apply my budding Ida knowledge!

Ida nodded and grinned.

Relieved, I fished around for a theme. Certainly, more people needed to know about Ida—I myself didn't learn a thing about her in school—primary, secondary, or post-secondary. And although lynching is an uncomfortable topic that lots of, if not most, Americans would rather not talk about, we can't afford to forget. If we forget, then Ida's labors were in vain.

In her introduction to *On Lynchings*, Collins states: "Ida B. Wells-Barnett was neither fully accepted nor recognized during her lifetime, and until recently, was generally neglected within historiography of African American social and political thought . . . For Wells-Barnett, those who failed to take a stand against lynching, or who remained silent and looked away, were as culpable as those committing the acts."[17]

***

Ida looked over my shoulder.

I was propelled forward, buoyed by an expectant energy.

Seeking out other Ida sources, I hit the mother lode at the local library, finding her pamphlets—*Southern Horrors*,[18] *A Red Record*,[19] and *Mob Rule in New Orleans*.[20] Finally, fortified with a specific purpose, I began to write.

***

On my small teacher's salary
When I was only a child myself,
I taught school,
Helped take care of my family,
And saved money
While managing to better myself
By attending Fisk University.

Now, I taught,
And I was a very good teacher.
But my heart wasn't really into it.
Journalism *was my real love.*
I wrote for small church bulletins,
And some of my writings were published in Black newspapers.
Finally, I was asked to work for the Memphis Free Speech.
But I agreed to do so only on the condition that I could be part owner.
So I invested some of my savings in order to do this.
Then, I could be free to write what I *wanted to write.*
Now, during this time
I still earned my living primarily as a teacher.[21]

***

I stared at the page. My hands cramped. Finding the words was torture; they just didn't flow. I was intimated, overwhelmed, for how do I say all that needs saying? What words would do justice to Ida's "crusade for justice"?[22] Indeed, Miller and Taylor argue:

> One major challenge of representing the historical figure in the autobiographical mode involves a careful selection process as the writer-performer chooses which layers of a complex, multifaceted persona to weave into a narrative. We label this process *auto/ biography*, as this kind of historical presentation represents a negotiation between the autobiographical self of the writer-performer and the biographical record of the histori-cal personage.[23]

Furthermore, I found that although the facts I've weaved together thus far are sound, as far as it goes, they weren't particularly interesting to read. All in all, I'm just not feeling Ida's presence anymore.

Thus blocked, I stopped writing.

As the contest submission deadline approached, I began to, once again, panic. I knew you can't rush creativity, and that the words would have to come to me on their own. Ida would have to come back, but I couldn't force her.

So I got distracted by other, less challenging activities.

Then one day, inexplicably and decidedly unannounced, she returned from hiatus. I trashed what I'd written up to that point and started over. This time, the words flowed.

Once again, I felt Ida watching.

***

Imagine.[24]

***

I couldn't seem to type fast enough. The words flew off the keyboard. And this time around, I knew that the majority of my largely white audience wouldn't be familiar with Ida. At best, they may have a passing knowledge. But this didn't mean that I needed to inform them of every facet of her life. Indeed, given that my time limitation was ten minutes, this would be impossible, anyway. Miller states: "As in any historically based solo production, there is an equally pressing temptation—and thus danger—to reduce a human being to a neatly packaged 'authentic' or 'essential' self."[25] I decide to focus on Ida's life passion and purpose—the abolition of lynching.

***

Extra! Extra! Read all about it!
The Memphis Free Speech *newspaper is burned to the ground!*
Destroyed!
Because I—
Its editor and part owner—
As an Afro American woman
Dared to tell the truth
As is my First Amendment right
But how dare I
The daughter of former slaves
Write in my *newspaper*
What I *know to be true*
That three innocent Black men
Were lynched
Only because they dared to stand up for themselves.
How dare I
In the Southern United States

In 1892
Exercise my First Amendment right!

But I did!
I used the power of the pen
To let the world—
Or, at least Memphis, Tennessee—
Know what had been done to three innocent Black men in that city.
I didn't try to pretty it up
Or make anybody feel good.
Again—
I simply exercised my First Amendment right.[26]

***

This first-person narrative felt natural. When satisfied with my first draft, I gave it to my friend L., an award-winning Toastmaster and community speaker, to critique. I expressed to L. my concern that the entry may be too short.

Slow down, she suggested. This is a very dramatic piece. Be sure to emphasize key points. If you do that, then this speech may very well last ten minutes.

So I relaxed and reveled in the fact that the hardest part was over. But only for a minute.

Then, L. asked what I will wear when giving the speech. I hadn't thought about this at all. She told me I needed to dress as Ida might have—a Victorian-era long-sleeved blouse and long skirt. Of course.

There's a whole lot more to this than I realized.

I let G. know that I'd written the speech. We then scheduled a date to videotape my presentation with the enthusiastic help of the local vocational school's audiovisual/broadcasting program. But first, I needed to practice.

Since I was a Toastmaster, I already had the perfect practice audience. I told my fellow club members that I needed constructive feedback, as this was a contest entry, and they obliged.

My first practice speech came in at seven minutes, two seconds. Acceptable.

I wrote down the comments:

D.: Try dropping voice, or hissing, where appropriate. Now a "blast" the whole time. Be "down" a little bit before you blast.
J.: Add body language, especially w/the word "jolt," and bring other elements of words to life (change character where appropriate).
B.: More body language. Let the fear get into your voice in the introduction.[27]

Grateful for the feedback, I took their comments and incorporated them into the presentation—adding here, tweaking there.

***

Now, I've never considered myself an orator
Like my contemporary and idol,
Frederick Douglass.
But I've always spoken my mind,
Even when it got me into trouble.
I've always believed in
Using my voice.

Yet, I was so afraid
When I addressed my first audience in New York in 1892.
My hands trembled (note to self—show hands trembling)
My heart raced (note to self—touch chest)
As I surveyed the scores of expectant faces before me (note to self—look around)
But I just said what I had to say.
I hadn't practiced beforehand
And I wasn't even aware of the tears streaming down my face (note to self—indicate tears)
Until they were later pointed out to me.
The audience was so moved by my presentation
That it gave me a standing ovation (note to self—clap and look around).
Thus, my public speaking career was launched.[28]

***

For the taping, although I would be filmed from the waist up only, I wore a long, dark, straight skirt, along with a long-sleeved white blouse and cameo brooch. And although my frizzy hairstyle was decidedly non-Victorian, I made do.

After a couple of false starts, the video was done, and G. mailed it to the national AWC.

Satisfied now that I'd managed to bring my creation from "Ida/idea" to fruition, I went on with my life, not really wondering about the ultimate outcome of my efforts.

A little while later, in an e-mail about something else entirely, G. mentioned that "a little birdie" told her that I'd placed second in the national contest. For this, AWC would give me $300 and the opportunity to present the speech at its annual convention in Tulsa, Oklahoma.

While elated, I didn't seriously ponder the possibility of actually attending the conference—money was tight. Still, I relished the fact that I was being recognized at all.

Ida scratched her head.

Soon thereafter, G. and I met for coffee. I explained my situation, extended my regrets to her and the local AWC branch that I wouldn't be able to present at the convention.

Wait, G. said. There may be a way for the local chapter to pay for your ticket, and I've already paid for my room—a double—so you could share with me.

My heart leapt.

Ida smiled.

Since going to Tulsa now appeared to be a certainty, I went into planning mode. First on my agenda was a proper outfit to perform in—one that would do Ida proud. I began to assemble the bits and pieces of my look. Foremost on my list were dark lace-up boots, along with a skirt that would be more evocative of Ida's era—the one I wore for the videotaping was much too contemporary.

Ida looked, too.

Where could I find a long, dark, old-fashioned skirt? Would I need to borrow from a local theater? Would they even let me? It's probably way too late for that.

Doubtful but desperate, I tried my luck at the nearest mall. And, not really planning on going to JC Penney, I found myself there anyway.

There, I found the perfect skirt—brown and ruffled—in my size, for six dollars—marked down from forty dollars! It's the only one like it on the rack, and it even came with a belt!

Now for shoes. There wasn't much time before I departed for Tulsa.

The weekend before the trip, I went to my neighborhood's annual yard sale—really just for fun, but I'd been on the lookout for anything that I could possibly use as part of my ensemble.

And there they were—slightly scuffed, dark brown lace-up ankle boots—again, in my size—for two dollars!

Ida laughed.

The week of my departure, when I shared with my co-workers why I'd be taking a few days off, they applauded my achievement. And the day before my flight, my supervisor brought flowers and food for a good-luck sendoff. Other higher-ups sent congratulatory notes, wishing me well.

As I boarded the plane early the next morning, I considered with awe the serendipitous events that had conspired to bring me to this point. To my amazed delight, support from unexpected sources had lubricated my efforts. All the while, in fact, I seemed to have been pushed along by unseen hands.

Ida's?

Throughout this experience, my affinity for Ida had grown. As Pineau states, I felt I "came to 'know'" my subject deeply, "as an interpersonal touchstone whose rites of passage . . . seemed to coalesce with my own experiences of interpersonal and intellectual maturation."[29] But yet . . .

Why Ida?

Sure, she's an interesting historical figure with whom I share a couple of professional commonalities. But this doesn't fully explain the connection I feel—after all, there are others closer to my own time, and even contemporaries, with whom I have much more in common.

Why me?

Yes, I have a certain dramatic flair when I choose to exercise it. But I know many others who are much more talented in this area, and some who even look more like

Ida. And let's not mention all the other aspects of my life that, when taken together, leave me with little time, and with even less energy, for any extraneous activities apart from work and family.

Thus, I'm not particularly special.

So, why Ida and *me*?

Did she, seemingly contrary to reason and across time and space, somehow decide on me? Was I called to perform Ida? And, if so, how could I have ever asked her to wait, and for so long?

When finally seated on the plane to Tulsa, as I fastened my seatbelt, I knew only this: Buoyed by Ida and hope, I was ready to fly.

POSTSCRIPT: MORE SERENDIPITY?

About two years after the contest, in March 2005, I decided to attend an African film festival after work one evening. After first meeting G. for coffee and chatting for several hours, I was exhausted, and considered ditching the festival to go straight home and to bed. But a little voice told me, faintly, yet clearly, "Yes, you're tired, but go to this thing anyway." And G. (key in so many pivotal moments of my life) told me quite assuredly, "You absolutely need to go." Fine, then.

Not exactly sure of the building where the theater was located, I circled the block several times before finding the right parking garage. Just as I was getting out of my van, a woman and man got out of a car not far from me. Since they were both dressed in African attire, I assumed they also were attending the festival. And since I still wasn't sure exactly where the theater was, I decided to follow them, since they didn't look lost at all.

I struck up a conversation with the couple; the woman and I really hit it off. In fact, we continued our conversation all the way from the parking garage to the theater lobby. As we were getting acquainted, I happened to mention that I'd given a performance of Ida B. Wells; why, I don't know.

"Who said, 'Ida B. Wells'?" asked a young woman I'd seen walking past us out of my peripheral vision. She had backed up and stopped in front of us. "I did," I replied. "I was just saying how I've written and performed a one-woman show based on her."

"Really? I'm from Holly Springs."

"Holly Springs, Mississippi? You're kidding—that's where Ida was born—I've never met anyone who's actually from there!"

"I know. But I was born there. My father's the president of Rust College."

"Rust College—that's where she went to school—I didn't even know it still existed! I just thought it had closed down, like a lot of the Freedmen's Bureau schools."

"No. As a matter of fact, Holly Springs puts on an Ida B. Wells festival every year. You should give your show there. I'll give you the chairwoman's contact information."

And that's how I came to perform at the 2005 Ida B. Wells Birthday Celebration and Museum Grand Opening in Holly Springs, Mississippi, that year, meeting Ida's grandchildren, great-grandchildren, and great-great-grandchildren.

***

I performed "Through Voice and Pen" at the National Communication Association and Florida Communication Association annual meetings in fall of 2005, immediately following the summer during which I'd met Ida's descendants; at Wesleyan College in 2006; and at the American Journalism Historians Association's Southeast Symposium in 2007. Since Ida had remained quiet after that, I had assumed that my Ida sojourn was over—until the fall of 2014, that is, when I happened to come across an announcement for the Association for Education in Journalism and Mass Communication's Southeast Colloquium Pre-Conference: "Ida B. Wells and Beyond," scheduled for the following spring at the University of Tennessee-Knoxville. Without a doubt, I knew I had to submit this essay and attend, and I did. Meeting other "Ida" devotees and scholars was incredibly rewarding and inspiring. In this age of "stand your ground," mass incarceration, Black Lives Matter, and violence perpetrated upon African Americans, her legacy is more relevant than ever, and I am honored to play a small part in keeping it alive.

NOTES

1. Chandra Clark, performer and writer. "Through Voice and Pen: Ida B. Wells-Barnett and the First Amendment." Association for Women in Communications annual meeting. Tulsa, Okla., October 2003.

2. Alice Walker, "Advancing Luna—and Ida B. Wells." In *You Can't Keep a Good Woman Down—Stories* (New York: Harcourt, [1977] 1981).

3. After careful consideration, the editors of this volume decided to look to historic leaders of the Black press as a model—to refer to African Americans in text primarily as Black individuals and groups (in upper case), except when discussing the experiences of the African-American community, especially in the last half of the twentieth century, while referring to European Americans as white individuals and groups (in lower case). See, Tema Okun, *The Emperor Has No Clothes: Teaching About Race and Racism to People Who Don't Want to Know* (New York: IAP, 2010), xi.

4. Lisa Watts, "A Personal Journey toward Authenticity: Recognizing and Reclaiming my Origins." In *Journey to the Ph.D.: How to Navigate the Process as African Americans,* edited by Anna L. Green, LeKita V. Scott, and Brenda Jarmon (Sterling, VA: Stylus Publishing, 2003), 180–95.

5. Clark, "Through Voice and Pen: Ida B. Wells-Barnett and the First Amendment."

6. Lerone Bennett, Jr., *Ebony Pictorial History of Black America* (Chicago: Johnson Publishing, 1971–1973).

7. Billie Holiday, "Strange Fruit," by Abel Meeropol (Lewis Allan), originally recorded 1939, re-released on *The Best of Billie Holiday: 20th Century Masters* (New York: Millennium Collection, 2002), CD.

8. Malcolm X and Alex Haley, *The Autobiography of Malcolm X* (New York: Grove Press, 1966).

9. H. Rap Brown, *Die Nigger Die!* (New York: Dial Press, 1969).

10. Ida B. Wells, *Crusade for Justice: The Autobiography of Ida B. Wells.* Edited by Alfreda M. Duster (Chicago: University of Chicago Press, 1970).

11. Clark, "Through Voice and Pen: Ida B. Wells-Barnett and the First Amendment."

12. Linda O. McMurry, *To Keep the Waters Troubled: The Life of Ida B. Wells* (New York: Oxford University Press, [1998] 2000).

13. Clark, "Through Voice and Pen: Ida B. Wells-Barnett and the First Amendment."

14. Ibid.

15. Ibid.

16. Clark, Chandra, personal communication, 2002.

17. Patricia Hill Collins, "Introduction." In *On Lynchings*, by Ida B. Wells-Barnett (Amherst and New York: Humanity Books, 2002).

18. Ida B. Wells, *Southern Horrors: Lynch Law in All Its Phases* (Salt Lake City, UT: Project Gutenberg Literary Archive Foundation, [1892] 2005).

19. Ida B. Wells, *A Red Record: Tabulated Statistics and Alleged Causes of Lynchings in the United States, 1892–1893–1894* (Chicago: Donohue & Henneberry, 1895).

20. Ida B. Wells, *Mob Rule in New Orleans* (New York: Firework Press, [1900] 2015).

21. Clark, "Through Voice and Pen: Ida B. Wells-Barnett and the First Amendment."

22. Wells, *Crusade for Justice.*

23. Lynn C. Miller, "Gertrude Stein Never Enough," 47–65.

24. Clark, "Through Voice and Pen: Ida B. Wells-Barnett and the First Amendment."

25. Lynn C. Miller, "Gertrude Stein Never Enough." In *Voices Made Flesh: Performing Women's Autobiography*, edited by Lynn C. Miller, Jacqueline Taylor, and M. Heather Carver (Madison: University of Wisconsin Press, [2000] 2003), 47–65.

26. Clark, "Through Voice and Pen: Ida B. Wells-Barnett and the First Amendment."

27. Clark, personal communication, 2003.

28. Clark, "Through Voice and Pen: Ida B. Wells-Barnett and the First Amendment."

29. Elyse Lamm Pineau, "Intimate Partners: A Critical Autobiography of Performing Anais." In *Voices Made Flesh: Performing Women's Autobiography*, edited by Lynn C. Miller, Jacqueline Taylor, and M. Heather Carver (Madison: University of Wisconsin Press, 2003), 35.

BIBLIOGRAPHY

Bennett, Lerone, Jr. *Ebony Pictorial History of Black America.* Chicago: Johnson Publishing, 1971–1973.

Brown, H. Rap. *Die Nigger Die!* New York: Dial Press, 1969.

Collins, Patricia Hill. "Introduction." In *On Lynchings*, by Ida B. Wells-Barnett. Amherst, New York: Humanity Books, 2002.

Holiday, Billie. "Strange Fruit," by Abel Meeropol (Lewis Allan), originally recorded 1939, re-released on *The Best of Billie Holiday: 20th Century* Masters. New York: Millennium Collection, 2002, CD.

MacKay, Carol Hanbery. "Performing Historical Figures: The Metadramatics of Women's Autobiographical Performance." In *Voices Made Flesh: Performing Women's Autobiography*, edited by Lynn C. Miller, Jacqueline Taylor, and M. Heather Carver, 152–64. Madison: University of Wisconsin Press, 2003.

McMurry, Linda O. *To Keep the Waters Troubled: The Life of Ida B. Wells.* New York: Oxford University Press, [1998] 2000.

Miller, Lynn C. "Gertrude Stein Never Enough." In *Voices Made Flesh: Performing Women's Autobiography,* edited by Lynn C. Miller, Jacqueline Taylor, and M. Heather Carver, 47–65. Madison: University of Wisconsin Press, [2000] 2003.

Miller, Lynn C., and Taylor, Jacqueline. "Editors' Introduction." In *Voices Made Flesh: Performing Women's Autobiography,* edited by Lynn C. Miller, Jacqueline Taylor, and M. Heather Carver, 3–14. Madison: University of Wisconsin Press, 2003.

Pineau, Elyse Lamm. "Intimate Partners: A Critical Autobiography of Performing Anais." In *Voices Made Flesh: Performing Women's Autobiography,* edited by Lynn C. Miller, Jacqueline Taylor, and M. Heather Carver, 33–46. Madison: University of Wisconsin Press, 2003.

Walker, Alice. "Advancing Luna—and Ida B. Wells." In *You Can't Keep a Good Woman Down—Stories.* New York: Harcourt, [1977] 1981.

Watts, Lisa. "A Personal Journey Toward Authenticity: Recognizing and Reclaiming my Origins." In *Journey to the Ph.D.: How to Navigate the Process as African Americans,* edited by Anna L. Green, LeKita V. Scott, and Brenda Jarmon, 180–95. Sterling, Virginia: Stylus Publishing, 2003.

Wells, Ida B. *Southern Horrors: Lynch Law in all its Phases.* Salt Lake City, UT: Project Gutenberg Literary Archive Foundation, [1892] 2005.

———. *A Red Record: Tabulated Statistics and Alleged Causes of Lynchings in the United States, 1892–1893–1894.* Chicago: Donohue & Henneberry, 1895.

———. *Mob Rule in New Orleans* (1900). New York: Firework Press, 2015.

———. *Crusade for Justice: The Autobiography of Ida B. Wells,* edited by Alfreda M. Duster. Chicago: University of Chicago Press, 1970.

X, Malcolm, and Haley, Alex. *The Autobiography of Malcolm X.* New York: Grove Press, 1966.

Introduction

Lori Amber Roessner and Jodi L. Rightler-McDaniels

On March 8, 1913, an above-the-fold, front-page article in the *Chicago Defender* informed readers that "the Modern Joan [of] Arc," Mrs. Ida B. Wells-Barnett (1862–1931), had marched in the inaugural Woman Suffrage Parade in Washington despite the protests and the "scorn of her Southern sisters."[1] Robert S. Abbott's *Chicago Defender* celebrated Wells-Barnett as both the greatest "race . . . leader among the feminine sex" and an individual of the "highest type of womanhood." "She is always to be found along the firing line in any battle where the rights of the race are at stake," the *Defender's* correspondent concluded. On this day, Wells-Barnett was hailed as a conquering heroine.

That was far from the case more than fifty years earlier, on July 16, 1862, when Ida Bell was born to Elizabeth "Lizzie" and James "Jim" Wells of Holly Springs, Mississippi. Still six months prior to Abraham Lincoln's Emancipation Proclamation, the arrival of a first-born child of the Wells family received little communal fanfare and no notice in the press of a region that was ravaged by the Civil War.[2] Born into slavery, Ida struggled to survive that first year as Confederate and Union forces fought over the strategic supply post en route to Vicksburg, Mississippi. But survive she did, and she would soon come to thrive.

In the immediate aftermath of the Civil War, like so many freed people, Ida's parents retained their jobs as a cook and carpenter for their former masters, but they had higher aspirations for their first-born and her seven siblings. They insisted that all of their children attend classes at nearby Shaw University (now Rust College). Ida obliged and was in the process of completing her education when her parents and youngest brother Stanley died in a yellow fever outbreak in 1878. Determined that her family would not be separated, sixteen-year-old Wells followed the path of so many women who were thrown upon their own resources. She accepted the responsibility of raising her remaining younger siblings, and after passing her teacher's exam, she earned her first job at a one-room, rural schoolhouse six miles outside Holly Springs. Resolute, Ida continued her education at Shaw University until a fiery altercation with then-President W.W. Hooper led to her dismissal from the school.[3] In the early 1880s, she moved with three of her younger[4] siblings to Memphis, Tennessee, to be closer to other family members, and became a teacher for the segregated Shelby County (Tennessee) School System.

Although the value of an education was instilled in all the Wells children from an early age, Ida's expulsion left her with little formal education herself. While she did pass the teacher's exam, she had "no normal training,"[5] nor formal preparation, for teaching. Like many women of the time, Wells struggled in "the winter of [her] discontent"[6] to earn a living *and*[7] to assert herself as an independent young woman. Carolyn Heilbrun described this struggle as the "female moratorium," where "[n]early every woman who has had dreams of a career and a life outside the boundaries prescribed for women reports this same sense of psychological stasis . . . a period in which the young woman feels strongly that she has the vocation but is unable to recognize it or name it or move forward toward developing her career."[8] Despite the boost in socioeconomic status associated with being a public school teacher and the ability to gain access to the Black middle class, Wells often envisioned herself outside of teaching's monotonous, "gentle, confined world."[9]

Although little is known of Wells' brief teaching career, as she seldom described her work as a teacher,[10] the first glimpse of the single recurring theme of her life is revealed during this time: the struggle of "a highly gifted and talented woman. . . . In constant conflict with conventional female roles, which undermine and restrict a woman's desire for work and achievement."[11] Though Wells considered herself fortunate to be one of only twenty or so Black public school teachers, she was not immune from the substantially unequal treatment of segregation. Her work was made more difficult, as it was often compounded with overcrowded classes, unruly students, irregular pay, and inadequate facilities. Wells expressed her disdain several times in her diary, even going so far as to later say she "never cared for teaching."[12]

Casting her passion for teaching aside, it was during her time as a teacher in Shelby County that Wells began to fight for equal treatment for her race under the law. Her first stand against racial inequity came on September 15, 1883, when she refused to relinquish her ticketed seat in the ladies' coach while on board a train owned by the Chesapeake & Ohio Railway Company. Wells later remembered the incident in her memoir:

> I refused, saying that the forward car [closest to the locomotive] was a smoker, and as I was in the ladies' car, I proposed to stay. . . . [The conductor] tried to drag me out of the seat, but the moment he caught hold of my arm I fastened my teeth in the back of his hand. I had braced my feet against the seat in front and was holding to the back, and as he had already been badly bitten he didn't try it again by himself. He went forward and got the baggage-man and another man to help him and of course they succeeded in dragging me out.[13]

Wells had taken a stand against the repeal of the 1875 Civil Rights Act, which had banned discrimination on the basis of race, creed, and color in public accommodations and transportation. After being forcibly removed from the train, she returned to Memphis and hired an attorney to sue the Chesapeake & Ohio Railway. Wells won her suit in the local court system, but the Tennessee State Supreme Court eventually overturned the case. In the aftermath of the episode, the twenty-five-year-old schoolteacher began writing for faith-based newspapers and the Black press about this incident as well as her experiences with Jim-Crow segregation in the local school systems. Wells may have lost her first battle over racial discrimination in the legal system, but the incident served as a signpost of her journey into political activism and sparked a journalistic career that would span more than four decades.

Over the next eight years, Wells would achieve a degree of local and regional fame as a staunch advocate of racial equity, but it was not until the months and years following the 1892 Memphis lynchings of her friends Thomas Moss, Calvin McDowell, and William Stewart that Wells would gain a national reputation as a social justice crusader. In the aftermath of the racism-fueled atrocity, Wells, now the editor of the *Memphis Free Speech and Headlight*, would turn to investigative journalism to expose the barbaric practice of lynching and the cruel terror that reigned over the Black male race. When the presses of the *Free Speech* were burned later that year, Wells persevered in her battle against racism and discrimination. After relocating to New York and then to Chicago, she turned to antecedent public relations techniques in her campaign against lynching. Still relying on investigative journalism and muckraking techniques, Wells penned articles for Thomas Fortune's *New York Age* and published two influential pamphlets—*Southern Horrors* (1892) and *A Red Record* (1895). She also turned to her voice, waging a national and international battle against the atrocity in the form of one domestic and two transnational lecture tours from 1892 until 1894. During this period, Wells continued to write about racial inequities, most notably with Frederick Douglass and her future husband Ferdinand Barnett in the 1893 pamphlet *Reasons Why the Colored American Is Not in the World's Columbian Exposition*, but she also became involved in the woman's club movement and the woman's suffrage movement.

By 1895, when the thirty-three-year-old social justice advocate married Barnett, a prominent Chicago-based lawyer, editor, and activist, Wells-Barnett had reached the height of her national fame, alongside other prominent leaders of her race, such as Booker T. Washington and W.E.B. Du Bois, and despite concern from individuals such as Susan B. Anthony that marriage and motherhood might shift her focus, Wells-Barnett would remain active as a political advocate for social justice.

In 1913, when Abbott's *Defender* praised her as the "Modern Joan of Arc," she maintained an activist presence at the national and local levels as the editor of the *Chicago Conservator* (1895–1914); one of the co-founders of the National Association for the Advancement of Colored People (1909); the creator of the Negro Fellowship League (1910), a local Chicago settlement house which offered employment assistance to the working-class Black community; and an organizer of the first Black woman's suffrage club—the Alpha Suffrage Club (1913). Throughout much of her life and career as an advocate for equity, the political pioneer of the press often encountered more scorn than praise from a society scarred by a centuries-long legacy of slavery, racism, and patriarchy. Despite the derision and mockery that

Wells-Barnett experienced—at times, even from her own race and sex—she committed her voice and her pen to her transnational crusade for social justice. From 1913
until her untimely death of kidney disease at age sixty-eight on March 25, 1931, she
would remain an active political crusader, advocating for suffrage, investigating and
campaigning against lynching, participating in the National Equal Rights League
(1913), serving as an adult probation officer (1913–1916), and even running for
an Illinois State Senate seat (1930). In each of these endeavors, she would use every
communication technique available to her, from interviews and articles in the white
and Black presses at both the local and national levels to public relations tactics such
as pamphlets, protests, and marches. Despite her activist presence, by the time of
her death, Wells-Barnett had largely faded from the national limelight.[14] She would
remain a relatively forgotten figure in American history until the 1970s.

***

Known most prominently as a daring anti-lynching crusader, Ida B. Wells-Barnett
worked tirelessly throughout her life and career as a communication practitioner
as a political advocate for the rights of women, minorities, and members of the
working class. Despite her significance, until the 1970s, the life, career, and legacy
of Wells-Barnett—like so many prominent women in American journalism and
politics—was relegated to the footnotes of history. Beginning with the posthumously published autobiography edited and released by her daughter Alfreda M.
Duster in 1970, a handful of biographers and historians—most notably, Patricia
Schechter, Paula Giddings, Mia Bay, Gail Bederman, and Jinx Coleman Broussard—have begun to place the life of Wells-Barnett within the context of the
social, cultural, and political milieu of the nineteenth and twentieth centuries.
This edited volume seeks to extend the discussions that they have cultivated over
the last four decades and to provide insight into the communication strategies that
the political advocate turned to throughout the course of her life as a social justice
crusader. In particular, scholars such as Schechter, Broussard, and many more will
weigh in on the full range of communication techniques—from lecture circuits
and public relations campaigns to investigative and advocacy journalism—that
Wells-Barnett employed to combat racism and patriarchy and to promote social
equity; her dual career as a journalist and political agitator; her advocacy efforts
on an international, national, and local level; her own failed political ambitions;
her role as a bridge and interloper in key social movements of the nineteenth and
twentieth centuries; her legacy in American culture; and her potential to serve as
a prism through which to educate others on how to address lingering forms of
oppression in the twenty-first century.

As our foreword, the personal essay of Chandra D. Snell Clark, illustrates, the life
of Ida B. Wells-Barnett has had a powerful impact on those who have encountered her
story. After stumbling across accounts of the social justice crusader, many individuals
have been compelled to fight injustice on all fronts; others—like the contributors to
this volume—have been called to amplify the record of the "Modern Joan [of] Arc."

In chapter 1, "Training the Pen: Ida B. Wells' Journalistic Efforts to Combat Emerging Jim Crow Laws in Transportation," Norma Fay Green explores the legal and moral stand taken by twenty-one-year-old Wells that contributed to her transition from a reluctant schoolteacher to a journalistic crusader for social justice. In the chapter, which weaves together legal decisions with accounts from Wells' diaries and the popular press, Green examines "the elements of race, gender, social class, religion, age, education, and ambition" that intersected like railroad lines that crisscrossed Memphis to form Wells' "identity and her ultimate calling."

In chapter 2, "'A Hearing in the Press': Ida B. Wells' Lecture Tour of 1893–1894," Joe Hayden considers Wells' transatlantic lecture tour as a conscious public relations strategy designed "to widen her reach and to amplify her voice." Hayden contends that Wells was compelled to embark on the tour by the lack of fair coverage of lynching in white-owned mainstream newspapers, and he provides insight into an overlooked aspect of the international lecture circuit—an analysis of press criticism, the "hearing in the press" that accompanied the anti-lynching crusade. Although the public speaking tour did not generate favorable publicity in the American press, especially in the South, Wells did succeed in generating public discourse surrounding the topic through her public relations strategies, which involved sending marked-up copies of British newspapers to American publishers, among other tactics. In light of her role as a "press critic and journalistic reformer," Wells should be considered as one of the nation's first muckrakers, Hayden suggests.

In chapter 3, "Communicating an Anti-Lynching Crusade: The Voice, The Writings, and the Power of Ida B. Wells-Barnett's Public Relations Campaign," Jinx Coleman Broussard explores the nascent public relations strategies that Wells-Barnett incorporated during her anti-lynching crusade. She contends that Wells-Barnett is a "neglected public relations pioneer" overlooked by early public relations historians who constructed a "great [white] men's]" history by focusing on the implementation of public relations strategies in corporate environments and neglecting the efforts of leaders of social movements. In the chapter, she offers evidence of Wells' incorporation of public relations strategies in her campaign against lynching, including her use of advocacy journalism, speaking tours, and pamphlets.

In chapter 4, "'The Modern Joan [of] Arc'": Press Coverage of Ida B. Wells-Barnett's Campaign for Women's Suffrage," Roessner considers the early involvement of Wells-Barnett in the women's suffrage movement in the late nineteenth century, her establishment and participation in the Alpha Suffrage Club in the second decade of the twentieth century, and her subsequent activity in politics in the 1920s, the last full decade of her life, focusing particular attention on her engagement in the Alpha Suffrage Club and the press attention that the publicity-savvy social justice crusader garnered on behalf of the club. The chapter involved the close examination of primary source documents housed at the University of Chicago and 140 articles published from 1894 to 1931 in prominent nationally circulating newspapers, including the *Chicago Defender*, the *Chicago Tribune*, and the *New York Times*, through a combination of narrative and discourse analysis. Through her examination, Roessner found that Wells-Barnett stressed in newspaper accounts the Alpha

Suffrage Club's function as a site of united womanhood, empowering the gender by educating women about their potential as political actors, and as a site of resistance, acknowledging the organization's role in demanding recognition for Black women and ensuring the welfare of their local community.

In chapter 5, "The Life of a Political Agitator: Ida B. Wells-Barnett's Transition from a National Activist to a Local Reform Expert," Kris DuRocher explores a largely overlooked portion of Wells-Barnett's life, her career as a social justice crusader after the formation of the NAACP in 1909. Past scholars have offered a declension narrative when considering the last two decades of Wells-Barnett's life, but DuRocher provides an alternative account, contending that Wells-Barnett turned to local reform efforts—using many of the same successful communication strategies that she had earlier in her career—when she was pushed out of the national arena by contemporaries that increasingly preferred less controversial activists with a college education. As a Black female political activist in Chicago, Wells-Barnett encountered limited success, establishing the Negro Fellowship League in 1910 to support the efforts of Black men to avert poverty, organizing the Alpha Suffrage Club in 1913 to advocate for the right of Black women to vote, and forming the Women's Forum in 1926 and the Third Ward Women's Political Club in 1927 to encourage Black women to fight "social injustices beyond racial violence" and to run for higher office, but these victories were not heralded by her peers—individuals such as W.E.B. Du Bois and Addie Waites Hunton—who actively omitted the political accomplishments of the "Princess of the Press," including accounts of her anti-lynching efforts, from the narrative of Black history. With this in mind, Wells-Barnett would begin writing her memoirs in 1927, and she would seek higher office, running for Illinois State Senate in 1930. Although she did not see the fruits of either of these final efforts before her death in 1931, Wells-Barnett's works would inspire future generations of political activists and social crusaders, after her story was retrieved from the footnotes of history by her daughter Alfreda, who published her autobiography in 1970, and the first generation of women's historians who sought to end the cultural amnesia surrounding her life.

In chapter 6, "Constructing Monuments to the Memory of Ida B. Wells-Barnett: Institutionalization of Reputation, Memory Distortion, and Cultural Amnesia," Roessner considers the intangible, abstract monuments that have been built by individuals and communities of journalists, scholars, documentarians, and grassroots organizations over the last eight decades alongside the tangible tributes and memorials housed in disparate spaces across the nation. As we will see, these monuments to the memory of Ida B. Wells-Barnett were constructed in distinct phases to chronicle, commemorate, or otherwise honor the legacy of the social justice crusader—the first version of history primarily was told by journalists of the Black press, such as Rebecca Stiles Taylor, in the decades after Wells-Barnett's death in 1931; after her daughter Afreda Duster's critical intervention as memory protector in 1970, historians, biographers, and documentarians reclaimed Wells-Barnett's story from the footnotes of Black history; and in the most recent years, a relatively monochromatic narrative of the historical legacy and public memory of Wells-Barnett has been reprinted and institutionalized in digital spaces and museums. In the chapter, Roessner contends that the majority of these remembrances have taken place outside of mainstream media outlets, where narratives of Wells-Barnett largely have been omitted and subjected to cultural amnesia by a white Western culture that has struggled to come to terms with its colonializing impulses and its dark history of racial violence and discrimination.

In chapter 7, "Ida B. Wells-Barnett and the Carceral State," Patricia Ann Schechter, a professor of history at Portland State University and the author of *Ida B. Wells-Barnett and American Reform, 1880–1930*, connects Ida B. Wells-Barnett's anti-lynching campaign and her greater crusade for justice with efforts to dismantle the modern American carceral state, one in which the government functions to confine and administer surveillance and punishment on minorities. Schechter's thoughts were prepared for a plenary session at the 97th annual Association for the Study of African American Life and History in September 2012, but her remarks remain salient in a culture that witnessed the rise of President Donald Trump, who as a Republican candidate for the nation's highest office attracted supporters with a divisive message and energized them with his xenophobia, misogyny, and homophobia. Schechter's comments, in particular, focus on lessons that can be drawn from Wells-Barnett's work in the 1910 case of sharecropper Steve Green.

In chapter 8, "Pioneering Advocacy Journalism: What Today's Journalists Can Learn from Ida B. Wells-Barnett's Methodology," R. J. Vogt argues that in an era of information abundance that has become defined by "fake news," Wells-Barnett's brand of advocacy journalism is worth revisiting. Vogt contends that Wells-Barnett succeeded in convincing her audiences with ethical advocacy journalism that integrated raw, factual, and anecdotal evidence to demonstrate a cultural problem, implemented messaging through diverse mediums, and proposed or embodied solutions. By studying her method, Vogt asserts, the modern advocacy journalist might achieve similar success.

"She would blog. She would tweet. She would take to the streets," suggests Chandra D. Snell Clark in chapter 9, "What Would Ida Do? Considering the Relevancy of Ida B. Wells-Barnett's Legacy to Journalism Students at an HBCU," a discourse analysis of student papers that considered the relevancy of Wells—as a journalist and anti-lynching crusader—to the recent violence perpetrated toward African-American men, in particular the cases of Trayvon Martin, Jordan Davis, and Michael Brown. In their essays, Clark's students at Florida A&M University, one of the top-ranked historically Black colleges and universities (HCBUs) in the nation, found Wells-Barnett's "crusade for justice" to be relevant not only to the recent civil rights cases, but also useful for modern-day journalists to consider. One student grappled with the difficulty of considering lingering racial oppression in American culture:

> This is a hard paper to write! Reading the *Red Record, The Memphis Diary* and *On Lynchings* made me sick in the stomach for a while, and I still don't get it—What?
>
> You ask me if there is any relevancy of Sister Ida Wells' "crusade for justice" to the Michael Brown case, and, are there any implications for today's journalist—What?

So we take this little excursion on the time machine and arrive at the conclusion that post-Reconstruction has lingered on into 2014, and with that, comes another calling for another "crusade for justice." Blacks as well as Whites knows [*sic*] all of this all ready [*sic*]—What? (Student Response #1, 2014)

Although the students used a variety of rhetorical strategies, they all came to the overwhelming conclusion that Wells' crusade is more than relevant in today's political climate.

In the afterword, Kathy Roberts Forde places this work against the backdrop of white supremacist New South ideology and suggests that journalism historians need to begin investigating the role of the white Southern press in building, nurturing, and protecting white supremacy and its brutal forms of racial domination from the Civil War through World War II. In the last instance, the editors and contributors to this volume hope that this book answers the call of *Chicago Defender* columnist Rebecca Stiles Taylor who "stress[ed] the importance of intangible, abstract, moral and spiritual monuments that are far more necessary than those of wood, brick, and stone."[15]

NOTES

1. "Marches in Parade Despite Protests," *Chicago Defender*, March 8, 1913, 1.

2. Based upon a Chronicling America search, records of only three area newspapers exist in the summer of 1862—the *Memphis Daily Appeal* (Memphis, Tennessee), the *Macon Beacon* (Macon, Mississippi), and the *American Citizen* (Canton, Mississippi). Various newspapers serving Holly Springs and Marshall County since 1838 (i.e., the *Marshall County Republican*, the *Southern Banner* and the *Holly Springs Gazette*) had ceased publication by the outbreak of the Civil War.

3. The circumstances surrounding Wells' dismissal from Shaw University are somewhat ambiguous, as is the exact year of her expulsion (1880 or 1881). Although there is no record of what actually transpired, Kristina DuRocher, professor of history at Morehead State University, provides some details of the incident in her book, *Ida B. Wells: Social Reformer and Activist* (New York: Routledge, 2016). According to DuRocher, Wells observed the university's president, W. W. Hooper, singling out Annie Talbot, a light-skinned classmate. Wells summized Talbot was receiving Hooper's extra attention as a result of her lighter complexion, and Wells challenged this inequality by confronting the college president. He responded by expelling Wells. In the immediate years after her dismissal, she resented President Hooper. However, according to a June 1886 entry in her personal diary, she admitted that her own "tempestuous, rebellious, hard headed wilfulness" was to blame, and she "no longer cherish[ed] feelings of resentment, nor blame[d] him that my scholastic career was cut short" (cited in DuRocher, 16–17).

4. In 1881, Wells' younger brothers James and George began apprentice work as carpenters, leaving her to care for her three younger siblings, Eugenia, Annie, and Lily.

5. Ida B. Wells, *Crusade for Justice: The Autobiography of Ida B. Wells*, edited by Alfreda M. Duster (Chicago: University of Chicago Press, 1970), 22.

6. The digitized diary can be viewed at the University of Chicago Online Archives of the Ida B. Wells Papers 1884–1976 at https://www.lib.uchicago.edu/ead/pdf/ibwells-0009-008.pdf. See, Wells, Ida B. Papers. [Box 9, Folder 8], Special Collections Research Center, University of Chicago Library; See also, Miriam DeCosta-Willis, ed., *The Memphis Diary of Ida B. Wells* (Boston: Beacon Press, 1995), 19.

7. Emphasis added.

8. As quoted in DeCosta-Willis, *The Memphis Diary of Ida B. Wells*, xi.

9. Ida B. Wells, as quoted in DeCosta-Willis, *The Memphis Diary of Ida B. Wells*, 6.

10. Extensive research was conducted for primary source documents referencing Wells' own education and her early career as an educator; results were minimal. Various library databases and primary source documents at the Univeristy of Chicago and the University of Memphis yielded a total of only six articles.

11. DeCosta-Willis, *The Memphis Diary of Ida B. Wells*, x.

12. Quoted in Wells, *Crusade for Justice*, 31.

13. Wells, *Crusade for Justice*, 18.

14. The only major national newspaper to run an obituary announcing Wells-Barnett's unexpected passing was the *Chicago Defender*. "Ida B. Wells-Barnett Passes Away," *Chicago Defender*, March 28, 1931, 1.

15. Taylor, "A Review of the Lives of Three Magnificent Women," *Chicago Defender*, January 15, 1938, 17.

BIBLIOGRAPHY

Bay, Mia. *To Tell the Truth Freely: The Life of Ida B. Wells*. New York: Hill & Wang, 2009.

Davidson, James West. *"They Say": Ida B. Wells and the Reconstruction of Race*. New York: Oxford University Press, 2007.

DeCosta-Willis, Miriam. *The Memphis Diary of Ida B. Wells*. Boston: Beacon Press, 1995.

DuRocher, Kristina. *Ida B. Wells: Social Reformer and Activist*. New York: Routledge Historical Americans, 2016.

Giddings, Paula. *Ida: A Sword among Lions, Ida B. Wells and the Campaign against Lynching*. New York: Harper Collings, 2008.

McMurry, Linda O. *To Keep the Waters Troubled: The Life of Ida B. Wells*. New York: Oxford University Press, 1998.

Schechter, Patricia A. *Ida B. Wells-Barnett and American Reform, 1880–1930*. Chapel Hill: University of North Carolina Press, 2001.

Wells, Ida B. *Crusade for Justice: The Autobiography of Ida B. Wells*, edited by Alfreda M. Duster. Chicago: University of Chicago Press, 1970.

———. *The Light of Truth: Writings of an Anti-Lynching Crusader*, edited by Mia Bay. New York: Penguin Books, 2014.

———. *The Memphis Diary of Ida B. Wells: An Intimate Portrait of the Activist as a Young Woman*, edited by Miriam Decosta-Willis. Boston: Beacon Press, 1995.

———. *Southern Horrors: Lynch Law in All Its Phases*. CreateSpace Independent Publishing Platform, 1892. http://www.gutenberg.org/files/14975/14975-h/14975-h.htm.

Wells-Barnett, Ida B. and Jacqueline Jones Royster. *Southern Horrors and Other Writings: The Anti-Lynching Campaign of Ida B. Wells, 1892–1900*. Boston: Bedford Books, 1997.

I

IDA B. WELLS & "THE STRANGE CAREER" OF A POLITICAL PIONEER OF THE PRESS: COMMUNICATING A SOCIAL JUSTICE CRUSADE

1

Training the Pen

Ida B. Wells' Journalistic Efforts to Combat Emerging Jim Crow Laws in Transportation

Norma Fay Green

Long before Rosa Parks' stand against Jim Crow on a Montgomery bus in 1955 or even before Mohandas Gandhi's efforts to desegregate mass transit in South Africa in 1893, Ida Bell Wells bought a first-class ticket for a Tennessee train ride in 1883 and took a legal and moral stand against racial discrimination by refusing to switch seats. Wells' defiance and subsequent fame soon contributed to her transition from a reluctant schoolteacher to a forty-year journalistic crusader for civil rights and social justice. This chapter, which weaves together legal decisions with accounts from Wells' diaries and the popular press, will explore how Wells trained her pen to combat racism and discrimination.

Paralleling the various railroad lines that crisscrossed late-nineteenth-century Memphis, elements of race, gender, social class, religion, age, education, and ambition intersected to form Wells' emerging identity and ultimate calling. In the 1880s, African Americans comprised nearly half the thirty-three thousand Memphis residents.[1] They were caught between the recently repealed federal Civil Rights Act legislating equal accommodations and the state's new laws allowing transportation companies to provide separate accommodations for different races.[2] Black middle-class women passengers, in particular, could never be sure what to expect when they boarded trains. While they were able to sit in what was designated as the "ladies' car" of trains early in the decade, railroad policies continued to shift, and though charged a first-class fare, they later were told routinely they were not allowed to sit in that particular coach with white ladies and their gentlemen escorts. Instead, they were told they had to sit in the "smoking car," alongside members of various races and classes, who often exhibited what was considered to be crude behaviors.[3] Thus twenty-one-year-old Ida, as a well-dressed model of bourgeoisie womanhood, traveling from Memphis to outlying Woodstock where she taught,

3

decided to challenge Tennessee's law and argue her constitutional rights to ride in a designated "ladies' car" in a state that became the first in the nation to enact what later became known as Jim Crow laws[4] of de jure racial segregation.

In September 1883, Wells bought a first-class ticket in Memphis and boarded an eastbound Chesapeake, Ohio and Southwestern train. Dressed in commonplace attire of a lady, Wells wore a floor-length corseted dress with a coat, hat, and gloves and carried a parasol and satchel.[5] There was only one distinction—the color of her skin. For that trait, a conductor told her she only qualified for transport in the "smoking car." She did not smoke and deemed the car full of drinkers and smokers engaging in generally uncouth behavior as decidedly second-class and unacceptable. She expected to be recognized as a lady worthy of respect and to receive the accommodations that she had paid for with her hard-earned teacher's salary. The conductor may have thought it would be easy to intimidate and physically remove the five-foot-tall member of the "weaker sex," but Wells refused to be moved. In her autobiography, she recalled her less than genteel defense as the incident quickly turned violent:

> When the train started and the conductor came along to collect tickets, he took my ticket, then handed it back to me and told me that he couldn't take my ticket, there. I thought that if he didn't want the ticket I wouldn't bother about it so went on reading. In a little while when he finished taking tickets, he came back and told me I would have to go in the other car. I refused, saying that the forward car was a smoker, and as I was in the ladies' car I proposed to stay. He tried to drag me out of the seat, but the moment he caught hold of my arm I fastened my teeth in the back of his hand. I had braced my feet against the seat in front and was holding to the back, and as he had already been badly bitten he didn't try it again by himself. He went forward and got the baggage-man and another man to help him and of course they succeeded in dragging me out. They were encouraged to do this by the attitude of the white ladies and gentlemen in the car; some of them even stood on the seats so that they could get a good view and continued applauding the conductor for his brave stand. By this time the train had stopped at the first station. When I saw that they were determined to drag me into the smoker, which was already filled with colored people and those who were smoking, I said I would get off the train rather than go in—which I did. Strangely, I held on to my ticket all this time, and although the sleeves of my linen duster had been torn out and I had been pretty roughly handled, I had not been hurt physically.[6]

TESTING THE LAW

Wells was angry and humiliated and sought legal retribution for her treatment by suing the railroad. Her lawsuit was newsworthy due to changes in laws and shifting judicial interpretations of equity for various races as she later explained:

> It was the first case in which a colored plaintiff in the South had appealed to a state court since the repeal of the [1875] Civil Rights Bill by the United States Supreme Court [in 1883]. The gist of the decision was that Negroes were not wards of the nation but citizens of the individual states, and should therefore appeal to the state courts for justice

instead of to the federal court. The success of my case would have a precedent which others would doubtless have followed. In this, as in so many other matters, the South wanted the Civil Rights Bill repealed but did not want or intend to give justice to the Negro after robbing him of all sources from which to secure it.[7]

Wells undoubtedly heeded the words of Benjamin Imes, the minister of her Memphis African Methodist Episcopal church, Avery Chapel, who in the wake of the repeal told his congregation "to agitate and discuss and in every proper way to contend for these rights and privileges inherent to us as men and citizens, and which have been and are still denied us."[8] Also, perhaps emboldened by previous victories of other Black women rail passengers in Tennessee, Wells continued her pursuit of transportation equity well after filing the initial suit.[9]

In 1884, she had another confrontation on the same rail line about the same issue and filed a second suit charging discrimination as well as assault, claiming the conductor pushed her back from entering the "ladies' car" when she refused to sit in the "smoking car." She returned to the platform on her own and promptly filed a second lawsuit. In May 1884, that second case was heard in the Tennessee Circuit Court, and while the assault charge was dismissed, Wells was awarded two hundred dollars in damages.[10] After more than a year's delay in the first case coming to trial, Wells suspected that the politically prominent Black lawyer she initially hired had been paid off by the railroad.[11] Her subsequent lead lawyer, "Judge [James] Greer, who kept his pledge [to defend her in court]"[12] happened to be white. His family was from Holly Springs, Mississippi, where Wells was born and had formed her strong sense of social justice. Later that year, her initial case stemming from the 1883 incident was finally heard by the same judge who had presided over the second, more recent case, James O. Pierce, an ex-Union soldier from Minnesota. Court transcripts indicate the railroad and its conductors acknowledged that races typically sat in different cars and that prohibiting "mixed car" drinking and smoking was not easily enforced. Based on that testimony, the Memphis circuit court judge ruled in favor of Wells a second time and awarded her five hundred dollars in damages noting that the transit company "had not complied with the 1881 and 1882 Tennessee statutes requiring railroads to provide accommodations for Negroes 'equal in all respects' to those set aside for whites."[13]

News of that award was published in local Memphis and national newspapers, and the Black press widely reprinted news of the ruling while the railroad appealed the verdict. In her autobiography, begun in 1927 and published posthumously in 1970, Wells recalled the alliterative attention she had received decades before in a local white-owned newspaper: "I can see to this day the headlines in the *Memphis Appeal* announcing DARKY DAMSEL GETS DAMAGES." The full headline included the lines: "What It Cost to Put a Colored Teacher in a Smoking Car . . . $500."[14] Buoyed by the legal triumphs and subsequent publicity, Wells became a regional celebrity. Among her friends and colleagues, she was encouraged to share the story of her transportation traumas and refusal to be relegated to a less desirable "separate but unequal" car. While frustrated by legal delays, she was heartened by the reception of the retelling of her story at local venues. She soon was asked to write about her experience—something she had never done publically—but was open to trying. She did not enjoy working in overcrowded, underfunded schools and was chafing under the tedium of teaching, one of the few acceptable occupations for nineteenth-century women and worthy of the strong work ethic instilled by her parents.

ROOTS OF TENACITY

Wells was the oldest of eight children, and she absorbed the religious, educational, and political values of her parents, James "Jim" and Elizabeth "Lizzie" (née Boling) Wells, in the early aspirational days of post-Civil War Reconstruction when a generation of Black children was taught to believe the promise of more opportunities to better themselves as individuals, as professionals, and as citizens. Literacy was revered (her mother accompanied the children to school to learn to read the Bible), and education was seen as a key to upward social mobility. Wells later wrote "my earliest recollections are of reading the newspaper to my father and an admiring group of his friends. He was interested in politics and I heard the words Ku Klux Klan before I knew what they meant."[15] James Wells was one of the trustees of Shaw University (now called Rust College), a grade-school-to-college institution established by the Freedmen's Aid Society of the Methodist Church in 1866. The expectations for his family were clear: "Our job was to go to school and learn all we could," Ida stated.[16]

As a church-going modest young woman, her world of infinite possibilities was tempered by Victorian-era gender boundaries on a woman's sphere of influence outside the home and soon to be further diminished by personal tragedy. Those nineteenth-century "cult of true womanhood" ideals, notions of a demure and prim comportment, undoubtedly were imparted by her Christian missionary teachers and heroines of library books she voraciously read including the novels of Louisa May Alcott, Charlotte Brontë, and Charles Dickens.[17] As one Wells' biographer noted, "Ida had had a special affection for the instructors, the 'consecrated teachers' from the North, as she described them, a number of whom were devout white women who demonstrated great courage in their determination to teach former slaves of the South even when doing so subjected them to slanderous innuendo and physical threats."[18]

When she was sixteen, however, she was forced to abandon her own education to keep her family together after her mother, father, and youngest brother died in a mosquito-borne yellow fever epidemic that swept her hometown. She was visiting her grandmother in Tippah County when she learned of the deaths. The grief-stricken teenager ended up riding in the caboose of a freight train back to Holly Springs to be with her younger siblings as passenger trains had ceased to run there due to fear of the virus. Overnight the self-described light-hearted "butterfly . . . schoolgirl who had never had to care for herself was trying to do what it had taken the combined effort of father and mother to do."[19] The social constraints of idealized Victorian femininity and her youth limited Wells' occupational choices.

With the help of family friends, she became a school-teacher in rural communities nearby her birthplace. Aware that appearances mattered, she pinned up her hair and lengthened her dresses to make herself appear older. She was determined to be taken seriously although she admitted, "As a green girl in my teens, I was no help to the people outside of the schoolroom, and at first, I fear, I was very little aid in it, since I had had no normal training."[20]

In her first teaching job, she had to ride "antiquated and slow-moving"[21] Ginger the mule to a school six miles outside of Holly Springs. Eventually she taught school at Marshall and Tate County Schools in Mississippi as well as in Cleveland County, Arkansas. After corresponding with her aunt, Fanny Butler, widowed by the yellow fever epidemic in Memphis, Ida and her siblings moved to the city, where the then twenty-year-old Wells landed a better teaching position at a Shelby County school in rural Woodstock, Tennessee. She later lived alone in rented rooms at various boardinghouses after her aunt and Ida's youngest sisters relocated to California and her brothers moved around the South as carpenter apprentices. Wells started keeping a diary in Memphis as a reflective outlet in which to record her thoughts and feelings and try out different types of written expression.

DIARY AS LITERARY LABORATORY

Wells practiced what the later editor of her diary described as "a direct, plain and down to earth style, wit, irony and wordplay, concrete details in descriptive passages, fictive devices including plot, denouement, dramatic tension in her expository writing and repetition of formulaic details."[22] Extant passages reveal a self-conscious woman struggling to be respected despite her youth. The editor of her diary observed that journal writing served as a "form of literary apprenticeship in which she consciously experiments with language, rhetorical strategies and narrative instructions as well as concepts and modes of [B]lack newspapers."[23] Wells was quite critical of her own writing as this August 26, 1886, entry indicates:

> Finished and at last mailed to the A.M.E. Church Review on the 24th my article on "Our Young Men" not because I was satisfied with it or thought it worthy publication by reason of the lucid exposition and connected arrangement, but as a trial to get the opinion of others. I never wrote under a greater strain, but kept at it until it was finished, anyhow. I think sometimes I can write a readable article and then again I wonder how I could have been so mistaken in myself. A glance at all my "brilliant?" productions pall on my understanding; they all savor of dreary sameness, however varied the subject, and the style is monotonous. I find a paucity of ideas that makes it a labor to write freely and yet—what is it that keeps urging me to write notwithstanding all?[24]

What kept her writing was the belief she could help others to see the inequities she saw in the world and lead them to do something about them. Her own actions, however, weren't always successful.

LOST SUIT, FOUND VOICE

In 1887, her initial lawsuit stemming from the 1883 incident was heard in the Tennessee Supreme Court. Chief Justice Peter Turney reversed the decision of the lower court, pronouncing the facilities accorded Blacks and whites to be "alike in every respect as to comfort, convenience, and safety." In the eyes of the court, the railroad company "had done all that could rightfully be demanded" in order to provide "accommodations equal in all respects."[25] Additionally, Wells' motivation for the suit was challenged. The court concluded: "We think it is evident that the purpose of the defendant in error was to harass with a view to this suit, and that her persistence was not in good faith to obtain a comfortable seat for the short ride."[26] Wells later wrote in her autobiography: "Before this was done, the railroad's lawyer had tried every means in his power to get me to compromise the case, but I indignantly refused. Had I done so, I would have been a few hundred dollars to the good instead of having to pay out over two hundred dollars in court costs."[27] That said, she would never have compromised her principles despite financial hardships. Her precedent-setting case would be cited in the landmark 1896 *Plessy v. Ferguson* "separate but equal" segregation ruling, which was not overturned until the *Brown v. Board of Education* case of 1954.[28]

Although Wells had lost her lawsuit on appeal, she found her editorial voice. By writing about the lawsuit she realized the power of words, and any further crusading that she performed was going to involve pen and ink and a larger, more adult audience than a single classroom. "I never cared for teaching, but I had always been very conscientious in trying to do my work honestly," she wrote in her autobiography. "There seemed nothing else to do for a living except menial work, and I could not have made a living at that."[29]

In the moment, drawing on her religious upbringing, she used a biblical metaphor in her diary to describe the legal defeat:

> I felt so disappointed because I had hoped such great things from my suit for my people generally. I have firmly believed all along that the law was on our side and would, when we appealed to it, give us justice. I feel shorn of that belief and utterly discouraged, and just now, if it were possible, would gather my race in my arms and fly away with them. O God, is there no redress, no peace, no justice in this land for us? Thou has always fought the battle of the weak and oppressed. Come to my aid at this moment and teach me what to do, for I am sorely, bitterly disappointed. Show us the way, even as Thou led the children of Israel out of bondage into the promised land.[30]

She was saddened by the seeming lack of support for her cause: "None of my people had ever seemed to feel that it was a race matter and that they should help me with the fight. So I trod the winepress alone."[31]

WRITING RELIGION

Well-versed in Christian traditions and in keeping with her upbringing and convictions, Wells' initial forays into journalism involved primarily religious publications. Upon her arrival in urban Memphis, she immersed herself in religious, social, and educational activities of the local Black bourgeoisie. One of her favorite cultural institutions was the Memphis Lyceum, a literary society of teachers like herself, that met at Vance Street Church and published the weekly journal, *The Evening Star*. A short while after she started participating in its weekly meetings, she was elected "editoress" of the publication in 1885. From that venue, under the penname Iola, she wrote letters and essays that were republished and caught the attention of newspaper editors and readers across the country. "I found I like the work," she wrote in her diary. "The lyceum attendance was increased by people who said they came to hear *The Evening Star* read. Among them one Friday evening was Rev. R. N. Countee, pastor of one of the leading Baptist churches, who also published a weekly called *The Living Way*."[32] Countee praised her work and offered her the opportunity to write a weekly column for his publication. She was flattered but insecure. Nevertheless, she was clearly ready for the new challenge of writing for an audience as she admitted:

> All of this, although gratifying, surprised me very much, for I had had no training except what the work on *The Evening Star* had given me, and no literary gifts or graces. But I had observed and thought much about conditions as I had seen them in the country schools and churches. I had an instinctive feeling that the people who had little or no school training should have something coming into their homes weekly which dealt with their problems in a simple, helpful way. So in weekly letters to The Living Way, I wrote in a plain, common-sense way on the things which concerned our people. Knowing that their education was limited, I never used a word of two syllables where one would serve the purpose. I signed these articles "Iola."[33]

Soon she not only had recognition from a following of readers but monetary compensation that came with her writing for one publication, the *American Baptist*:

> One day I had a caller who said he was passing through Memphis and could not resist the opportunity to look up "the brilliant Iola" whose writings he had read in various papers. He was Rev. William J. Simmons, DD., who was traveling for the American Baptist Home Missionary Society . . . he was the head of their work among the colored people, and was also president of the state university of Louisville, Kentucky, organizer and president of the National Baptist Convention, and editor of the Negro Press Association. . . . He wanted me as correspondent of his paper and offered me the lavish sum of one dollar a letter weekly! It was the first time anyone had offered to pay me for the work I had enjoyed doing. I had never dreamed of receiving any pay, for I had been too happy over the thought that the papers were giving me space.[34]

Her journalistic reputation and professional recognition continued to grow over the next three years when she became the first woman to represent the publication at a national press convention. She admitted to being "tickled pink over the attention I received from those veterans of the press."[35] No longer feeling the limitations of Victorian femininity, she reveled in the rarity that her gender represented in her newfound profession. Novel or not as one of forty-five Black women journalists working at the time,[36] she apparently impressed the group enough that in 1889 she was elected secretary to the National Press Association. In January 1885, the *New York Freeman* reprinted "Woman's Mission," an essay of thanks Ida wrote to a white newspaper editor in Memphis who defended the virtue of Black women:

> What is, or should be woman? Not merely a bundle of flesh and bones, nor a fashion plate, a frivolous inanity, a soulless doll, a heartless coquette—but a strong, bright presence, thoroughly imbued with a sense of her mission on earth and a desire to fill it; an earnest, soulful being, laboring to fit herself for life's duties and burdens, and bearing them faithfully when they do come; but a womanly woman for all that, upholding the banner and striving for the goal of pure, bright womanhood through all vicissitudes and temptations. Her influence is boundless. Only the ages of eternity will serve to show the results of woman's influence. . . . The masses of women of our race have not awakened to a true sense of the responsibilities that devolve on them, of the influence they exert; they have not realized the necessity for erecting a standard of earnest, thoughtful, pure, noble womanhood, rather than one of fashion, idleness and uselessness.[37]

Her well-reasoned opinions were valued and her writing, practiced initially in a diary she kept to herself, soon found a new public outlet. People started to pay attention to what she wrote. Thus, in a relatively short period, Ida had journeyed from commuting to teach on a mule to one of the "iron horse" trains that revolutionized travel in the nineteenth century and put her on track to a whole new career. The transportation vehicle became a catalyst, demonstrating a young woman's metamorphosis from a self-described "butterfly girl" to whom admirers came to call "Princess of the Press."

VOCATIONAL VALIDATION

In 1891, I. Garland Penn, secretary of the Freedmen's Aid Society of the Methodist Episcopal Church, chronicled the history of the Black press and Wells' foray in journalism stating: "Miss Wells' first article was a 'write up' of a suit for damages at the request of the editor of the *Living Way*, and to which she contributed for two years. This introduced her to the newspaper fraternity as a writer of superb ability and demands for her services began to come in."[38] Another prominent male journalist, Thomas Fortune of the *New York Age*, met Ida at a press convention and declared, "She has become famous as one of the few of our women who handle a goose quill with diamond point as easily as any man in newspaper work. If Ida were a man she would be a humming independent in politics. She has plenty of nerve and is as sharp as a steel trap."[39] Lucy W. Smith listed more than a dozen publications to which

Wells had contributed and praised her in an 1895 entry in the book titled *The College of Life or Practical Self Educator: A Manual of Self Improvement of the Colored Race*:

> Miss Ida B. Wells, "Iola" has been called the Princess of the Press, and she has well earned the title. No writer, the male fraternity not excepted, has been more extensively quoted none struck harder blows at the wrongs and weaknesses of the race. Her readers are equally divided between the sexes. She reaches the men by dealing with the political aspect of the race question, and the women she meets around the fireside. She is an inspiration to the young writers and her success has lent an impetus to their ambition. When the National Press Association, of which she was elected assistant secretary, met in Louisville, she read a splendid paper on "Women in Journalism, or How I would Edit." By the way it is her ambition to edit a paper. She believes there is no agency so potent as the press in reaching and elevating a people.[40]

Soon Wells' wish came true when she was offered the editorship of a local newspaper, *The Memphis Free Speech and Headlight*. There, she negotiated a one-third partnership with the Rev. Taylor Nightingale, minister of the Beale Street Church, where the newspaper was published and his business manager, J. L. Fleming, who had merged his *Marion* [Arkansas] *Headlight* after he fled political violence in Arkansas.[41] Thus she achieved another first by becoming "the only [B]lack woman of record to be an editor in chief and part owner of a major city newspaper."[42] Wells thrived in her new leadership role and quickly increased readership along train routes:

> My travels were so successful that I felt I had at last found my real vocation. I thoroughly enjoyed my work because the people were so kind and helpful. It was quite a novelty to see a woman agent who was also an editor of the journal for which she canvassed. The *Free Speech* began to be in demand all up and down the Delta spur of the Illinois Central Railroad. So much was this so that the news butcher on one of the trains on which I traveled came and asked me for a copy of it. He said he had never known so many colored people to ask for a newspaper before. I told him we would be glad for him to handle it. Our circulation had increased in less than a year from fifteen hundred to four thousand, and my salary came to within ten dollars of what I had received as teacher.[43]

As we have seen in this chapter, Wells' career as a crusading journalist was launched by her firsthand experiences combatting the emerging conditions of Jim Crow segregation in her daily life traveling the rails to teach. During this period, she had trained her pen through her personal writings as a diarist and as a contributor to the religious and Black presses; now in her new journalistic post, Wells implemented all sorts of editorial changes, big and small, from shortening the publication's name to *The Free Speech* to printing the newspaper on pink paper to make it stand out. But death and devastation that haunted her early life returned with vengeance as her journalistic popularity and power grew. "While I was thus carrying on the work of my newspaper, happy in the thought that our influence was helpful and that I was doing the work I loved and had proved that I could make a living out of it, there came the lynching in Memphis which changed the whole course of my life."[44]

MEMPHIS TRAGEDY SPURS TRANSIT CRISIS

While Wells was out of town on business, three Black entrepreneurs, including a friend who was the father of her godchild, were murdered. She later eloquently wrote about the March 1892 incident:

> Three young colored men in an altercation at their place of business, fired on white men in self-defense. They were imprisoned for three days, then taken out by the mob and horribly shot to death. Thomas Moss, Will Stewart and Calvin McDowell were energetic business men who had a built up a flourishing grocery business. This business had prospered and that of a rival white grocer named Barrett had declined. Barrett led the attack on their grocery which resulted in the wounding of three white men. For this cause were three innocent men barbarously lynched, and their families left without protectors. Memphis is one of the leading cities of Tennessee, a town of seventy-five thousand inhabitants! No effort whatever was made to punish the murderers of these young men. It counted for nothing that the victims of this outrage were three of the best known young men of the population of thirty thousand colored people of Memphis. They were the officers of the company which conducted the grocery. Moss being the President, Stewart the Secretary of the Company and McDowell the Manager. Moss was in the Civil Service of the United States as letter carrier, and all three were men of splendid reputation for honesty, integrity and sobriety. But their murderers, though well known, have never been indicted, were not even troubled with preliminary examination.[45]

Wells' final fiery editorials in *The Free Speech* in the spring of 1892 condemned the white residents for the murder and encouraged the Black community to save its money and move out of Memphis—even out of state. Apparently her readers took that advice to heart and stopped riding the streetcar even though mule-driven streetcars had long been integrated. Soon trolley officials from the City Railway Company visited her newspaper office. The officials said they were worried about the drop in ridership and attributed it to a fear of the newly electrified cars. The company's superintendent and treasurer asked her to write an editorial urging Black people to return to the streetcar. Instead, she wrote about the transit officials' naïve and false assumption that Black community members were afraid of electric trolleys rather than the more palpable fear of continued violence and death. After the murder of her friends, she surmised that there would be no justice for Black community members who stayed. She knew the consequences of her writing as she had lost her teaching job when she criticized the local education system. After the murders and her editorial call for action, she received death threats and started carrying a pistol to protect herself. When she went to a convention in Philadelphia, a mob broke into *The Free Speech* office and burned it to the ground. No extant copies of the publication exist, but her writing could not be extinguished. Thanks to her newfound portable profession with its network of journalistic support as well as her indomitable spirit and potent pen, Wells soon resumed her editorial campaigns to expose injustices and advocate for reforms in her continuing journeys all over the United States and Great Britain.

NOTES

1. Paula J. Giddings, *Ida: A Sword among Lions* (New York: Amistad, 2008), 40.

2. James West Davidson, *"They Say": Ida B. Wells and the Reconstruction of Race* (New York: Oxford University Press, 2007), 66. Davidson quoted the federal law wording from Civil Rights Cases, 109 U.S. 3 (1883): "Citizens of every race and color [were] entitled to the full and equal enjoyment of the accommodations, advantages, facilities, and privileges of inns, public conveyances on land or water, theaters, and other places of public amusement."

3. Cartwright noted railroads operating in Tennessee in the 1880s were often in violation of the law requiring them to provide first-class accommodations for first-class fare payers. He noted that some railroads [like C&O] complied via a three-car system including a white car, one for Black passengers and a third smoking car. But he pointed out "in practice, however, the car set aside for Negroes also was occupied by second class white passengers whose smoking, profane language and drinking went largely unchecked." Also Davidson noted "when [B]lacks took seats in the lady's car, the reception they received depended on the character of the conductor, the mood of white patrons or the resolve of the [B]lack passenger." Davidson, *They Say*, 67.

4. The use of the phrase, Jim Crow, was traced to "Jump Jim Crow," a caricature performed at minstrel shows in the 1830s by Thomas Rice, a white actor in blackface making fun of President Andrew Jackson's policies. It eventually became code for racial segregation, according to C. Vann Woodward and William S. McFeely, *The Strange Career of Jim Crow* (New York: Oxford University Press, 2001), 7.

5. Giddings, *Ida*, 61.

6. Ida B. Wells, *Crusade for Justice: The Autobiography of Ida B. Wells*, ed. Alfreda M. Duster (Chicago: University of Chicago Press, 1970), 18–19.

7. Ibid., 20.

8. Giddings, *Ida*, 64.

9. Ida B. Wells recorded a June 7, 1886, entry about going with three friends on one of the educational excursions for teachers: "Of course, we had the usual trouble about the first-class coach, but we conquered." The digitized diary can be viewed at the University of Chicago Online Archives of the Ida B. Wells Papers 1884–1976 at https://www.lib.uchicago.edu/ead/pdf/ibwells-0009-008.pdf. See, Wells, Ida B. Papers. [Box 9, Folder 8], Special Collections Research Center, University of Chicago Library; see also, Miriam DeCosta-Willis, ed. *The Memphis Diary of Ida B. Wells*, 76. The well-informed Wells was no doubt aware of previous lawsuits against Tennessee railroads for unequal accommodation brought by Black women including Mrs. Richard Robinson, who was denied access on Memphis & Charleston Railroad but subsequently lost her 1879 case; Jane Brown, who was ejected from same rail line and awarded three thousand dollars in federal court in 1880 (cited in *Brown v. Memphis & C. R. Co.*, 5 Federal Reporter 499–503 [1885]); and Ada Buck, who received seven hundred and fifty dollars in damages for discriminatory seating on a Louisville & Nashville Railroad car in 1880 (cited in Linda O. McMurry, *To Keep the Waters Troubled* [Oxford University Press, 1998], 26–27). Also a suit contemporaneous to Wells' involved a Black woman being denied a first-class ride [cited in *Logwood and Wife v. Memphis & C.R. Co.*, 23 Federal Reporter 318-9 (1885); Quoted in Cartwright, *The Triumph of Jim Crow*, 189].

10. McMurry, *To Keep the Waters Troubled*, 27; Quoted in *New York Globe*, May 24, 1884.

11. DeCosta-Willis, *The Memphis Diary of Ida B. Wells*, 56. Giddings, *Ida*, 63. Giddings noted that while bribery was possible given the business practices of railroad owner Collis Huntington, her initial lawyer, a Black legislator and former assistant attorney general who

attended her church, may have been heavily influenced by the shifting political winds, especially when he added co-counsel James Phelan, white owner of the *Memphis Avalanche* newspaper.

12. Wells, *Crusade for Justice*, 19.

13. *Ida Wells v. Chesapeake, Ohio, and Southwestern RR C*, 1884 MS court record (Archives Div., Tennessee State Library); cited in Cartwright, *The Triumph of Jim Crow*, 190.

14. Giddings, *Ida*, 64. Giddings quoted from *Avalanche* November 3, 1884 (no page number given). Duster cited a similar headline "A Darky Damsel Obtains a Verdict for Damages Against the Chesapeake & Ohio Railroad—What It Cost to Put a Colored School Teacher in a Smoking Car—Verdict for $500" from *The Memphis Daily Appeal*, December 25, 1884, 4.

15. Wells, *Crusade for Justice*, 9.

16. Ibid.

17. McMurry, *To Keep the Waters Troubled*, 23.

18. Giddings, *Ida*, 30.

19. Wells, *Crusade for Justice*, 16.

20. Ibid.

21. Mia Bay, *To Tell the Truth Freely* (New York: Hill & Wang, 2009), 46.

22. DeCosta-Willis, *The Memphis Diary of Ida B. Wells*, 11.

23. Ibid.

24. The digitized diary can be viewed at the University of Chicago Online Archives of the Ida B. Wells Papers 1884–1976 at https://www.lib.uchicago.edu/ead/pdf/ibwells-0009-008.pdf. See, Wells, Ida B. Papers. [Box 9, Folder 8], Special Collections Research Center, University of Chicago Library; see also, Miriam DeCosta-Willis, ed. *The Memphis Diary of Ida B. Wells*, 100.

25. *Chesapeake, Ohio and Southwestern RR Co v Wells*. 85 Tennessee Reports 613-5 (1887); cited in Cartwright, *The Triumph of Jim Crow*, 191.

26. *Chesapeake & Ohio & Southwestern Railroad Company v. Wells*. Tennessee Reports: 85 Cases Argued and Determined in the Supreme Court of Tennessee for the Western Division, Jackson, April Term, 1887, 615; cited in Wells, *Crusade for Justice*, xvi.

27. Wells, *Crusade for Justice*, 20.

28. Giddings, *Ida*, 671 footnote cited Railroad Co. v. Wells 85 Tenn. 613, 4 S.W. 5.

29. Wells, *Crusade for Justice*, 31.

30. The digitized diary can be viewed at the University of Chicago Online Archives of the Ida B. Wells Papers 1884–1976 at https://www.lib.uchicago.edu/ead/pdf/ibwells-0009-008.pdf. See, Wells, Ida B. Papers. [Box 9, Folder 8], Special Collections Research Center, University of Chicago Library; see also, Miriam DeCosta-Willis, ed. *The Memphis Diary of Ida B. Wells*, 140–1.

31. Wells, *Crusade for Justice*, 21. Some Wells biographers noted that people in the community were not necessarily convinced that her lawsuits were purely about race segregation more than gender or socio-economic class divisions. Indeed, testimony in her case revealed that Black nurses and maids were allowed to ride in the "ladies" car with no objection while her attorneys argued that, "If a Negro had to be a servant or nurse in order to obtain first-class accommodations, [B]lacks faced the ludicrous prospect of finding that their privileges increased as they sank lower in the social scale. . . . We had as well say that the colored men should not be allowed to buy the best article of groceries, though he pays in full for such and we pretend to sell him only the best. Might as well say we will ask him the same price for the best and then deliver him the inferior grade." *Chesapeake, Ohio and S.W. Railroad v. Ida Wells*, April 1885, "Brief of Greer and Adms." (Archives Div., Tennessee State Library); Quoted in Cartwright, *The Triumph of Jim Crow*, 191. And the circuit court judge noted in his initial verdict Ida's "lady-like appearance and deportment, a school teacher, and one who might be expected to object to traveling in the company of rough or boisterous men." *Ida B. Wells v.*

Chesapeake, Ohio & South Western Railroad Company, Circuit Court of Shelby County, manuscript court record, February 16, 1885, Tennessee State Library and Archives, Nashville, Tennessee, 61–62; Quoted in Giddings, *Ida*, 63.

32. Wells, *Crusade for Justice*, 23–24. Her reason for the adoption of the pen name "Iola" is unclear but in Greek it means "violet."

33. Ibid.

34. Ibid., 31–32.

35. Ibid., 32.

36. Bay, *To Tell the Truth Freely*, 44.

37. The digitized diary can be viewed at the University of Chicago Online Archives of the Ida B. Wells Papers 1884–1976 at https://www.lib.uchicago.edu/ead/pdf/ibwells-0009-008.pdf. See, Wells, Ida B. Papers. [Box 9, Folder 8], Special Collections Research Center, University of Chicago Library; see also, Miriam DeCosta-Willis, ed. *The Memphis Diary of Ida B. Wells*, 180–81.

38. Wells, *Crusade for Justice*, 32; Penn as quoted in *Afro-American Press and Its Editors* (Springfield, Mass.: Wiley & Co., 1891), 407.

39. Wells, *Crusade for Justice*, 33.

40. Ibid. Henry Davenport Northrop, Joseph R. Gay, and I. Garland Penn, *The College of Life; or, Practical Self Educator: A Manual of Self-Improvement of the Colored Race* (Chicago: Chicago Publication and Lithograph Company, 1895), 100.

41. Davidson, *They Say*, 112–13.

42. Wells, *Crusade for Justice*, 35.

43. Ibid., 41.

44. Ibid., 47.

45. Wells, "Southern Horrors: Lynch Law in All Its Phases," an 1892 pamphlet published by the *New York Age*, where Ida sought refuge after her Memphis newspaper was destroyed. Reprinted in Michelle Duster, ed. *Ida in Her Own Words* (Chicago: Benjamin Williams Publishing, 2008).

BIBLIOGRAPHY

Bay, Mia. *To Tell the Truth Freely: The Life of Ida B. Wells*. New York: Hill & Wang, 2009.

Cartwright, Joseph H. *The Triumph of Jim Crow: Tennessee Race Relations in the 1880s*. Nashville, TN: University of Tennessee Press, 1985.

Davidson, James West. *"They Say": Ida B. Wells and the Reconstruction of Race*. New York: Oxford University Press, 2007.

DeCosta-Willis, Miriam, ed. *The Memphis Diary of Ida B. Wells: An Intimate Portrait of the Activist as a Young Woman*. Boston: Beacon Press, 1995.

Duster, Michelle, ed. *Ida in Her Own Words*. Chicago: Benjamin Williams Publishing, 2008.

Giddings, Paula J. *Ida: A Sword among Lions: Ida B. Wells and the Campaign against Lynching*. New York: Amistad, 2008.

McMurry, Linda O. *To Keep the Waters Troubled: The Life of Ida B. Wells* New York: Oxford University Press, 1998.

Wells, Ida B. *Crusade for Justice: The Autobiography of Ida B. Wells*, edited by Alfreda M. Duster. Chicago: University of Chicago Press, 1970.

Woodward, C. Vann and William McFeely. *The Strange Career of Jim Crow*. New York: Oxford University Press, 2001.

2

"A Hearing in the Press"

Ida B. Wells' Lecture Tour of 1893–1894

Joe Hayden

When a Memphis mob threatened Ida B. Wells' life and destroyed her printing press in the spring of 1892, her weekly newspaper, *The Free Speech*, was permanently silenced. She, however, was not. Her campaign against lynching and for the rights of African Americans was just getting started. Over the next couple of years, she would find her voice in publicizing a cause that until then many people hesitated to address publicly. She also discovered a receptive audience, a slender but growing one in the North and a larger and more fervent one in the United Kingdom.

Her transatlantic audience was no accident. She constructed and developed it as part of a conscious strategy to widen her reach and to amplify her voice, a goal she was blocked from achieving in the United States. As she wrote in her autobiography, "[t]he press and pulpit of the country are practically silent with a silence which means encouragement. . . . Only in one city—Boston—had I been given even a meager hearing, and the press was dumb. I refer, of course, to the white press, since it was the medium through which I hoped to reach the white people of the country, who alone could mold public sentiment."[1] What the anti-lynching movement required was publicity, "a modern-era public relations war, not just a moral one."[2] This is why Wells went to Britain—not merely to enlist new international allies and support, but also to force American newspapers and, by extension, the American public back home to pay attention. Just as the press played a vital role in the abolitionist movement,[3] anti-lynching crusaders understood they had an information war to win as well. When Wells returned to the United States in the summer of 1894, she urged Black individuals in the North to create a news bureau that would carefully document lynchings and other assaults all across the country. Ending lynching, she recognized, could not happen without an overhaul of American journalism.

This chapter examines Wells' lecture circuit in Britain in 1893 and 1894 and the publicity it generated. Its focus is on one aspect of her transnational tours that usually goes unremarked or underplayed in the historiography about her career: the explicit press criticism such an undertaking entailed. In trying to win more hearts and minds in the crusade for civil rights, Wells' untiring itinerancy was compelled by a lack of fair coverage of lynching in newspapers. Her speaking tour was one of the few methods available to her to force the white-owned press to take notice. Her speeches represented a rebuke of current journalism practices and assumptions. A committed advocate, she nonetheless used objective methods to shed light on lynching and on the inability of many journalists to cover it honestly. Facts were important to her, and she was quick to correct inaccurate newspaper reports. Historian David Mindich contends that objectivity failed Wells' cause, but it seems fairer to say that most American journalists at the time failed objectivity.[4] In a dispatch from a *New York Times* foreign correspondent identified only as "H. F.," for instance, the writer introduces Wells by saying, "she has a lurid two-column interview in to-day's [London] *Chronicle*, in which sensational charges, unhappily true in the main, are very skillfully mixed with stuff which I feel sure is not true."[5] Wells did not usually indulge in references to herself or her feelings. This was her frustration with so many newspapers of the era: They shrank from the truth about lynching, while she confronted it head-on. Decades before Will Irwin engaged in his muckraking critique of the press, Ida B. Wells subjected it to her own merciless scrutiny, a process she initiated by going abroad.

Many clues for this time in Wells' life appear in her autobiography and other writings, but the most voluminous record attesting to her impact remains the press coverage she inspired—the announcements, articles, and editorials that often excerpted her remarks and those of allies and organizers, even when they disagreed with her mission. Newspapers consulted for this analysis include the *Atlanta Constitution, Boston Globe, Chicago Tribune, Detroit Free Press, Los Angeles Times, Manchester Guardian, Memphis Appeal-Avalanche* (which became the *Commercial Appeal* in July 1894), *New Orleans Times-Picayune, New York Times, New York Tribune, The Scotsman*, and the *Washington Post*. What this publicity most clearly reveals is the importance of her trip and the indispensability of her overture to the British press and public.

Wells was relatively unknown before 1892. The *New York Times* noted her presence at an anti-lynching meeting in New York in April 1892, a month after her friends were murdered but before her notorious editorial appeared. The mention bore little fanfare. Her name was simply included in a list of twenty-one other people who sat on the platform at Cooper Union that day. Even when she published "The Truth about Lynching" in May, the ensuing furor in Memphis occasioned no coverage in the *Times*, and indeed no mention whatsoever of her name was published there for more than two years.[6] Other northern newspapers were less stingy. The *Boston Globe* provided sympathetic treatment in a short profile in November 1892, the writer's admiration obvious from the headline alone: "Energetic Miss Ida Wells. A Colored Young Woman Who Is Not Afraid to Express Her Opinion."[7] The article, a mix of interpretation and storytelling, recounted Wells' background and offered readers a glowing review of her character: "One of the smartest and most talked of colored women in this country today is Miss Ida B. Wells. Her history is an eventful one, and speaks volumes for her pluck and enterprise."[8]

A trickle of other stories about Wells appeared that year, but they amounted to little more than a momentary drip. A fuller flow came the following year, when the thirty-one-year-old ex-editor traveled to Scotland and England at the invitation of reformers Catherine Impey and Isabella Fyvie Mayo and began giving lectures and meeting with journalists, politicians, and social activists. Often titled "Lynch Law in the Southern States," her speeches in Aberdeen, Huntly, Glasgow, Edinburgh, Newcastle, Birmingham, Manchester, and London explained the South's brutal system of oppression, the nature and frequency of lynching, and problems exacerbating the lawlessness. One of these factors, she made clear to a Scottish journalist, was the press: "The reports of the lynching cases, she said, were always biassed [*sic*] by the perpetrators or their friends so as to represent the negro victims as desperate and immoral characters, and the lynchers of the south had grown bolder and bolder as the time went on."[9] The challenge, then, was not just political will. It was fair representation and a firm fidelity to facts in the nation's newspapers. The *Manchester Guardian* published a 2,600-word account, which quoted lavishly from the "cultivated and interesting lady" and in doing so revealed Wells' crucial purpose:

> *Interviewer:* Do you think that British opinion and protest will have any weight in the matter?
> *Wells:* Yes, the Americans express their views on the conduct of other nations, and they will feel the force of the condemnation of other nations[.][10]

After her exile from Memphis, the story continued, Wells

> complained that neither the press nor the pulpit in America exposed the outrages that were constantly being committed against the coloured [*sic*] race. The press, indeed, was almost exclusively against the negroes, with the result that when reports of those outrages went forth to the world they invariably described the culprit as a brutal specimen of humanity, no matter how innocent he might be or how doubtful his guilt.[11]

What Wells believed she was doing abroad, then, was trying to gain attention for a subject that was either ignored or distorted in the mainstream American press. She wanted to correct the record. Wells was engaging in a publicity battle, a war of words, one that she feared she could not win in the US, at least not without leverage. The weight of British public opinion would be her leverage. In large measure, that strategy worked. Indeed, according to one historian:

> Mrs. Wells' lectures were a smashing success. For one thing they inspired the English to form an anti-lynching league with a treasury of five thousand pounds for the purpose of investigating and publishing the persecution of Southern negroes in America. Naturally the merchants back in Memphis were alarmed at the impact of Ida Wells' lectures; for being among the largest cotton exporters in the world, they depended upon the English textile industry for much of their business.[12]

Even more telling, perhaps, was the influence of the British press on the American press, which up until that point had ignored Wells' campaign. Most mentions in US newspapers, particularly in the South, prefaced coverage of Wells with references to what the British newspapers were saying already. The *Memphis Appeal-Avalanche*, for example, studiously ignored Wells in its news columns, running no articles about her in 1893, but it did run several editorials that year, most of which started with lengthy excerpts from sympathetic foreign newspapers. A May 11 editorial that ran 237 lines in length included 109 lines from a newspaper from Aberdeen, Scotland, the *Daily Free Press*.[13] And excerpts sometimes overshadowed the *Appeal*'s own commentary. "Ida Wells Abroad," published on May 23, typified this treatment. It criticized Wells for "continuing her triumphant mendacity,"[14] for not telling the whole story and duping her listeners. Yet almost sixty percent of the editorial consisted of a reprinted *Manchester Guardian* story, with ample quotes and much of Wells' argument kept intact.[15] A few weeks later, another editorial in the Memphis paper bore similar characteristics. Titled "Ida, the Fakir [*sic*] Abroad," it again fulminated against Wells, calling her a "liar" and a con artist, but not before running fifty column lines from the *Liverpool Post*, half the entire editorial.[16] Perhaps the most interesting part was the introduction, explaining how the *Appeal-Avalanche* obtained the report in the first place: "Marked papers from Great Britain continue to reach this office, telling of the triumphant march of Prophetess Ida Wells through the softheads of that country."[17] Who was "marking the papers"? Wells and her allies in Britain. In her autobiography, she disclosed the method she and her British allies employed:

> After every meeting the [temperance] committee purchased not less than one hundred copies of whichever paper had the best report. The next morning's work was to gather around the table in the breakfast room and mark and address these newspapers. They were sent to the president of the United States, the governors of most of the states in the Union, the leading ministers in the larger cities, and the leading newspapers of the country. In that way the United States was kept fairly well informed as to the progress of the "Negro Adventuress and her movements."[18]

Undoubtedly, these stories with loud denunciations of American morals must have cut hard at some newspaper proprietors who fancied themselves the consciences of their communities, prompting them to respond to Wells' accusations. "According to the reports in the Birmingham newspapers," a *Washington Post* editorial dourly noted, "Miss Wells' lectures are liberally punctured by cries of 'shame,' 'abominable,' and other words that express the English indignation over her stories of outrages."[19] The *Post*'s piece was triggered by a copy of the *Birmingham Gazette*, which was mailed to its offices at the end of May, following a lecture by the anti-lynching crusader in that city. The editorial, "Not a Nation of Lynchers," appeared on May 31, accusing Wells of libeling her country and insisting that the American people and the American press did not condone mob violence.[20]

Even when American editors held somewhat mixed reactions to Wells' arguments, the inclusion of references to her cause sparked discussion and exchange, especially in northern publications, where debate on the issue was more likely to be countenanced. Less than a week after the *Post* editorial, a reader named George Jackson sent a letter to the paper defending Wells:

> [W]hen we remember that . . . the leading newspapers and periodicals in the United States give unstinted space to Mr. Bryce, of the English Parliament, to discuss the American negro, and deny the latter the right to reply through the same channel, is it not about time for Miss Wells and every other lover of fair play to strive for the establishment in America of a sentiment which will discriminate between Fred Douglass and the "big, burly negro (!)" who is now his equal?[21]

Like Wells, Jackson was championing equal time, fair coverage. He was engaging in press criticism. He took the paper to task for saying Wells ignored white victims of lynching:

> If THE POST, along with its contemporaries, were not given to the habit of printing excerpts, instead of publishing in their entirety, the writings, speeches, and lectures of prominent colored men and women, or even of white men and women who discuss the negro's side of the race question, the public would discover that, in their condemnation of lynching and lynch law, they include the outrages perpetrated against the whites as well as [B]lacks.[22]

Determined to participate in the discussion, Wells sent a letter to the *Post* herself, criticizing the original editorial. As to the *Post*'s complaint that she went to Britain to agitate, she writes,

> For six months before the invitation came to me to go to Great Britain I tried to get a hearing in the white press and before white audiences in this country, because they could do something to check this evil. Boston was the only city in which I succeeded in doing this, and on three of the occasions I spoke to white audiences there. I paid my own expenses there and back from Washington.[23]

She also noted that she had reported the same outrages in Washington as in England, but the *Post* in its article covering the DC speech failed to find fault then. "If it were not a 'misrepresentation' in Washington City, how could it be so in Birmingham and London?" She added that she got the original information from the *Post*'s coverage itself (of Henry Smith's lynching in Texas). And she said that is what caused British audiences to yell "Shame!" and "Abominable!"[24]

She was not through exposing the failings of journalism in the United States, and she went further than most reformers by placing blame squarely on newspapers. "The American press, with few exceptions, either by such editorials or silence, has encouraged mobs, and is responsible for the increasing wave of lawlessness which is sweeping over the States,"[25] she was quoted as saying. Reporters and editors were not only guilty of cowardice but of dereliction of duty:

> In no case have the lynchers been punished, in few cases has the press said anything in favor of law and order, the religious and philanthropic bodies of the country utter no

word of condemnation, nor demand the enforcement of the law, and still I am charged with mispresenting my native country. If the pulpit and press of the country will inaugurate a crusade against this lawlessness, it will be no longer necessary to appeal to the Christian, moral, and humane forces of the outside world. And when they do so, not out of sympathy with criminals, but for the sake of their country's good name, they will have no more earnest helper than Ida B. Wells.[26]

Wells' focus on the press was clear enough to a writer in the *Chicago Tribune* that month. An article about a meeting to raise funds for a Columbian Exposition pamphlet told where Wells had traveled and why: "She has recently returned from Scotland, where she delivered many addresses showing the condition of her people in this country, and correcting erroneous statements which have been made to the Scotchmen in reference to them, wherein they had been described as a worthless class."[27] Wells was trying to counter propaganda with facts, logic, and moral principles, weapons with which she was well-armed, but in the United States she was outgunned in terms of sheer publicity. Attention to her cause improved the following year, when she returned to England and Scotland. She added new stops in Liverpool and Bristol to the previous year's itinerary and increased the number of lectures she gave, in Manchester, speaking a dozen times in ten days, and in Bristol, twice a day for a week, a rarity for a woman of the era, who was still subject to mockery and castigation for the act of public speaking.[28]

Coverage of Wells in the American newspapers surveyed for this analysis jumped four-fold from 1893 to 1894. Coverage included many more news articles, not just editorials, at least for Northern and Midwestern newspapers. Southern periodicals maintained their preference for editorials about Wells, continuing to assert that she was lying and perpetrating a fraud, therefore undeserving of news coverage. In 1894, the *New York Times* ran ten items mentioning Ida B. Wells: one ad, two editorials, three articles, and four briefs (announcements of fewer than twenty words). The briefs noted Black leaders' defense of Wells' campaign, as well as their recognition of the publicity fight at hand:

T. Thomas Fortune, President of the Afro-American League of the United States, has directed the Presidents of all local leagues of the organization to call mass meetings for the evening of July 16 to protest against the "action of white citizens of the Southern States to break down the testimony given by Miss Ida B. Wells to the British public as to the extent of race prejudice and mob violence in the United States."[29]

Back in the US by late July, Wells spoke before a large gathering at New York's Bethel African Methodist Episcopal Church to describe what she had been doing in Britain. In terms echoing the letter she sent to the *Washington Post* a year before, she outlined the context of her strategy and made the clearest explanation yet of her purpose:

After trying for two years to get a hearing in the press, after I was banished from my home, I met an Englishwoman who had been in the South and knew something of the real state of affairs. She asked me if I would go to England and tell the people how the negro was treated in America, and I said I would.

My reception in Liverpool was a most gracious one, and after holding ten meetings there we started on a tour. Wherever we went we were greeted by large crowds, who listened to my tale of how innocent men were lynched, burned at the stake, and shot down without a trial, and how half-grown boys were allowed to fire bullets into the bodies of dying men. They were horrified to hear these things.

Newspapers containing the vilest articles about me were sent to England from America to stop my work. At one time I thought I would have to remain in England to defend my own character, but the London Anti-Lynching League decided that my character needed no defense. They also decided that the time was ripe for me to return and make an appeal to the American people, and that is why I am here tonight. I may say that never since the days when *Uncle Tom's Cabin* was first published has the English public and people been stirred as they were by my tales of Southern lynchings.[30]

A "hearing" is what an *audience* literally does and what an *audition* is literally for, and both ideas are connoted by Wells' term. She was looking for an opportunity to be heard and a constituency with which to share her message. This lecture circuit was an alternative to publishing, therefore, but also a foray that stimulated publishing. And, as in 1893, the ripple effect of her lectures was obvious in nearly all coverage, including the *Times* article quoting her so extensively above. Wells' own words ran twice as many column lines as the rest of the article, an illustration of the power of her publicity tour. One of those few passages in the writer's own words paraphrased an intriguing idea proposed by the speaker: "Miss Wells made an appeal to the colored people of the North to organize, and urged that a bureau be established to procure authentic news of the outrages perpetrated on negroes in the South, and see that whenever the story of an outrage was sent out by white men in the south the negro's side be told also."[31]

Notice from American newspapers, even in the North, did not lead to editorial support. More often the opposite resulted. The *New York Times* opinion page consistently was hostile to Wells, as typified by this short July 27 editorial:

> Miss Ida B. Wells, a mulatress who has been "stumping" the British Islands to set forth the brutality of Southern white men and the unchastity and untruthfulness of Southern white women, has just returned to these shores. On the same day on which an interview with her was reported it was also reported that a negro had made an assault upon a white woman for purposes of lust and plunder, not in Texas or Mississippi, but in the heart of the city of New-York. The wretch is probably safe from lynching here, which is to the credit of the civilization of New-York. Thus far he seems to have escaped the clutch of the law. But the circumstances of his fiendish crime may serve to convince the mulatress missionary that the promulgation in New-York just now of her theory of negro outrages is, to say the least of it, inopportune.[32]

Editorial criticism was similar, if briefer, in the *Washington Post*, where Wells was usually portrayed as a grifter taking advantage of British gullibility: "And Miss Ida B. Wells may be very sure that in no part of this country, where the facts are of general knowledge, will she find or be able to excite any great amount of public indignation."[33] But as with previous *Post* editorials, this one triggered a response from readers. In a long, impassioned letter, sociologist Kelly Miller of Howard University defended Wells, saying she might not speak for all Blacks but deserved credit for her determination and effort. He compared her to Henry Ward Beecher and his journey to Britain during the Civil War. "Why," he asked, "should we condemn in Miss Wells what we applaud in Mr. Beecher? Is it because the one is a man and the other is a woman? Or because the one is white and the other is [B]lack?"[34] Miller then turned his attention to the press:

> The newspapers have much to say about the gain which Miss Wells is supposed to gather from her crusade. It is not customary for persons carrying on a benevolent or humanitarian campaign to refuse gratuitous contributions for the furtherance of their work. It is not fair to condemn Miss Wells for following a universal practice. The pro-lynching press has studiously and persistently striven to convince the world that negroes are lynched for one offense only, viz: Rapeful assault upon white women. The apologists for lynching know fully well that if they succeed in convincing mankind that lynching is resorted to only in case of rape, the victim can expect no sympathy from the civilized world.[35]

Regardless of the editorial content, the *Post*, like the *Times*, often ran even-handed articles summarizing Wells' activities and quoting her at length, evidence that by the end of the nineteenth century a wall had begun to develop between the news and editorial functions of some American newspapers.

Midwestern newspapers such as the *Chicago Tribune* and the *Detroit Free Press* usually eschewed editorials in favor of news items about Wells, often just mentioning her presence as a member or speaker at various political or civic meetings in the US Their most extensive coverage followed her speech at Bethel AME Church in New York at the end of July. Both newspapers ran the same wire service copy that quoted Wells generously and again depicted a substantial part of the issue as one of information control:

> When she was in England copies of southern newspapers containing articles attacking her personal character were spread and everything was done to influence the British public against her. "We want the colored race to be placed in the proper light before the people of this country," Miss Wells concluded, for there is in literature no true type of the negro as he is to-day. The lawless lynchings in the south for alleged crimes against the whites are in ninety-nine cases out of 100 simple outrages against our race. The press is in control of the whites and the attacks upon us are colored to suit themselves. The colored people of this country should organize themselves from one end of the country to the other. They should at least contribute the sinews of war with which to fight the battle. The south knows that we are very much disorganized. It is our duty to see that every story published from the south in which a negro is accused of some fiendish act and lynched for it, is run down by our own detectives, if necessary, and the other side of it published. There are two sides to every lynching.[36]

"Two sides to every lynching": The last line was a lightning bolt. Of course, many American newspapers had expressed their unease with lynching because it threatened law and order. The *Atlanta Constitution* conceded instances when "negroes are the victims," and the *Memphis Appeal-Avalanche* claimed in an editorial that it had never condoned the practice.[37] But the assumption held by most Americans in that era, even by many Black individuals, including Frederick Douglass, was that, however regrettable the actions of a mob, the person lynched was probably guilty.[38] In contending that there were "two sides," in questioning the culpability of the accused, Wells was issuing a forensic challenge to the people reporting the story—journalists—and she was saying that they were getting the story wrong. Her notion of a battle for public opinion meant that more truth-tellers were needed in the fray, an idea she pursued in a lecture she gave in Washington, DC: "The remedy for all this is to get the facts and publish them to the world. We want a wave of public sentiment against these outrages from one end of the world to the other. Get the facts of every lynching as it occurs and some wonderful revelations will be made."[39] Journalists in the former Confederate states were not free to publish those facts, she argued, and this was why outside pressure was so necessary: "We cannot arouse sentiment in the South, because the lyncher's own the newspapers and have too strong an influence over the authorities. Is it not a terrible commentary on the government of this country when the authorities are powerless to put down these outrages?"[40]

In general, southern coverage of Wells was hostile and contemptuous. In 1893, newspapers from this region largely ignored her. In 1894, when they paid more attention to her, they primarily expressed themselves through angry or sarcastic editorials. The striking imbalance between news and commentary was altered slightly by the involvement of governors who eventually weighed in on the subject. In the meantime, the region's press contented itself with attacking either Wells or the country she was visiting. Southern newspapers regularly criticized England for hypocrisy. "Lynching is a bad thing," noted an *Atlanta Constitution* editorial, "but it is not confined to the south."[41] The writer pointed to the brutality of British colonists in South Africa "who take the law into their own hands, and slaughter negro criminals wherever they find them, with the certainty of being acquitted by the courts and sustained by public opinion."[42] Another editorial criticized British behavior in India, "where Britons themselves keep up the most abominable phase of race distinction," before addressing the matter of publicity: "There are evils in the United States, and evils more than there should be in the southern part of the union, but when England protects her own women by law from 'noble' ruffians, it will be time enough for her meddlesome propagandists to have something to say about the shortcomings of either people or law on this side of the Atlantic."[43] But the essay begins by grumbling over the circumstances of the information it received about Wells: "The *London News* comes to *The Constitution* marked—first on the editorial page, where much is made of a communication itself, which appears to have been sent by a number of negro preachers and teachers, who are desirous of breaking the white line."[44] Mention of *The London News* throughout the piece indicates the successful abrasion caused by a professional rival goading its American counterpart.

Newspapers such as the *Constitution*, the *New Orleans Times-Picayune*, and the *Appeal-Avalanche* often characterized Wells' overseas tour as a publicity stunt by western merchants and manufacturers, as well as the "big mortgage syndicates of New England," supposedly conspiring to discourage migration to the South and divert it to the West.[45] The *Times-Picayune*, affecting some degree of indifference, floated the economic theory, criticizing Wells, her audience, and her supposed backers:

> For some time past a colored woman has been lecturing in England on the lynching of negroes in the Southern States of the Union. The Picayune has paid but little attention to the matter, although it has been largely commented on in the English press, and often to the extreme disadvantage of the people of the Southern States.
>
> It is useless to meet slanderous charges with counter statements. There are always people who prefer to believe the slanders no matter how unreasonable they may be; but, fortunately, these do not make up a majority. The world has been for so long treated to sensational stories that there is scarcely any dish of horrors that is not largely discounted. Extravagant stories may amuse, but they do not convince.
>
> As to the Ida Wells slanders, however, there has gone out a notion that they are part of a scheme to turn English capital away from the Southern States. The recent disastrous collapse of many large investments in the Western States has had the effect to direct attention to the Southern States of the Union as offering favorable opportunities and fields for the use of capital, and a desperate effort to save the West is being made in the propagation of slanderous statements in England against the Southern people.
>
> Governor [William J.] Northen, of Georgia, holds that the slanders were inspired by capitalists whose money is invested in the West, who view with well-founded apprehension the growing importance of the South, and who fear that foreign emigrants and capital may be attracted to that section to the disadvantage of that in which they have placed their money.[46]

The *Memphis Appeal-Avalanche*'s coverage was almost entirely composed of editorials, which were filled routinely with ad hominem attacks on Wells' character and motives. The first mention of Wells by the *Appeal* in 1894 was apparently an effort to make up for lost time, as the newspaper turned over five of seven columns on the opinion page to the subject, more than 6,500 words. Much of it consisted of reprinted reports from the *Westminster Gazette* and the *London News*, along with letters about and by Wells to the *Gazette*. The Memphis paper's own stance was clear: Wells was a liar who was smearing the reputation of the region. She "is merely another Lucy Parsons—a woman unusually shrewd, with a passion for incendiarism" and also [B]lack people's "worst enemy."[47] Why was the newspaper paying attention to Wells at this time? Apparently because of reaction to the British lectures:

> The *Appeal-Avalanche* has been in receipt of letters from prominent persons in England and the United States, asking if the utterances of Ida B. Wells in England and the United States are based upon facts. She has surely made a sufficient impression in England to justify some response. In her scheme of propagandism she has been seconded by the Republican political press of our Northern States and since the *Appeal-Avalanche* has been asked to reply by persons in England who are responsible, it will undertake to do so, trusting that its home readers will forbear complaint because of the space consumed in order that the reply may be thorough.[48]

The newspaper did not relent in its denunciation. An editorial in June denigrated Wells and her audience alike: "The ignorance and gullibility of some classes in England is beyond all comprehension. The receptions given the sharp negro adventuress, Ida Wells, in London is a striking illustration of English stupidity and mawkish sentimentality. It makes very little difference over here what such people think of us."[49] The writer noted the "marked" copy of the May 31 edition of the *London Sun*, which had been sent to the Memphis office.

In the summer of 1894, two factors sparked the slight increase of news articles about Wells in the southern press. One of these triggers was official endorsements by various religious or political groups, such as New Jersey's Colored Republican State Central Committee.[50] Other organizations, which publicly congratulated Wells, included the Missionary Convention of the North Mississippi Annual Conference, an assembly of "Negro Methodists," which publicly saluted Wells in mid-July and offered a defense against previous or would-be critics:

> Our condition in this particular section is becoming more largely the focus of enlightened public opinion than ever before, this situation is destined to be productive of good results in the course of time, and has to a great extent been brought about by the labors of that able and persistent representative of her race, Ida B. Wells (in foreign lands), and we find it our duty to accord her a generous meed of praise, and we sincerely deprecate any expressions on the part of our race representatives or friends, calculated to reflect upon her character or unselfish labors.[51]

This constituted rare positive news about African Americans in the newly renamed *Commercial Appeal*. Until then, Black readers could find their race mentioned only in crime stories, and sensationalistically racist ones at that.[52] In September, a convention of Black Baptists passed a resolution confirming that though rape was a "diabolical crime," no one should be killed for it "without adequate proof of guilt established by due process of law," and that

> our thanks are due, and the same are hereby extended, to Miss Ida B. Wells, and to all other justice and liberty-loving people, north and south, at home and abroad, for the efforts which they have made and are making to create a sentiment which has for its object the restoration to favor and to power that which is noblest in human nature and that which brings peace and prosperity in the south, and who are more and more inclined to extend to us the helping hand and to voice the spirit of justice and fairness through the pulpit and the press.[53]

The group also thanked state authorities for the successful prosecution of lynchers in West Tennessee. This summary of the convention's business was printed in the *Atlanta Constitution* in a neutral, straightforward manner—two paragraphs objectively summarizing the resolutions. The only editorial comment came in the headline: "Stop the Crime/And the Lynching Will Cease—Resolutions of Colored Baptists,"[54] a cause-and-effect point the conventioneers manifestly were not making.

The other factor prompting additional news coverage in the South was the involvement of several governors in the discussion about lynching, men whose letters defending the region were widely circulated in the press there. In June 1894, Governor Benjamin Tillman of South Carolina issued a letter to the press explaining his views on lynching:

I beg to say that I am correctly reported to this extent: I said in my canvass two years ago and I say now that, Governor as I am, I would lead a mob to lynch any man, white or [B]lack, who had assaulted any woman, white or [B]lack.

I am on record as having asked the Legislature to give me power to remove any Sheriff who allowed a prisoner to be lynched within his custody.

I have ordered out the militia to protect prisoners whenever called on by Sheriffs. I am opposed to lynch law for anything but this particular crime. That is a crime which, in my opinion, places any man beyond the pale of the law, and puts him below the brutes. The Southern people are not blameless in dealing with the question of lynching, but all our lynchings are not of negroes, and but for the fact that every outbreak of the kind is used as a text by Republican newspapers to slander and misrepresent our people they would excite no more comment than elsewhere in the United States. I think statistics will show that lynchings occur as often in Western and Northern States as they do in the South.[55]

This excerpt appeared in the *Chicago Tribune*, and reprints of the letter also appeared in many other newspapers as well.

The same month, Missouri Governor William J. Stone penned a lengthy reply to the *London News*, one that was reprinted and lavishly praised by the *Memphis Appeal-Avalanche*. After addressing Wells' accusations one at a time, the governor launched his defense:

Taking these statements as a basis and assuming them to be true, you proceeded in your editorial comments to prefer a severe indictment against all the Southern states of the Union. Your paper has a world-wide circulation, and the appearance of this article in your columns, especially in your editorial columns, is calculated to do immeasurable and most unmerited harm to those against whom it is directed, in the opinion of the good people of all Europe.[56]

Stone goes on to argue that Blacks in his own state have extensive rights and opportunities, and that these conditions prevailed in the southern states as well. He questions the statistics, ones that the British newspaper, and not Wells, had actually misreported:

The arraignment of the Southern states by the organizations mentioned in your editorial is unjust, because wholly unwarranted by the facts. The statement by Miss Wells that out of 138 lynchings occurring under her own notice only 30 were even accused of crime, is absurd; and equally absurd is the statement that she has been "exiled under a threat of mob violence for protesting in her own paper against these crimes." I have not a shade of doubt that the entire statement of this "colored lady from Memphis" is a pure fabrication. I deny it with the same authority and assurance that you would deny a similar charge if made against any highly reputable community in England.

The story is absurd. It is surprising that any intelligent person could be found willing to credit the statement of this woman that over [one hundred] cases had come under personal notice within a year of innocent people being murdered by lawless mobs without even being accused of crime. If the good ladies of the British Women's Temperance Association will reflect somewhat they can not [sic] fail to see that they have been imposed upon. Equally has Dr. Bradford, whoever he may be, and the "other Americans who are appealing to public opinion at home," whoever they may be, have imposed the Baptist and Congregational unions. Is it not a little strange that Dr. Bradford and his colleagues should "appeal to public opinion at home" by going away from home to make these monstrous accusations?[57]

The rest of Stone's letter consisted of his theory that an industrial conspiracy had inspired Wells' trip, that rival capitalists in the North or West were fighting dirty by encouraging the controversy. Under the headline "A Manly Act," the 1,200-word column said Stone had "earned the affection of all the Southern people, and especially those of Memphis, for a manly and voluntary reply to the libelous utterances of Ida B. Wells in England."[58] It ended on the same note as well, declaring "the Southern people will always hold Gov. Stone in grateful remembrance."[59]

The *Chicago Tribune* was quick to pounce on Stone's letter. It pointed out the falsehoods in it—namely the assertion that Black people in the South enjoyed the same rights of citizenship as did whites there. The *Tribune* said that Stone also was wrong about the nature of lynching: "The vast majority of persons lynched in the South is composed of [B]lacks, and this is a fact which the Governor of Missouri cannot controvert. The Governor of Arkansas attempted it recently, and when confronted with the facts held his peace."[60] The newspaper, which according to Wells was the source of her statistics, included some in the end of the editorial, a reminder to the governor that the data were well-documented: "These are the cold facts in the case and they do not sustain Gov. Stone's arguments. The Tribune invites him to a contest of these figures."[61] The newspaper ended the editorial with a stern assignment for all southern governors: they needed to "reform their processes of justice so that offenders against the laws can be punished by the law instead of by mobs."[62]

An editorial in the *Manchester Guardian* noted the complaints and protests by the press in the US were odd considering they themselves regularly reported on the atrocities:

Some of the American papers were uneasy at English disapproval of lynching, and thought to smooth over the difficulty by talking of the "Ida Wells slanders." But they forget the evidence afforded by their own news columns. That Miss Wells focussed [sic] some of this evidence and brought it to the notice of thousands of English men and English women who rarely or never see an American newspaper is quite true. She did not invent, but spoke from data that were and are open to all the world. What she had to say from personal knowledge was interesting and telling, but her case against lynching was established without the evidence of her own persecution.[63]

After resolutions were passed in Bradford, England, in August, Arkansas Governor William Meade Fishback sent a letter to officials there and also released it publicly to the press. Fishback started the letter by dismissing any notion that Wells knew what she was talking about and even questioned that she had lived in Memphis:

> Although the negro woman, Ida Wells, is reported to have been a resident of Memphis, I have never heard of her except through reports coming from England. I know nothing of her character, but judge from your resolutions that she is a shrewd adventuress, who has found a fit field for her impositions in British credulity and British ignorance of this country. It is a matter of regret to all right-thinking people that there should exist such a thing as lynch law in any community, and our regret is not lessened by the fact that there are more negroes lynched in the northern states of our union in proportion to the negro population than in the southern states. This barbarous method of punishing crime receives our unqualified condemnation, whether in America or in England or elsewhere.
>
> The motives which prompted your resolutions are doubtless sincere and entitled to respect, but, pardon me for suggesting that if you would obtain your information from a credible source, such as our census bulletins, rather than from such persons as Ida Wells, your benevolence would be much more intelligently directed and productive of much beneficial results.[64]

Whether or not Fishback truly had never heard of Wells before her British trip, the important point is the publicity. The "reports" she was generating there had become too loud and influential for him to ignore, and he felt forced to respond publicly. And although he challenged her trustworthiness, it still must have struck some readers as odd that after a dearth of coverage about Wells' trip, it took someone as powerful as a sitting governor to attempt to repudiate her.

Northen engaged in the debate the same month as well, writing letters and submitting to interviews on the subject, and his involvement in the discourse stirred still more publicity for Wells. The *Detroit Free-Press* reprinted a *Baltimore Sun* editorial:

> Ida Wells, the colored woman, who has recently returned to this country from her crusade in England against the south, is beginning to be understood abroad. Governor Northen's refutation of the wholesale slanders put forth by the woman has already had good effect, and the further statements that will be made in answer to letters received by him from abroad will probably do much to dissipate the false impressions produced. Governor Northen does not think the woman was actuated entirely by hate of the southern white people in her harangues. He thinks there was a business motive behind them.[65]

Although the involvement of protesting governors or congratulatory civic groups led to more news coverage, many newspapers continued their preference for editorial comment alone. Still, the fact that the press was compelled to respond at all, to discuss lynching and mob violence, and to defend the region's legal order forced them to pay more attention to instances of lynching generally. Many American journalists may have continued to believe that Black victims were guilty, but that faith could not have been as unassailable as it was before 1893-1894. Wells' accusations and

British reproaches had angered and embarrassed them. Her press criticism exacted a cost for lynching and for those supporting lynching. She changed the debate in England, too. There, historian Sarah L. Silkey writes, Wells' campaign "permanently altered the way in which the British public understood and discussed American lynching. Henceforth, British journalists discarded romantic notions of frontier justice and accepted Wells' assertions that lynching was a racially motivated act of violent oppression."[66] The criticism of Wells took a toll on her as well. In the US, her reputation suffered as a result of the backlash. In Britain, however, where tougher libel laws probably spared her from the most egregious personal attacks, her fame may have grown stronger.[67]

Aside from her role as a press critic and journalistic reformer, Wells can be seen from two other perspectives that have received less attention from scholars and that are related to the focus used in this chapter. First, Ida B. Wells deserves to be viewed as an early muckraker, a journalist who, like that other Gilded Age documentarian, Jacob Riis, was as determined to investigate and catalogue society's problems as to persuade and reform.[68] Just as Lincoln Steffens uncovered widespread graft in modern municipalities and Upton Sinclair laid bare the horrific workings of the twentieth-century slaughterhouse, Wells exposed the ways in which mob violence and lawlessness directed at Black Americans actually transpired. She did so, not as she often alluded, in the manner of Harriet Beecher Stowe, but with cool, hard data. Her pamphlet *A Red Record* offered so exhaustive a classification system that it was a veritable taxonomy of lynching.[69] She investigated cases and gathered details, "replaced the language of gentility with reality and dispensed with the 'false delicacy' of 'the unspeakable crime.' She was one of the few women reformers who actually used the word *rape*, and had learned to do so without apology."[70] Observers in the US and abroad frequently noted her calm, dispassionate presentation, her logic and, above all, her statistics. She was not an orator, and she did not thunder from the dais. She was a thorough clinician who modestly set forth her findings. She was an investigative reporter sharing what she knew.[71]

Her demeanor on the stage points to another unexamined aspect of her campaign—the fact that it coincided and benefited from the professionalization of journalism at the time, the commercial and social marketplace afforded to writers who wanted or needed to amplify the work they did and to broaden its reach and appeal. During the late nineteenth century, journalists were not just penmen and -women; many took up the cause of reform, social justice, and political change, and they used journalism as a tool to help them accomplish these goals. But their purpose and their means were not always easily separable. Many editors disparaged Wells for what they assumed was a self-promoting, mercenary agenda—the theory that she was more interested in enriching herself than in helping her less fortunate countrymen, that her trip to Britain was, as one writer put it, about "an income rather than an outcome."[72] Although racial animosity probably fueled much of their criticism, these editors also may have harbored professional jealousy and class resentment. Reporters were on the rise, and increasingly dissatisfied with being anonymous "brain workers." Within a decade, bylines would become more common. Journalists' success would increasingly rely, in part, on their ability to market themselves. Wells fit into the profile of the type of author described by historian Christopher Wilson—someone who "engaged the market directly and attempted to master its primary motives and methods"; whose career "involved close interaction with book, newspaper, and magazine environments"; and who "explored . . . the role of the literary marketplace as a crucible and vehicle of democratic values."[73]

Ida B. Wells was a rising star in the intellectual universe of the era, someone who left the US in relative obscurity and returned "a celebrity."[74] She was not the first American to turn to the lecture circuit, of course. It was a well-established publicity tool during the nineteenth century, employed by renowned writers such as Mark Twain, little-known speakers in the Chautauqua or Lyceum movements, and reformers hoping to catch a break. A decade before Wells journeyed to the East Coast, Sarah Winnemucca, a Paiute author and activist, made a similar journey and for similar reasons. A Native American from Nevada, Winnemucca sought help for her people, and with a combination of letters, articles, lectures, and performances she won the support of people like Oliver Wendell Holmes and even President Rutherford B. Hayes.[75]

In addition to practical objectives, such as political or financial support, both Winnemucca and Wells also were trying to negotiate the public sphere and change the narrative in the mainstream press. In so doing, of course, they attracted fierce criticism and personal abuse, with writers often attacking their femininity, their virtue, their intelligence, and their integrity. Southern white men viewed themselves as chivalrous heroes protecting their vulnerable women and regarded Black men as brutal "ravishers" unable to help themselves.[76] Through her writing and speeches, Wells reversed the formula, flipping the script. "In refuting this discourse of civilization," historian Gail Bederman writes, "Wells was trying to stop lynching by producing an alternative discourse of race and manhood."[77] The "alternative discourse" she sought was a different type of journalism, one that was more accurate and less emotional, more scientific and less judgmental. This was the hearing she wanted. Remediating the problem could not happen without reforming the profession; the two challenges were urgent and interrelated. In establishing herself as a renowned if controversial authority on lynching and its coverage in the press, Wells exposed both. She was the first American to muckrake mob violence and newspaper complicity.

NOTES

1. Ida B. Wells, *Crusade for Justice: The Autobiography of Ida B. Wells*, edited by Alfreda M. Duster (Chicago: University of Chicago Press, 1970), 131, 86.

2. Paula J. Giddings, *Ida: A Sword among Lions* (New York: Amistad, 2008), 227.

3. Ford Risley, *Abolition and the Press: The Moral Struggle against Slavery* (Evanston, IL: Northwestern University Press, 2008), 188.

4. David T.Z. Mindich, *Just the Facts: How "Objectivity" Came to Define American Journalism* (New York: New York University Press, 1998), 136.

5. Untitled dispatch, *New York Times*, April 29, 1894, 1.

6. "Fortune Stirred Them Up; Excitement at the Colored Mass Meeting," *New York Times*, April 5, 1892, 1.

7. "Energetic Miss Ida B. Wells," *Boston Daily Globe*, November 29, 1892, 3.

8. Ibid.

9. *The Scotsman*, April 29, 1893, 9.

10. "Lynch Law in the United States," *Manchester Guardian*, May 9, 1893, 9.

11. Ibid.

12. David Tucker, "Miss Ida B. Wells and Memphis Lynching," *Phylon* 5.32 (1971): 121.

13. "A Memphis Negro Abroad," *Memphis Appeal-Avalanche*, May 11, 1893, 4.

14. "Ida Wells Abroad," *Memphis Appeal-Avalanche*, May 23, 1893, 4.

15. Ibid.

16. "Ida, The Fakir Abroad," *Memphis Appeal-Avalanche*, June 2, 1893, 4.

17. Ibid.

18. Wells, *Crusade for Justice*, 213–34.

19. "Not a Nation of Lynchers," *Washington Post*, May 31, 1893, 4.

20. Ibid.

21. George W. Jackson, letter, *Washington Post*, June 5, 1893, 4.

22. Ibid.

23. Ida B. Wells, letter, "Lynch Law and the Color Line," *Washington Post*, July 3, 1893, 7.

24. Ibid.

25. Ibid.

26. Ibid.

27. "Progress of the Colored Race," *Chicago Tribune*, July 24, 1893, 9.

28. Wells, *Crusade for Justice*, 148, 154.

29. "City and Vicinity," *New York Times*, July 7, 1894, 8.

30. "Miss Wells' Plea for the Negro," *New York Times*, July 30, 1894, 8.

31. Ibid.

32. Editorial, *New York Times*, July 27, 1894, 4.

33. "British Anti-Lynchers," *Washington Post*, August 2, 1894, 4.

34. Kelly Miller, letter, "Ida Wells' Crusade," *Washington Post*, August 5, 1894, 7. For more on Miller, see Giddings, *Ida*, 326, 554.

35. Ibid.

36. "Friend of the Colored People," *Detroit Free Press*, July 30, 1894, 1.

37. Mindich, *Just the Facts*, 121–22.

38. "The 'threadbare lie' as Wells called it, the belief that [B]lack men were lynched because they raped white women, was believed by practically everyone. . . . This impression, that [B]lacks were culpable, was conveyed by the journalism of the elite newspapers." Quoted in Ibid.

39. "A Very Quiet Lecture," *Washington Post*, December 21, 1894, 2.

40. Ibid.

41. "What the English Think of Us," *Atlanta Constitution*, June 23, 1894, 4. See also "The British and the Negroes," *Atlanta Constitution*, May 23, 1894, 4.

42. Ibid.

43. "A Word to The London News," *Atlanta Constitution*, August 8, 1894, 4.

44. Ibid.

45. "The Ida B. Wells Crusade," *Atlanta Constitution*, July 29, 1894, 18.

46. "Bootless Slanders About the South," *New Orleans Times-Picayune*, August 7, 1894, 4.

47. "A Libel Upon a Country," *Memphis Appeal-Avalanche*, May 29, 1894, 4.

48. Ibid.

49. "A Gullible English Public," *Memphis Appeal-Avalanche*, June 12, 1894, 4.

50. "Colored Republicans in Line," *New York Tribune*, October 25, 1894, 3.

51. "Boost for Ida B. Wells," *The Commercial Appeal*, July 15, 1894, 9. The newspaper changed its ownership and its name on July 1.

52. One May news article was headlined "A Colored Child Rapist." The man was not lynched, according to the story, "as his victim was not seriously injured." *Memphis Appeal-Avalanche*, May 16, 1894, 5.

53. "Stop the Crime," *Atlanta Constitution*, September 17, 1894, 5.

54. Ibid.

55. "Gov. Tillman Favors Lynch Law," *Chicago Tribune*, June 2, 1894, 3.

56. "A Manly Act," *Memphis Appeal-Avalanche*, June 19, 1894, 4.

57. Ibid.

58. Ibid.

59. Ibid.

60. "Mob Law in the South," *Chicago Tribune*, June 20, 1894, 6.

61. Ibid.

62. Ibid.

63. No title, *Manchester Guardian*, September 4, 1894, 7.

64. "Ida Wells' Dupes," *New Orleans Times-Picayune*, August 10, 1894, 2.

65. "The Ida Wells Crusade," by the *Baltimore Sun*, reprinted in the *Detroit Free-Press*, August 5, 1894, 10.

66. Sarah L. Silkey, *Black Woman Reformer: Ida B. Wells, Lynching, & Transatlantic Activism* (Athens: University of Georgia Press, 2015), 113.

67. Silkey, 139–41.

68. Riis, a reporter and photographer on the police beat for the *New York Sun*, published his classic exposé of poverty in New York City, *How the Other Half Lives*, in 1890.

69. Ida B. Wells-Barnett, *On Lynchings: Southern Horrors; A Red Record; Mob Rule in New Orleans* (Salem, NH: Ayer Co., 1993), 16–20.

70. Giddings, *Ida*, 228–29.

71. A Liverpool pastor, Richard Acland Armstrong, was impressed by Wells. He said in a letter to a religious newspaper in America: "She spoke with singular refinement, dignity, and self-restraint, nor have I ever met any 'agitator' so cautious and unimpassioned in speech. But by this marvelous self-restraint itself, she moved us all the more profoundly." Quoted in *Crusade for Justice*, 146.

72. "British Anti-Lynchers," *New York Times*, August 2, 1894, 4.

73. Christopher P. Wilson, *The Labor of Words: Literary Professionalism in the Progressive Era* (Athens: University of Georgia Press, 1985), xiii.

74. Gail Bederman, "'Civilization,' the Decline of Middle-Class Manliness, and Ida B. Wells's Antilynching Campaign (1892–1894)," *Radical History Review* 52.4 (1992), 5.

75. Cari M. Carpenter and Carolyn Sorisio, eds. *The Newspaper Warrior: Sarah Winnemucca Hopkins's Campaign for American Indian Rights, 1864–1891* (Lincoln: University of Nebraska Press, 2015), 1–348.

76. A news brief about a lynching in South Carolina illustrates this rather plainly. "Lynched a Ravisher," *Memphis Appeal-Avalanche*, May 7, 1893, 1.

77. Bederman, "'Civilization,'" 15.

BIBLIOGRAPHY

Bederman, Gail. "'Civilization,' the Decline of Middle-Class Manliness, and Ida B. Wells's Antilynching Campaign (1892–1894)," *Radical History Review* 52.4 (1992).

Carpenter, Cari M. and Sorisio, Carolyn, eds. *The Newspaper Warrior: Sarah Winnemucca Hopkins's Campaign for American Indian Rights, 1864–1891.* Lincoln: University of Nebraska Press, 2015.

Giddings, Paula J. *Ida: A Sword among Lions.* New York: Amistad, 2008.

Mindich, David T. Z. *Just the Facts: How "Objectivity" Came to Define American Journalism.* New York: New York University Press, 1998.

Risley, Ford. *Abolition and the Press: The Moral Struggle against Slavery.* Evanston, IL: Northwestern University Press, 2008.

Silkey, Sarah L. *Black Woman Reformer: Ida B. Wells, Lynching, & Transatlantic Activism.* Athens: University of Georgia Press, 2015.

Tucker, David. "Miss Ida B. Wells and Memphis Lynching," *Phylon* 5.32 (1971).

Wells, Ida B. *Crusade for Justice: The Autobiography of Ida B. Wells,* edited by Alfreda M. Duster. Chicago: University of Chicago Press, 1970.

———. *On Lynchings: Southern Horrors; A Red Record; Mob Rule in New Orleans.* Salem, NH: Ayer Co., 1993.

Wilson, Christopher P. *The Labor of Words: Literary Professionalism in the Progressive Era.* Athens: University of Georgia Press, 1985.

3

Communicating an Anti-Lynching Crusade

The Voice, the Writings, and the Power of Ida B. Wells-Barnett's Public Relations Campaign

Jinx Coleman Broussard

On March 10, 1892, the *Memphis Appeal-Avalanche*, a white local newspaper, included a woodcut sketch, "Into the Hands of the Mob," that represented the fate of People's Grocery store owner Thomas Moss and his business partners, Calvin McDowell and William Stewart. The accompanying article described their March 9 lynching, the barbaric retribution for a confrontation enflamed by racial tensions and violence that had taken place several days prior: "There was no hooping [*sic*], no loud talking, in fact, nothing boisterous. Everything was done decently and in order . . . the vengeance was sharp, swift, and sure . . . The avengers swooped down last night and sent the murderous souls of the ring leaders in the Curve riot to eternity."[1]

Proponents of the abhorrent, violent act contended that it had been justified by the "Curve riot," a gunfight that had occurred between William Barrett, the white owner of a rival grocery store nearby, and McDowell, and had resulted in three injuries on March 5. The gun fight had been triggered three days earlier by a scuffle over business interests between Barrett and Stewart. Members of the Black community had backed Moss' business venture, but it competed with and thus threatened the profits of the store owned by Barrett, a determined white man who wanted to maintain his monopoly. In the aftermath of the initial scuffle, Moss—a letter carrier by day, and store proprietor by night—had been taken from his home, hauled off to jail, and shortly thereafter, dragged from his cell and lynched alongside his partners McDowell and Stewart at the hands of a vigilante group of whites. By most accounts, Moss was a decent and hardworking man.[2] He was not involved in the confrontation that occurred when whites descended on the People's Grocery and when Blacks took up arms to protect themselves. His only offense, according to

Ida B. Wells, the budding local journalist and godmother to Moss' child, was opening the People's Grocery Store in a predominantly Black neighborhood outside the
city limits.[3]

In the three days leading to that fateful 3 a.m. removal of Moss and his partners
from a cell that a sheriff deputy had left unlocked, many Blacks were arrested, the
People's Grocery was looted, and the homes of Black community members were
damaged.[4] These activities and Moss' death crystallized for Wells that the public was
being misled into believing that lynching was a necessary punishment for Black men,
who according to era logic were inclined to rape white women and to commit violent
acts. But Moss was not accused of rape, or any crime for that matter. This argument
provided the cover that allowed people such as Moss to be murdered, often at the
whim of mobs, for any manner of perceived indiscretions. In reality, race prejudice
and economic reprisal and intimidation were the incentive, Wells argued, as she
offered in her autobiography: "Thus, with the aid of the city and county authorities
and the daily papers, that white grocer had put an end to his rival Negro grocer as
well as his business."[5]

Until Moss' death, Wells believed she was advocating for social justice for her
race and gender adequately through the *Free Speech* weekly newspaper she edited
and published in Memphis.[6] After the lynching of her close friend, her eyes were
opened to the ineffectiveness of her current approach. She launched a social justice
campaign that sought to influence public opinion and ultimately end lynching
in the United States. The campaign was initiated in her efforts with the pen as a
muckraking advocacy journalist, but she soon turned to other communications
methods—nascent public relations strategies—to advocate, persuade, and bring
about meaningful change in the lives of Black individuals and women in the US.
This chapter will explore the public relations strategies that Wells employed in her
transnational anti-lynching crusade.

THE "GREAT [WHITE] MEN'S" HISTORY OF PUBLIC RELATIONS

The names of "great [white] men"—Ivy Ledbetter Lee, George Creel, Edward
Bernays, Arthur W. Page, and Carl Byoir— often are invoked in the conversation
about the pioneers of public relations. Many historians consider Lee to be the first
professional public relations practitioner and even the father of the field.[7] John D.
Rockefeller, the majority owner in the Colorado Coal and Fuel Company, hired
Lee to neutralize public opinion toward the Rockefellers during the coal miners'
strike of 1913-1914,[8] and according to one scholar, Lee "provided many of the
modern public relations ideas that Rockefeller eventually adopted to alleviate tensions and improve labor relations."[9]

Like Lee, the other four pioneers were former journalists who also used strategies
and tactics associated with the modern professional practice of public relations to
mobilize favorable public opinion for their clients during the early 1900s. George

Creel, for instance, was a well-respected investigative journalist before he was tapped to chair the Committee on Public Information, a publicity agency designed to release government news, to administer voluntary press censorship, and to develop transnational propaganda during World War I. For the task, Creel enlisted the efforts of both Byoir, an "effective manager" who "directed a brilliant propaganda campaign to sell America's war aims at home and abroad,"[10] and Bernays, who took public relations to another level by linking attitude formation and behavior to public opinion and utilizing research based on psychology rather than intuition to guide his work.[11] Known as the first corporate public relations practitioner, Page professionalized the field by incorporating research, issues management, and speech-making, among other techniques, for his employer AT&T in the 1920s. He also gave speeches, wrote letters, and made presentations on behalf of his client. Early public relations historians, such as Scott Cutlip, aptly identified these "great [white] men" as the architects of professional public relations, but they failed to recognize era individuals engaged in similar strategies that operated outside of the bounds of governmental organizations and corporate structures. As a result, although they acknowledged that antecedent public relations techniques had been implemented in a transnational context as early as the seventeenth century, they failed to identify era leaders of social movements as pioneers in public relations. This chapter contends that Wells pre-dated the early giants identified above in the implementation of professional public relations strategies and tactics to mold public opinion. Although Wells took a prominent role in the woman suffrage movement from 1893 until her death in 1931, her anti-lynching campaign more succinctly fits the paradigm of a public relations campaign and will serve as the focus of the remainder of the chapter.

IDA B. WELLS: A NEGLECTED
PUBLIC RELATIONS PIONEER

Public relations scholar Robert Kendall writes that "the advocacy of a cause is a socially important function that we call public relations."[12] Wells focused on the greater good of society.[13] She addressed an issue—a problem—that was destructive to the fabric of society and her race's existence. Thus, in the aftermath of the lynchings of her friends, she launched a campaign that sought to influence public opinion in the US. With a focus on advocacy and change, her ultimate goal was to end lynching in all its forms in the US, to press for political and economic equity, and to encourage educational opportunities for Black individuals. To accomplish that end, she set out to expose and discredit the myth surrounding the murders of Black men, women, and children.

As articulated by John Marston in an early public relations text in 1932, research is the first step in the public relations process, followed by action, communication, and evaluation.[14] Research lends credibility and helps guide in identifying and clarifying the issue, problem, challenge, or opportunity.[15] Wells engaged in this important first step throughout her public relations campaign by painstakingly conducting primary and secondary research, and armed with statistics and her firsthand observations, she presented and buttressed her arguments. For instance, in her initial inquiry into regional lynching in 1892, Wells investigated the lynching of a Black man in Tunica, Mississippi. The Associated Press had labeled the man a "brute" for allegedly raping a seven-year-old girl, but Wells "visited the place . . . and saw the girl, who was a grown woman more than seventeen years old. She had been found in the lynched Negro's cabin by her father, who had led the mob against him in order to save his daughter's reputation."[16] Following the murder of Henry Smith in Paris, Texas, on February 1, 1893, Wells read mainstream newspaper accounts of the preparation for the lynching and the gruesome details about the manner in which he was killed. "I said in newspaper articles and public speeches that we should be in a position to investigate every lynching and get the facts ourselves. If there was no chance for a fair trial in these cases, we should have facts to appeal to public opinion," Wells explained years later.[17] Such an approach aligns with the practice of public relations, where research enables the practitioner to craft campaign messages and make credible and persuasive arguments.

In 1984, James E. Grunig and Todd S. Hunt identified four models of public relations, including press agentry or staged events aimed at garnering publicity; public information or dissemination of factual and favorable information; two-way asymmetrical communication, which utilizes research to develop messages aimed at persuading; and two-way symmetrical communication, which seeks to establish and maintain relationships that benefit the organization and its publics and in which negotiated agreement and conflict resolution occur.[18] Throughout her anti-lynching campaign, Wells incorporated strategies associated with these models. Armed with her research, she took action and communicated, the second and third steps of the public relations process and the equivalent of the public information and asymmetrical models. With a goal of informing and countering the prevailing narrative, the first issue of *Free Speech* after the lynching of her friends outlined the sequence of events leading to the actual shooting, and concluded that Moss "was murdered with no more consideration than if he had been a dog."[19]

Several articles appeared before Wells issued her scathing editorial in the *Free Speech* on May 21, 1892, asserting that of the eight Black men who [recently] had been lynched, three were charged with killing white men and five were charged with raping white women. Wells then challenged the notion that the lynching was needed to protect white womanhood, and she emphasized: "Nobody in this section believes the old thread-bare lie that Negro men assault white women."[20] To drive home her point, she admonished: "If Southern white men are not careful they will over-reach themselves and a conclusion will be reached which will be very damaging to the moral reputation of their women."[21] For the first time ever, Wells also charged that economic reprisal was the real reason for the lynching.[22]

Incorporating professional public relations tactics, Wells enlightened and proposed an action. She urged Black community members to save their money and to leave Memphis because the town would not protect their lives and property or give them a fair trial. Instead, it murdered them "in cold blood" when a white person accused them of a crime.[23] Black individuals were powerless to protect themselves because they were outnumbered and had no weapons, the editorial charged. They could, however, take Wells' advice and leave Memphis. Wells also exhorted them to boycott the segregated railway system that primarily took them to their domestic jobs in white households.

Realizing their untenable situation, approximately two thousand Black men, women, and children heeded Wells' call, moving to Kansas City and Oklahoma during the first three months following the lynching. Those who remained not only boycotted the rails, but returned furniture and other goods they had purchased on credit at white businesses. "Business had ground to a halt," Wells said.[24]

Even when Memphis leaders and Black preachers beseeched Wells to end the campaign, she did not relent. "When I asked why they came to us, the reply was that colored people had been their best patronage. . . . They wanted us to assure our people that there was no danger and to tell them that any discourtesy toward them would be punished severely."[25] This is an example of the attitude and behavior change Wells was seeking from influential stakeholders. Nevertheless, she continued to urge Black community members to leave Memphis because an end to lynching was her ultimate goal. The issue of the *Free Speech* that Wells published after the visit of the white leaders carried an account of their meeting and a renewed call for Black community members to "keep up their good work" and to "stay off the cars."[26] Implementing public-speaking techniques still discouraged by the strictures of gender norms, she also told the congregants of the two largest churches in the city about the exchange with the white leaders the next Sunday. This tactic aligns with Grunig's press agentry, public information, and two-way asymmetrical models. Wells' efforts crippled the railway system and the Memphis economy, and accomplished the first of Wells' behavioral goals that followed her informational goal.[27]

The white press reacted to the articles in the *Free Speech* and castigated the writer. "There are some things the Southern white man will not tolerate and the obscene intimations of the foregoing have brought the writer to the outermost limit of patience," the *Memphis Appeal-Avalanche* wrote on June 8, 1892.[28] Going so far as to incite violence, the Memphis *Commercial Appeal* wrote: "If the Negroes do not apply the remedy without delay it will be the duty of those he attacked to tie the wretch who utters those calumnies to a stake at the intersection of Main and Maddison Sts., brand him on the forehead with a hot iron and perform on him a surgical operation with a pair of shears."[29]

Whites also attempted to counter Wells' campaign with articles and editorials that urged Blacks to remain, suggesting that life would be harder where they were planning to move. On March 23, 1892, the *Weekly Avalanche-Appeal* reported that the weather would not be conducive for Blacks. A month later, the newspaper ran a long story under the headline: "The New Promised Land, Unlike Old Canaan. It Doesn't Flow with Milk and Honey."[30] These pieces had no impact as Wells presented additional messages based on statistic and strategized with race leaders. Failing in their efforts, some members of the white community and a number of newspapers called for the death of the individual who wrote the editorials. On May 27, 1892, a mob destroyed the *Free Speech*.

Wells, who was traveling at the time, did not return to the city. Instead, she accepted the offer of the *New York Age's* T. Thomas Fortune to move to that city where she continued her anti-lynching campaign. The *Age* was an excellent medium through which Wells could reach Black and white audiences. It was a well-respected publication, and Fortune was highly regarded.[31] "The Negro race should be ever grateful to T. Thomas Fortune and Jerome B. Peterson" because "they helped me give to the world the first inside story of Negro lynchings," Wells once wrote.[32] The white press also took note of the newspaper, which was on the "exchange list" of white publications in the North.[33]

A little more than a week after her arrival, Wells kicked off a new phase of her anti-lynching campaign. Historian Mia Bay offers that "Wells crafted a new identity as a refugee forced to flee the 'Southern horrors' that countless [B]lacks still experienced."[34] Wells' seven-column, front-page article in a special edition of the *Age* attested to the authenticity of her editorial in the *Free Speech*, which was based on the "fact of illicit association between [B]lack men and white women."[35] Other articles, which detailed the number of lynchings and disproved the widely accepted lynching premise, followed. Even the *Memphis Appeal-Avalanche* reported that Wells was continuing her "week-to-week" campaign in the *New York Age*, adding that the newspaper now was circulating in Memphis.[36]

The success of public relations campaigns often depends on the appropriateness of the communication vehicles to reach the target audiences—the stakeholders.[37] The Black press was Wells' primary vehicle, and she employed the power of the pen in it because she believed in its value as a medium of advocacy, a champion of causes, and an instrument for racial elevation.[38] Throughout her career, Wells had tried to do just that in other Black newspapers such as the *Washington Bee,* the *Kansas City Gate City Press*, the *Little Rock Sun*, and the *Detroit Plaindealer*, and now, she was reaching both Black and white audiences, a primary goal of her campaign, through her writings in the *Age*. Whites who had subscribed to the *Free Speech* also received the *Age* and learned that Wells had written the editorial. "The rage escalated as she repeated her attack on the reputation of white women for a national audience."[39]

TRAVELING ABROAD: CULTIVATING OPINION LEADERS AND BUILDING SUPPORT VIA LECTURES AND THE PRESS

Wells did not remain stationary in New York for long. In April 1893, she arrived in Liverpool, England, hoping she could make strides in the anti-lynching campaign she had been waging in the US for almost a year. The trip abroad was important to Wells because the white audiences she hoped to attract were not materializing at her U.S. lectures.[40] As we observed in the previous chapter, she also was concerned that her efforts to disseminate her messages were diluted because the white mainstream press at home virtually had ignored her as she traveled in the North to call attention to the unlawful killing of Black citizens and to obtain support to stamp out the barbaric practice. The white press was the vehicle through which she hoped to reach whites and thus mold public opinion.[41] With that in mind, she designed an international public relations campaign that might attract notice in the British press and by extension, demand attention from US newspaper publishers and policymakers.[42] She eventually likened the experience in Great Britain to "being born again in a new condition," where she was treated as an equal to the women who were "doing so much for me and my cause."[43]

Relationship building is central to public relation campaigns,[44] and Wells began cultivating relationships with two prominent British reformers, Caroline Impey and Isabelle Fyvie Mayo, before she sailed abroad. Impey, the publisher and editor of the British journal, *Anti-Caste*, which addressed subjugated peoples in England, invited Wells to lecture in Great Britain after learning of the increased frequency of race-based lynchings. While visiting the US in September 1892, Impey, a leading British Quaker reformer whose parents had been abolitionists, had attended a meeting of the National Press Association, where Wells introduced an anti-lynching resolution, and two months later, while attending another meeting, Impey had interviewed Wells for an article in *Anti-Caste*.[45] Wells later wrote in her biography that the interview was "the beginning of a worldwide campaign against lynching."[46]

A few months later, Impey took note of the grisly details of the February 1893 lynching of a Black man in Paris, Texas. Due to the advocacy journalism of individuals such as Wells, the murder received attention in the national and international press, and in the aftermath of the lynching, Impey and Mayo invited Wells to England and Scotland to air "this intolerable condition."[47] The women agreed to fund the visit,[48] and Wells readily accepted the invitation.[49] Intent on managing the lynching issue for public consumption and action, Impey, Mayo, and "three protégés" prepared for Wells' tour. They wrote letters, scheduled meetings, sought attention in the press, and mailed ten thousand copies of Impey's *Anti-Caste*.[50] During her travels, Wells engaged in a transnational lecture tour, speaking at meetings, luncheons, teas, and other events. As a component of her international crusade against lynching, she also wrote articles for dissemination at home and abroad. Her activities and messages received broad transnational exposure through the British press.

This trip abroad gave Wells her first opportunity to spread her message about lynching in America to a broader, transnational audience and to obtain international support for her crusade against lynching. Wells had reason to be optimistic. She already had two influential women as allies in these prominent British reformers, and just as abolitionist Frederick Douglass believed his visit to Great Britain in 1846 would cause British public opinion to pressure the US to end slavery, Wells understood that international pressure on the US might be a powerful means of persuading the government to not only end lynching, but to bring about equal justice for Black citizens. A comment Impey made confirms Wells' intent: "[Wells] maintains that British opinion and protest will have a great force, and for this reason has determined to hold meetings in the principal cities here. She is delighted with the reception hereto accorded her, and feels greatly encouraged."[51]

Wells embraced her role as the guiding force behind the anti-lynching campaign, first meeting with "local celebrities" who formed a "new society" to assist in the cause. Her implementation of the two-way symmetrical public relations model is evident. "When introduced to speak, I told the same heart-stirring episodes which first gained for me the sympathy and good will of my New York friends. The facts [messages] I related were enough of themselves to arrest and hold the attention. They needed no embellishment, nor oratory from me," Wells recounted in her autobiography.[52]

Wells realized that message creation and dissemination are important steps in a public relations campaign. A practitioner first creates messages about an issue or problem aimed at causing an action. Stakeholders then have to pay attention to, understand, and accept the messages. In the process, those stakeholders can form, retain, or change an opinion or attitude, and possibly act.[53] Messages should be persuasive as they inform, and in order for persuasion to occur, messages must be based on solid, logical arguments, supported by facts and statistics. Emotional appeals also contribute to the persuasiveness of messages.[54]

At home, Wells had framed her message through the lens of debunking the moralistic myth that justified lynching. Applied to public relations, framing involves "inclusion, exclusion and emphasis," which is important when addressing issues and policy debates that can involve the treatment or portrayal of groups in society.[55] Social movements, grassroots organizations, and interest groups also employ framing in their advocacy activities.[56] Wells employed different tactics and messages overseas. The crusader had learned that the British perceived lynching as a kind of "frontier justice" committed by isolated communities that lacked access to an effective legal system.[57] "Whereas her American lectures frequently discussed lynching and Jim Crow as a betrayal of "American institutions," according to Bay,[58] Wells' recast message for English audiences countered that view by harkening to Britain's glorious antislavery movement to illustrate that conditions in the South betrayed abolition, and contending that lynching was an inhuman and brutal crime against all Blacks.[59] Such messages sought to not only capture attention but also to rouse the ire and indignation of her host country in order to change the status quo in her home country. Emotional appeals were evident in Wells' graphic details that directly addressed accomplishing an attitudinal goal of creating moral outrage. That, in turn, would lead to a behavior—condemnation of the barbaric practice and passage of legislation to end it.

The special issue of the *Anti-Caste* that preceded the visit was an equally useful and persuasive reinforcement. The editors published a vivid picture of the January 1893 lynching in Clanton, Alabama, where gleeful men, women, and children stood nearby. As Caroline Karcher offers, the editor's imagery "dramatized the brutality of lynching to powerful effect and contrasted the 'shameless satisfaction on the faces of the men' in the photograph with the 'innocent wonder of those of the children.'"[60] Such behavior conveyed to the children how a Black person should be treated, including not being afforded a trial or given the opportunity to present a defense.

Due to the actions of Wells and her host reformers, the press, indeed, paid attention to Wells' visit. For instance, the May 6, 1893, issue of the London-based publication, *Society*, reported about the expectancy of Wells' stop in that city and noted that she had spoken to fifteen hundred men as she opened her campaign in Aberdeen. Other publications chronicled her activities, including the meetings she attended, what she said, and the reaction of the audiences. Some publications ran her letters to the editor, and some offered commentary. For instance, the *Peterhead Sentinel and Buchanan Journal* reported on May 2, 1893, that Wells had spoken about lynchings at meetings the previous week, and it added the following:

> The facts that are set forth go to show very clearly that, although slavery in the Southern areas of America is believed to have been abolished when the American War closed, the lot of the colored people in these parts is little better than when slavery was in full force. The people are uniformly treated as people of an inferior caste, they are subjected to every possible indignity, they are denied all rights of citizens, and when they give any manner of offence to the white man, they are tried according to summary methods of Judge Lynch.[61]

Wells' message had gained traction and was reaching additional influential publics/ stakeholders.

Four days later, the *Newcastle Leader* reported that large audiences at two meetings had heard Wells give "some harrowing instances of the injustice to members of her race, of their being socially ostracized and frequently lynched in the most barbarous fashion by mobs on mere suspicion and without any trial whatsoever."[62] Accounts in the *Edinburgh Evening Gazette* used such adjectives as "influential" and "crowded assembly" to describe meetings where Wells had spoken on Friday, Saturday, and Sunday. Noting that Wells had spoken at more than one meeting on Saturday and that she was gaining more supporters on each stop, the article reported: "She has everywhere been heard with deep attention and interest, and has evoked unanimous expressions of sympathy."[63] The same tenor of reporting occurred prior to, during, and after Wells' visit to a particular city.

In England, her letters to the editor ran in the *Birmingham Daily Post* and the *Liverpool Daily Post*. These and other British papers also ran their own editorials and articles about Wells' trip. One particular article, titled "Breaking the Silent Indifference," detailed Wells' success in getting exposure in the British press, offering that newspapers devoted "columns of reports on her meetings, as well as splendid editorials."[64] The May 18, 1893, issue of the *Birmingham Daily Gazette* had a "wonderful, full-two column editorial, and another full-column news report of the Birmingham meeting."[65] The *Birmingham Daily Post* of the same date also carried a report of the meeting under the caption "LYNCH LAW IN AMERICA."[66]

The British people afforded Wells "a platform from which to tell the Negro's side of the gruesome story of lynching, and to appeal to Christian and moral forces for help in the demand that every accused person be given a fair trial by law and not by the mob."[67] As a result, they also became voices for the anti-lynching campaign

and their publications became advocates for ending the murders. The opinion leaders also were highly credible spokespersons for Wells' efforts.[68] Yet, although Wells'
efforts increased visibility about the issue and secured credible supporters of the
cause, the visit did not accomplish the goal of British pressure on the United States
to end lynching. The visit concluded abruptly because a major dispute between
Impey and Mayo that caused the collapse of organizational planning and financial
support for Wells.[69] Wells would travel to Great Britain less than a year later.

Back at home, Wells redoubled her efforts to continue her anti-lynching campaign with fervor. Robert L. Heath argues that public relations practitioners "design,
place, and repeat messages . . . that shape views of government," and that they
"speak, write, and use visual images to discuss topics and take stances on public
policies at the local, state, and federal levels."[70] Wells understood that in order to
influence public opinion, she would have to reach whites and government officials
and that her arguments would have to be credible and based on facts that could be
substantiated.[71] In the coming years, she continued to spread the word and tell the
truth on an international level.

CONTINUING THE CRUSADE: DOCUMENTING THE "SOUTHERN HORROR" THROUGH PAMPHLETS

Painstaking research by Wells led to the publication of three pamphlets in the coming years, the first of which appeared within weeks after Wells returned from her
first trip to Great Britain and within a year of the second sojourn abroad. *Southern
Horrors: Lynch Law in All Its Phases* presented in twenty-five pages of pamphlet form
even more evidence than Wells had through the press or in speeches in the United
States or abroad, and it reinforced her messages. As with her speeches and articles,
the goal was to provide documentation on the record about the barbarity of lynching
and its impact on Black citizens in the US. In professional public relations, producing pamphlets and brochures is a major means of conveying messages that are both
portable and sustainable. By design, pamphlets and brochures can be read multiple
times and transferred to multiple audiences.[72] That is what occurred with *Southern
Horrors*.

To produce *Southern Horrors*, Wells located and read hundreds of articles that
described the gruesome details of the murders as well as facts and figures, dates,
locations, and the number and names of Black men, women, and children killed
each year. Her sources included the Associated Press and credible white newspapers
such as the *Times-Picayune* in New Orleans and the *Chicago Tribune* that carried
official explanations for the killings. The latter began publishing lynching statistics in
1882.[73] Wells then crisscrossed the South to gather information about the murders
where they occurred. Firsthand information also came from people who knew individuals who had met that terrible fate or who had other pertinent details.[74]

As in previous communication, the content nullified the accepted rationale
for lynching. Raw data and news articles revealed that neither age nor gender

was a deterrent because thousands of Black men, women, and children were murdered between 1882 and 1892.[75] Because Wells had traveled to sites of the lynchings, interviewed relatives of victims or those aware of the crimes, and conducted other research, she was able to offer relevant examples. For instance, she included details about a woman who met the noose for allegedly killing her white female boss, and another who suffered the same fate after being accused of murdering a man identified as her abusive white lover.[76] It was clear that no Black person was safe, Wells noted, as she rhetorically asked silent "Christians" in the US why America failed to protect Black citizens and denied them human rights. Instead, the government sent "state troops to shoot them down like cattle when in desperation" when Black men tried "to defend themselves."[77] Reinforcing her message and arguably appealing to people's sensibilities to stir outrage, Wells described the brutal death of a Black man—also accused of rape. The mob tied him to a tree, chipped away his flesh, and doused him with coal oil before his alleged victim set him afire.[78]

Continuing to frame her argument that economic reprisal was the motive for lynching, Wells pointed to the circumstances surrounding Moss' murder. The pamphlet emphasized that the Memphis white community resented and feared the upwardly mobile and increasingly well-educated and financially secure Black community. Whites just would not stand for direct competition to their businesses.[79] Blacks "were horrified when they realized they had no protection under the law and the freedoms they once had was no longer available."[80]

Such thorough research gave Wells credibility and enabled her to respond to critics. She once told a writer who challenged her that he could check the same sources she had, including prominent publications in the nation, books, and journals that carried the information regularly. Wells argued that there was no excuse for anyone to accept the lie about lynching when the truth was so thoroughly well-documented. There was no assault upon white womanhood.[81] One man's crime was writing a note to a white woman that confirmed their intimacy.[82] The findings showed convincingly that Black men were "being branded as a race of rapists" of white women and "moral monsters" by those who sought "to justify these horrible atrocities to the world."[83] This horrible stereotype robbed them "of all the friends" they had and quieted "those who might have protested on their behalf."[84]

ACROSS THE POND AGAIN: A SECOND TRANSNATIONAL LECTURE TOUR

A year had not elapsed when Wells went back to Great Britain. Before leaving in March 1894, she arranged to chronicle her overseas campaign as a foreign correspondent for the *Chicago Inter-Ocean*, a white publication. She sent back letters that recapped her experiences and talks at various locations from March through July. The first correspondence to the *Inter-Ocean* asserted that Wells had gladly accepted the invitation to travel abroad again, and reiterated concerns about her unsuccessful attempts to gain attention in white publications at home and thus rally the American people against what was "fast becoming a national evil."[85]

Her *Newcastle Notes* of May 28, 1894, offered a report on British reaction to lynching. *Southern Horrors* had made Reverend Walter Walsh, minister of more than one thousand congregants, "ill with horror." The same letter revealed that all of the five newspapers in Newcastle had interviewed Wells "and given extended accounts of meetings."[86] Reflecting her overarching campaign goal again, Wells offered: "When my own countrymen and women take hold of the lynching matter in the same vigorous way, a means will be found to free our country from mob murder and lynching disgraces."[87]

Mainstream newspapers and others at home paid attention to Wells' activities. For instance, one of Wells' dispatches commented that the *Memphis Daily Commercial* had called her a "Negro adventuress" and "violently" castigated the British for giving her an audience. Wells countered: "If I am become [*sic*] an adventuress for stating the facts when invited to do so, by what name must be characterized those who furnish the facts, and those who give the encouragement of their silence to them. However revolting these lynchings, I did not commit a single one of them, nor could the wildest efforts of my imagination manufacture one to equal their reality."[88]

She referred to that newspaper in subsequent dispatches, including in the July 7 issue. Writing that the *Daily Commercial*'s May 26 edition referred to her in "vulgar and obscene" language,[89] Wells charged that it failed to prove anything it said about her. Pointing out that the editors of the newspaper had "flooded England with copies of the paper," Wells clearly was delighted that London newspapers "would not touch the *Commercial*'s articles with a pair of tongs. . . . That *Commercial* article has brought warmer friends and stronger supporters to the anti-lynching cause than it perhaps would have had otherwise."[90]

This second trip, indeed, accomplished Wells' goals of informing to shape public opinion, to mold or change attitudes, and to secure allies who exerted pressure on the US. She later wrote that she did so many interviews abroad that she had difficulty keeping track of them.[91] British journalists understood, reported on, and supported her cause. Their publications also condemned lynching. Her missives to the *Inter-Ocean* named influential individuals and groups in Great Britain that also condemned lynching.

During visits to Glasgow, Edinburgh, Manchester, Birmingham, London, and other cities, Wells spoke at meetings, luncheons, teas, and other events that provided an avenue through which she could disseminate her logical and persuasive messages in person and, by extension, through the British press. She also raised funds and cultivated relationships with opinion leaders in England and Scotland to win support for her cause.[92] She succeeded in garnering both, as a letter Impey wrote to a fellow supporter reflects: "Miss Wells has made an impression on the minds of thousands (perhaps ten thousand direct—beside those who read press accounts)."[93]

Wells returned to the US in July after having appeared before groups 102 times, and having secured "moral support" from across the pond.[94] "The Christian, moral, and social forces of Great Britain had nobly responded to our appeal, and caused the whole civilized world to acknowledge that it was the duty of civilized nations to exert moral force against the lynching infamy."[95] An invitation the South extended for Britons "to come see for themselves" backfired, because the Duke of Argyle and "the Anti-Lynching Committee" he headed accepted.[96] As we have seen in a previous chapter, negative reaction to the delegation by Southern governors received attention in such mainstream publications as the *New York World,* the *New York Times,* and the *Literary Digest.* The Black press chronicled the investigation and the committee's negative view of lynching. The manner in which those abroad perceived the South—as Wells had hoped—arguably had an impact, because soon after the visit, the *Memphis Commercial Appeal,* long a supporter of the status quo, criticized the lynching of a Black man. Sheriff's deputies who were in charge when the man was lynched were soon arrested.[97] The reaction to a letter of support Wells received from "leading ministers of all denominations" in Great Britain further indicates the success of her overseas campaign.[98] The missive paved the way for her to speak before white churches and other groups where she traveled. The future national lecture circuit included such cities as New York, Philadelphia, Washington, and Providence in the North, almost every area in the South, and two months in the West and Midwest. As Wells remembered, the letter was important "because our American ministers knew this powerful committee in London would receive reports as to their attitude on this burning question."[99]

THE REAL REASON: TERROR AND SUBJUGATION

Wells' on-going travels and research led to her second publication, which scholars called "the first comprehensive history of lynching."[100] *A Red Record: Tabulated Statistics and Alleged Causes of Lynching in the United States, 1892–1893–1894*[101] traced the genesis of the crime. The pamphlet elaborated on the spread of lynching, the political and economic rationale for the sanctioned murders, and the role racial prejudice played in the spread of lynching bees. That rationale began with the need to "stamp out alleged 'race riots,'" followed by the desire to take away Black suffrage, and then progressing to the protection of white womanhood narrative.[102] That was the real excuse, and organized terror against Blacks was the result.

Wells again reminded readers that the empirical data she presented were "gathered and preserved by white men," and they had "not been questioned."[103] Those statistics showed that "more than ten thousand Negroes have been killed in cold blood," primarily by white men, while not one white person had been lynched for killing a Black person.[104] Wells hoped she had presented a convincing and credible argument that could appeal to logic. As noted above, the use of credible sources as well as statistics in public relations contribute to the trustworthiness and persuasiveness of the argument, and as Bay noted, *A Red Record* "was written in accordance with the methodology advocated by the sociologists of her day."[105]

MOBILIZING FOR GOVERNMENT
ACTION: THE NEXT STEP

After marrying prominent Chicago lawyer and newspaper owner Ferdinand Barnett in 1895, Wells-Barnett continued writing in the press and producing pamphlets, but she also engaged in other public relations activities aimed at securing government action. In March 1898, for instance, she mobilized a mass meeting of Blacks in Chicago to protest the death of the newly appointed Black postmaster in Lake City, South Carolina. Frazier B. Baker, his wife, and three of their four children were killed.[106] In addition to collecting funds at a meeting for Baker's family, Wells-Barnett collected money to travel to the White House and meet with President William McKinley to press the federal government to investigate Baker's death.

Seven Congressmen and one state senator attended the meeting with Wells-Barnett, who presented a petition to the president titled "Justice Like Charity."[107] Her message was that before the US sent Black citizens to fight in the Spanish-American War, the country "should attend to the 'slaughter' of African Americans at home by punishing Baker's murderers and taking action against lynching."[108] The petition did not secure justice for Baker and his family, but the relentless pressure Wells-Barnett and other Black leaders put on President McKinley resulted in the first federal proceedings against a lynch mob, according to Bay. This was an example of Wells-Barnett working with and persuading crucial stakeholders to act.

In 1900, Wells-Barnett published another pamphlet titled *Mob Rule in New Orleans: Robert Charles and His Fight to the Death*. This publication was more in-depth than the previous two. Here, again, Wells-Barnett employed the persuasive technique of using credible, trustworthy sources to reinforce her argument. Referring to details from two white newspapers in New Orleans, she highlighted "accounts of brutality, injustice and oppression" in the city.[109] *Mob Rule* told the story of the lynching of Robert Charles, who defended himself while being pursued by a mob of white men after an altercation with the police wherein he shot and killed several men and wounded others who were trying to enter a house where he was hiding. Charles died in a hail of bullets, shot beyond recognition, according to Wells-Barnett, and was dragged through the streets of the city. Here is Wells-Barnett's chilling detail of Charles' predicament:

> In any law abiding [sic] community Charles would have been justified in delivering himself up immediately to the properly constituted authorities and asking for a trial by a jury of his peers. He could have been certain that in resisting an unwarranted arrest he had a right to defend his life, even to the point of taking one in that defense, but Charles knew that his arrest in New Orleans, even for defending his life, means nothing short of a long term in the penitentiary, and still more probable death by lynching at the hands of a cowardly mob.[110]

Also reinforcing the fallacy of the myth regarding white women, Wells-Barnett's message in this publication was that innocent people could be lynched at any time for any reason. Statistics again revealed that Blacks were lynched for such purported causes as "slapping a child," "colonizing Negroes," and "disobeying quarantine."[111] Black women and children were not spared. The precarious nature of Black existence was clear as Wells-Barnett related details she had read in the newspaper about the murder of a Black man who was walking down the street following Charles' death. The mob beat and shot the man for no other reason than the color of his skin, Wells-Barnett wrote.[112] Following the model of her previous works, Wells-Barnett offered updated empirical statistics on the number of people lynched and the reasons for the lynchings from 1896 through 1900. It was clear that the overarching rationale included racial intolerance and subjugation, race prejudice, and suppression of the Black vote in order to maintain the economic and political power of the dominant society.

Such messages were aimed at doing more than creating awareness, but at evoking emotion, even revulsion, among those who might have had a different view of how and why lynching was conducted. In public relations, there is often a call to action. Wells-Barnett issued several. She often called for the arousal of "public sentiment" against rampant lawlessness.[113] She cloaked her messages in love of country, patriotism, and how the world would view white civilization, pointing out that lynching had affected each of those areas. Lynching was "a blight upon our nation."[114] She also called the government to action, insisting that it hold a conference and establish a bureau to track lynching. She also charged the National Afro-American Council, a prominent Black organization, to create an Anti-Lynching Bureau to collect data on lynching and publicize its findings.[115] This was a role Wells-Barnett was almost alone in fulfilling. America also should commit to ending the lawless murders, pay restitution to the families of victims, and protect Blacks, Wells-Barnett contended.[116]

The death of a Georgia farmer in 1900 provided another opportunity for Wells-Barnett to spread her message and champion her cause. Sam Hose was burned alive, and the killers and their audience fought for samples of his flesh, Wells-Barnett wrote in "Lynch Law in Georgia."[117] She and other Black community members hired a white private investigator, Louis Levin, to look into Hose's death. The investigation found that Hose was murdered and was in the same category as four out of every five Black persons who were unjustly lynched without a jury trial.[118] For Wells-Barnett, it was important to refer to and discredit the concept of the Black moral monster.

The anti-lynching campaign continued in other locations. Following a three-day race riot in Springfield, Illinois, in August 1908, in which three Black men were lynched, Wells-Barnett began to lay the groundwork for the Negro Fellowship League (NFL) that, as we will see in a later chapter, would be another influential voice and valuable ally in her social justice crusade. As one of the speakers at a dinner the Congregation Union sponsored, Wells-Barnett not only provided statistics on lynching, she also pleaded for a fair trial for anyone accused of a crime.[119] Not long after the Springfield riot, a mob in Cairo, Illinois, with the sheriff's compliance, lynched William "Frog" James, a Black man accused of raping a white salesgirl. According to Bay, some ten thousand men, women, and children participated. Some even removed James' "heart and other organs to preserve as souvenirs. They also cut off his head—which they mounted on the fencepost nearest the scene of the crime."[120]

Wells-Barnett traveled to Cairo and learned that Black community members believed James was guilty of the crime. In other words, they accepted the narrative those in power offered, and they supported Sheriff Frank Davis, who was removed from his position. Wells-Barnett asked Black community members to consider that they had condoned "the horrible lynching of a fellowman who was a member of his race."[121] She also pointed out that the same fate could befall any one of them. She asked them to pass a resolution calling for the ouster of the sheriff who had not protected the man who was in his custody.

Visits to other Black community members in their homes followed as Wells-Barnett gathered evidence; before traveling to the site of the lynching, Wells-Barnett reported on her observations and made a persuasive argument against reinstating Sheriff Davis at a meeting the following day. One elderly man who had written a letter supporting the sheriff offered the following: "But now that the sister has shown us plainly the construction that would be placed on that letter, I want her to tell the governor tomorrow that I take that letter back and hereby sign my name to this resolution."[122] Wells-Barnett also had explained to the large gathering that she understood their circumstance as residents of the area who could face retaliation if they opposed the sheriff and lynching. "I said I had come down to be their mouthpiece," she wrote in her memoir.[123]

Springfield was the next stop because Wells-Barnett wanted to be present when the sheriff appeared before Governor Charles S. Deneen to appeal his dismissal from office. Following the lynching, Wells-Barnett had called on him to propose legislation that would remove any sheriff who allowed prisoners to be taken from him and lynched. Such measures were primarily symbolic because any sheriff could make his case before the governor and be reinstated. After Davis and a myriad of lawyers and other prominent people made their cases, Wells-Barnett outlined the facts she had uncovered, as well as the resolution the NFL had adopted. "It looked like encouragement to the mob to have the chief law officer in the county take that man up in the woods and keep him until the mob got big enough to come after him," Wells-Barnett told the governor, adding "if this man is reinstated, it will simply mean an increase of lynchings in the state of Illinois and encouragement to mob violence."[124] She successfully argued against reinstatement.

Her message was a solid argument that changed the attitude of key stakeholders and opinion leaders. As a matter of fact, following her address to the governor, "all of the white men came over," shook her hand, and congratulated her on a "wonderful speech."[125] Even Sheriff Davis told her he did not have a grudge against her. Finally, and most importantly, the governor ruled against reinstating the sheriff, agreeing with Wells-Barnett that Davis had not sufficiently protected the prisoner, and writing that "lynch law could have no place in Illinois."[126] No lynchings occurred in the state after 1909. Wells-Barnett accomplished her goal. As Bay notes, "Ida's work on the Cairo lynching helped her find new supporters."[127]

The foregoing example illustrates aspects of a public relations effort. Wells-Barnett became a credible spokesperson because, as was her usual method, she began with research to find the facts from trusted sources, convened and attended meetings, engaged in eyewitness observation, built relationships based on trust and the credible information she provided, made compelling and convincing arguments against lynching, and precipitated an action.

Not long after that, Wells-Barnett became a founding member of the National Association for the Advancement of Colored People, which made preventing lynching a major part of its platform. Hence, Wells-Barnett had taken her campaign to another level, enlisting the support of Blacks and whites. Scholars say the organization followed "Wells' proposed program almost to the letter," although as we will see in a later chapter, she received little of the credit.[128] As she continued her campaign, Wells-Barnett wrote other persuasive pieces that appealed to emotions and reason, again based on statistical and qualitative evidence. In "How Enfranchisement Stops Lynching," Wells-Barnett traced lynching from the fifty-two people murdered in 1882, showing a continued increase until 1892, then a decrease for the next decade, followed by a rise.[129] Throughout the campaign, Wells-Barnett's critique of lynching was far-reaching. "Long a critic of segregation, disfranchisement, and mob violence against Blacks, Wells linked them all in her discussion of the Memphis murders, fashioning a compelling new image of lynching as the 'Southern horror' that sustained Jim Crow," Bay wrote.[130]

As in public relations, where message repetition contributes to understanding and acceptance, Wells-Barnett's messages had a recurring theme—the fallacy of the notion that Black men raped white women. In fact, she continually wrote and said white women often initiated relationships with Black men, as the following excerpt indicates:

> The more I studied the situation, the more I was convinced that the Southerner had never gotten over his resentment that the Negro was no longer his plaything, his servant, and his source of income. . . . Hence came lynch law to stifle Negro manhood which defended itself and the burning alive of Negroes who were weak enough to accept favors from white women.[131]

"Lynching: Our National Crime" was an informational and persuasive message Wells-Barnett delivered. It later became part of the published proceeding of the National Negro Conference.[132] "Our Country: Lynching Record" called for a cessation of lynching and simultaneously exposed the fallacy of the accepted narrative.[133] Governor Deneen of Illinois had condemned lynching, but many others had "refused to deal sternly with the leaders of mobs or to enforce the law against lynchers."[134]

The South was a major focus of Wells-Barnett's messages, but events in the North did not escape her as she lamented the acceptance of the falsehood on which the murders were based. "In the thirty years in which lynching has been going on in the South," Wells wrote, "this falsehood has been offered by the thousands as universally accepted in all sections of our country."[135] People readily believed the propaganda, and no one spoke out "against these terrible outrages."[136] From a public relations perspective, this type of message can lead to action.

NO LONGER NEGLECTED

Wells, indeed, was a public relations pioneer in the tradition of the "great [white] men" whom historians have recognized since the beginning of the profession. She employed public relations strategies and tactics long before Lee, Bernays, and other pioneers did. Beginning in the 1890s and continuing into the twentieth century, she spearheaded numerous public relations initiatives and activities. Chief among them was the anti-lynching campaign she conceived of and skillfully implemented.

Campaigns can inform, create awareness, educate, reinforce, modify an attitude and behavior, or cause a behavior.[137] Wells' campaign, then, fit that mold. It was a comprehensive, coordinated, and on-going campaign, and it aligned with every element of public relations campaigns as we know them today. In that manner, she arguably surpassed the "great [white] men" pioneers who did not incorporate research, the first element in the public relations process.

Wells began with that element and uncovered the real truth about lynching. It was armed terrorism aimed at subjugating a race of people economically and politically. Equipped with that information, she solidified her major goal of ending the brutal murders of innocent Black men, women, and children by providing a compelling counter-narrative that revealed the fallacy of lynching. Through her efforts, whites could no longer justify their barbarism on the basis of fallacies.

Acting as an advocate—which public relations practitioners routinely do, Wells crafted persuasive messages and communicated them through articles, letters, and pamphlets. Public relations scholars argue that identifying and building dialogic relationships is central to the practice. That is what Wells did. She communicated with and built relationships with key stakeholders and public officials. She marshaled her organizational skills to coordinate and speak at events and meetings that influenced public opinion and attitude. She took her campaign on the road, lecturing at home and in Great Britain, where its press also ran her articles and covered her activities. Her transnational discourse garnered the international support that helped change the racial status quo in the US. She made compelling arguments before the public, the press, elected officials, and the president of the United States.

These strategies and tactics preceded many that "great [white] men" pioneers employed. Wells was more than a journalist-in-residence in the mode of Ivy Ledbetter Lee, known as the father of the field. Like Bernays and other early practitioners, Wells provided advice and counsel to her publics as she strategized to accomplish a goal. Unlike the early pioneers, she was not working for a client; rather, she was working on behalf of Blacks in a way she believed would benefit her race and her country by making it live up to its promise.

Largely because of her exposés and her public relations strategies and tactics, Wells accomplished her goal. Her efforts and leadership led to the creation of anti-lynching sentiments and action in the US and in England. Lynchings slowly declined from a high of 241 in 1892 to 107 seven years later.[138] The anti-lynching Blair Resolution was introduced in Congress in 1894, and six states passed anti-lynching measures between 1893 and 1897. Illinois, for instance, ended lynching in 1909, and although the Blair Resolution failed, North Carolina, Georgia, South Carolina, Ohio, Kentucky, and Texas passed legislation to end lynchings.[139] Wells, therefore, should be included in the cannons of literature as a consummate and successful public relations pioneer.

NOTES

1. "Into the Hands of the Mob," *Memphis Appeal-Avalanche*, March 10, 1892, 1.

2. Mia Bay, *To Tell the Truth Freely: The Life of Ida B. Wells* (New York: Hill & Wang, 2009), 87–88.

3. Ida B. Wells, *Crusade for Justice: The Autobiography of Ida B. Wells*, edited by Alfreda M. Duster (Chicago: University of Chicago Press, 1970), 47–57.

4. Ibid.

5. Ibid., 51–52.

6. Ibid., 47; Bay, *To Tell the Truth Freely,* 89.

7. Nevertheless, historians often ascribe the title of the first public relations counsel to Bernays. Maureen H. Beasley, "The Emergence of Modern Media, 1900–1945," in Wm. David Sloan, *The Media in America: A History,* ninth edition. (Northport, AL: Vision, 2014), 311; Karen Miller Russell, "Public Relations 1900-Present," in Wm. David Sloan, ed., *The Media in America,* eighth edition. (Northport, AL: Vision, 2011), 445–58.

8. Ibid.; For reference, see Scott M. Cutlip, *Public Relations from the 17th Century* (Hillsdale, NJ: Lawrence Erlbaum and Associates, 1995); Ray Eldon Heibert, *Courtier to the Crowd: The Story of Ivy Lee and the Development of Public Relations* (Ames: Iowa State University Press, 1966); Kirk Hallahan, "Ivy Lee and the Rockefellers' Response to the 1913–1914 Colorado Coal Strike," *Journal of PR Research* 14 (2002): 264–314. A former newspaper man who had worked for the *New York Times* and *New York World,* Lee co-founded the nation's third publicity bureau in 1905. The tactics he employed while working for the Pennsylvania Railroad Company and for John D. Rockefeller during the Colorado Fuel and Oil Company Strike in 1913 are considered milestones in public relations. Most notably, Lee published his "Declaration of Principles" that made presentation of factual information to the public the goal of public relations in order to bring about support, understanding, and acceptance.

9. Kirk Hallahan, "W.L. Mackenzie King: Rockefeller's 'Other' Public Relations Counselor in Colorado," *Public Relations Review* 29.4 (2003): 401–14.

10. Scott Cutlip, "Lithuania's First Independence Battle: A PR Footnote," *Public Relations Review* 16.4 (1990): 12–16, 2003.

11. Karen S. Miller, "Edward Bernays: Public Relations Pioneer," in Margaret A. Blanchard, ed., *History of the Mass Media in the United States: An Encyclopedia* (New York: Routledge, 1999), 57.

12. Robert Kendall, *Public Relations Campaign Strategies*, second edition. (New York: Addison Wesley Longman, 1996), 23.

13. See, for, example, Dean Newsom, Judy Vandyke Turk, and Dean Kruckeberg, *This Is PR: The Realities of Public Relations* (Independence, KY: Cengage Learning, 2013).

14. Research remains the first component regardless of whether the public relations model is RACE (Research, Action, Communication, and Evaluation), ROPE (acronym for Research, Objectives, Programming, and Evaluation), or other iterations. For reference, see Scott M. Cutlip, Allen H. Center, and Glen M. Broom, *Effective Public Relations* (Englewood Cliff, NJ: Prentice Hall, 1994); Ronald Smith, *Strategic Planning for Public Relations,* third edition. (New York: Routledge, 2009); W. Timothy Coombs and Sherry J. Holladay, *PR Strategy and Application* (Malden, MA: Wiley-Blackwell Publications, 2010); Dennis L. Wilcox, Glen T. Cameron, Bryan H. Reber, and Jae-Hwa Shin, *Think Public Relations* (Boston: Pearson, 2013).

15. Ibid.

16. Wells, *Crusade for Justice, 65.*

17. Ibid., 84.

18. James E. Grunig and Todd S. Hunt, *Managing Public Relations* (New York: Holt, Reinhart and Winston, 1984).

19. Ida B. Wells, editorial in *Free Speech*, as cited in Wells, *Crusade for Justice*, 52.

20. Wells, *Crusade for Justice*, 52.

21. Wells, editorial in *Free Speech*, as cited in Wells, *Crusade for Justice*, 65–66.

22. Ibid., 64.

23. Ibid., 52.

24. Ibid., 53.

25. Ibid., 54.

26. Ibid., 55.

27. Ibid., 52.

28. *Memphis Appeal-Avalanche*, June 8, 1891, as cited in Linda O. McMurry, *To Keep the Waters Troubled: The Life of Ida B. Wells* (New York: Oxford University Press, 1988), 147.

29. For reference, see, Trudier Harris, comp., *Selected Works of Ida B. Wells-Barnett* (New York: Oxford University Press, 1991), 18; Herbert Shapiro, *White Violence and Black Response: From Reconstruction to Montgomery* (Boston: University of Massachusetts Press, 1988), 55.

30. *Weekly Appeal-Avalanche,* March 23 1892, 4; *Weekly Appeal-Avalanche*, April 27, 1892, 1, as cited in Wells, *Crusade for Justice*, 57.

31. See, for example, Armistead S. Pride and Clint C. Wilson, *A History of the Black Press,* (Washington, DC: Howard University Press, 1997).

32. Ibid., 71.

33. Wells, *Crusade for Justice*, 78.

34. Bay, *To Tell the Truth Freely*, 108.

35. Ida B. Wells, "Exiled," *New York Age*, June 5, 1892.

36. *Memphis Appeal-Avalanche,* June 30, 1892, 5, is cited in Wells, *Crusade for Justice*, 77.

37. For reference, see, Cutlip, *Public Relations from the 17th Century*, ix; Wilcox, Cameron, Reber, and Shin, *Think Public Relations*.

38. See, for example, Pride and Wilson, *A History of the Black Press*; Jinx Coleman Broussard, *Giving a Voice to the Voiceless* (New York: Routledge, 2004); Jinx Coleman Broussard, *African American Foreign Correspondents: A History* (Baton Rouge, LA: LSU Press, 2013); Carl Senna, *The Black Press and the Struggle for Civil Rights*, (Danbury, CT: Scholastic Library Publishing, 1994).

39. McMurry, *To Keep the Waters Troubled,* 154. It would later appear in such white papers as the *Chicago Inter-Ocean,* as well as in the British press when she traveled abroad. For reference, see, Miriam DeCosta-Willis, *The Memphis Diary of Ida B. Wells* (Boston: Beacon Press, 1995).

40. Wells, *Crusade for* Justice, 86.

41. Ibid., 87.

42. Mia Bay, *To Tell the Truth Freely: The Life of Ida B. Wells* (New York: Hill & Wang, 2009), 133–34.

43. Ibid., 141.

44. For reference, see John A. Ledingham and Stephen D. Bruning, eds. *Public Relations Management: A Relational Approach to the Study of Public Relations* (Mahwah, NJ: 2000); Newsom, Turk, and Kruckeberg, *Realities of PR.*

45. Bay, *To Tell the Truth Freely*, 136.

46. Wells, *Crusade for Justice*, 82.

47. Ibid., 85.

48. Mayo was a novelist who wrote under the pen name Edward Garrett in Scotland and England. While visiting Impey, she asked if her host had found out on her trip to America the previous year that the country was burning people alive. For reference, see Wells, *Crusade for Justice*, 85.

49. Ibid.

50. Ibid., 89–90.

51. Ibid., 100.

52. Ibid., 90.

53. For reference, see Cutlip, Center, and Broom, *Effective Public Relations*, 359.

54. Robert Seiter and John S. Glass, *Persuasion, Social Influence, and Compliance Gaining*, fourth edition. (Boston: Allyn and Bacon, 2010), 33; Richard Perloff, *The Dynamics of Persuasion: Communication and Attitudes in the 21st Century*, fourth edition. (New York: Routledge, 2010).

55. Kirk Hallahan, "Seven Models of Framing: Implications for Public Relations," *Journal of Public Relations Research* 11.3 (1999): 217.

56. Kirk Hallahan, "Political Public Relations and Strategic Framing," in Jesper Stromback and Spiro Iiousis, *Political Public Relations: Principles and Applications* (New York: Routledge, 2011), 118.

57. Sarah L. Silkey, "Redirecting the Tide of White Imperialism: The Impact of Ida B. Well's Transatlantic Antilynching Campaign in British Conception of American Race Relations," In Angela Boswell and Judith N. McArthur, eds. *Women Shaping the South: Creating and Confronting Change*, (Columbia: University of Missouri Press, 2006), 100. As cited in Bay, *To Tell the Truth Freely*, 141.

58. Bay, *To Tell the Truth Freely*, 144.

59. Ibid., Bay cites *Anti-Caste* 3, nos. 7 and 8 (July and August 1890).

60. Carolyn L. Karcher, "Ida B. Wells and Her Allies against Lynching: A Transnational Perspective," *Comparative American Studies* 3.2 (2005); as cited in Bay, *To Tell the Truth Freely*, 142.

61. Wells, *Crusade for Justice*, 91–92.

62. Ibid., 95.

63. Ibid., 92.

64. Ibid., 95.

65. Ibid.

66. Ibid., 96.

67. Ibid.,101.

68. Ibid., 98–99. Also, for explanations of source credibility, see such references as Michael D. Slater and Donna Rouner, "How Message Evaluation and Source Attributes May Influence Credibility Assessment and Belief Change," *Journalism and Mass Communication Quarterly* 73.4 (1996): 974–91; Elliot Aronson and Bruce W. Golden, "The Effect of Relevant and Irrelevant Aspects of Communicator Credibility on Opinion Change," *Personality* 30.2 (1962): 135–46.

69. Ibid.

70. Robert L. Heath and Elizabeth Toth, *Rhetorical and Critical Approaches to Public Relations*, second edition. (Thousand Oaks, CA: 2009), 18.

71. Wells, *Crusade for Justice*, 86.

72. For reference, see Doug Newsom and Jim Haynes, *Public Relations Writing: Form and Style*, tenth edition. (Wadsworth Cengage Learning: Boston, 2011), 286.

73. Wells, *Crusade for Justice*, xxii.

74. Ibid., 272.

75. Ida B. Wells, "Lynch Law in All Its Phases," *Our Story* (May 1893): 333–37, reprinted in Mildred Thompson, *Ida B. Wells*, 171–87.

76. Ibid., 183.

77. Ibid.

78. Ibid.

79. Ibid., 176.

80. Ibid.

81. Ibid., 250.

82. Bay, *To Tell the Truth Freely*, 102.

83. Wells, *Crusade for Justice*, 71.

84. Ibid.

85. Ida B. Wells, *Inter-Ocean*, April 2, 1894, cited in Wells, *Crusade for Justice*, 128.

86. Ida B. Wells, *Inter-Ocean*, May 28, 1894, cited in Wells, *Crusade for Justice*, 168.

87. Ibid.

88. Ibid., 168–69.

89. Ibid., 181.

90. Ibid., 182.

91. Wells, *Crusade for Justice*, 168.

92. Ibid., 98–99.

93. Ibid., 145.

94. Ibid., 189.

95. Ibid. Bay provides the number of visits.

96. McMurry, *To Keep the Waters Troubled*, 226.

97. Ibid., McMurry cites accounts in the *Indianapolis Freeman*, September 15, 1804, and *Conservator*, which cites the *Washington Bee*, September 15, 1894.

98. Wells, *Crusade for Justice*, 220, as cited in McMurry, *To Keep the Waters Troubled*, 226.

99. Ibid.

100. Roger Streitmatter, *Raising Her Voice: African-American Women Journalists Who Changed History* (Lexington, KY: The University of Kentucky Press, 1994), 49–50, 56.

101. Ida B. Wells, *A Red Record: Tabulated Statistics and Alleged Causes of Lynchings in the United States, 1892–1893–1894*. Reprinted in Jacqueline Jones Royster, ed., *Southern Horrors and Other Writings: The Anti-Lynching Campaign of Ida B. Wells, 1892–1900* (Boston: Bedford St. Martin's, 2016), 73, 75–78, 80–81, 131–32, 138–30, 146–47, 153–55.

102. Ibid.

103. Ibid., 2.

104. Ibid.

105. Bay, *To Tell the Truth Freely*, 211.

106. Ibid., 236.

107. Ida B. Wells, "Petition on Behalf of Frazier Baker's Wife and Children, 1898," in Christopher Waldrop, ed., *Lynching in America: A History in Documents* (New York: New York University Press, 2006), 210, cited in Bay, *To Tell the Truth Freely*, 237–38.

108. Bay, *To Tell the Truth Freely*, 237–38.

109. Ida B. Wells, *Mob Rule in New Orleans* (Chicago: Self, 1900), 224–25.

110. Ibid.

111. Ibid., 263.

112. Ibid., 284.

113. Ibid., 243.

114. Ibid., 263–64.

115. Ida B. Wells, "Lynch Law in America," originally published in *Arena*, (January 1900):15–24, reprinted in Thompson, *Ida B. Wells*, 240.

116. Ibid., 240–44, 263–64.

117. Ida B. Wells, "Lynch Law in Georgia, 1899" (New York: Fbc Ltd., 2016).

118. Ida B. Wells, "Lynching and the Excuse for It," *The Independent* (May 1901): 1133–6, reprinted in Thompson, *Ida B. Wells*, 249.

119. Ibid., 26.

120. Wells, *Crusade for Justice*, 312.

121. Ibid., 312–13.

122. Ibid., 314.

123. Ibid., 313.

124. Ibid., 317.

125. Ibid., 318.

126. Ibid., 319.

127. Bay, *To Tell the Truth Freely*, 281.

128. Robert L. Zangard, *The NAACP Crusade against Lynching, 1909–1950* (Philadelphia: Temple University Press, 1980); Cited in Bay, *To Tell the Truth Freely*, 268.

129. Ida B. Wells-Barnett, "How Enfranchisement Stops Lynching," *Original Rights Magazine*, (June 1910): 42–53 and reproduced in Thompson, *Ida B. Wells*, 267–76.

130. Bay, *To Tell the Truth Freely*, 108.

131. Wells, *Crusade for Justice*, 70–71.

132. Ida B. Wells, *Lynching: Our National Crime* (*National Negro Conference Proceedings*, New York, 1909), 174–79, reprinted in Mildred I. Thompson, *Ida B. Wells Barnett: An Exploratory Study of an American Black Woman* (Brooklyn, NY: Carlson Publishing Inc.), 261 originally published in *Survey* (February 1913): 573–74, reprinted in Thompson, *Ida B. Wells-Barnett*, 277.

133. Ida B. Wells, *Our Country: Lynching Record*, reprinted in Thompson, *Ida B. Wells-Barnett*, 274.

134. Ibid.

135. Ibid., 279.

136. Ibid.

137. Ronald E. Price and William J. Paisley, eds., *Public Communication Campaigns: The American Experience*, in *Public Communication Campaigns* (Beverly Hills: Sage, 1984), 23.

138. DeCosta-Willis, *The Memphis Diary of Ida B. Wells*, 192.

139. Streitmatter, *Raising Her Voice*, 56. Streitmatter cites Lloyd W. Crawford, "Ida B. Wells: Her Anti-Lynching Crusades in Britain and Repercussions from Them in the United States," paper presented to the Association for the Study of Negro Life and History, October 1962, Xenia, Ohio, 17–20, 22–24.

BIBLIOGRAPHY

Aronson, Elliot and Golden, Bruce W. "The Effect of Relevant and Irrelevant Aspects of Communicator Credibility on Opinion Change," *Personality* 30.2 (1979): 135–46.

Bay, Mia. *To Tell the Truth Freely: The Life of Ida B. Wells*. New York: Hill & Wang, 2009.

Boswell, Angela and McArthur, Judith N. *Women Shaping the South: Creating and Confronting Change*. Columbia: University of Missouri Press, 2006.

Broussard, Jinx Coleman. *Giving a Voice to the Voiceless*. New York: Routledge, 2004.

———. *African American Foreign Correspondents: A History*. Baton Rouge, LA: LSU Press, 2013.

Coombs, W. Timothy, and Holladay, Sherry J. *PR Strategy and Application*. Malden, MA: Wiley-Blackwell Publications, 2010.

Cutlip, Scott M. "Lithuania's First Independence Battle: A PR Footnote," *Public Relations Review* 16.4 (1990):12–6.

———. *Public Relations from the 17th Century*. Hillsdale, NJ: Lawrence Erlbaum and Associates, 1995.

———, Center, Allen H., and Broom, Glen M. *Effective Public Relations*. Englewood Cliff, NJ: Prentice Hall, 1994.

DeCosta-Willis, Miriam. *The Memphis Diary of Ida B. Wells*. Boston: Beacon Press, 1995.

Grunig, James E., and Hunt, Todd S. *Managing Public Relations*. New York: Holt, Reinhart and Winston, 1984.

Hallahan, Kirk. "Political Public Relations and Strategic Framing," in Jesper Stromback and Trudier Harris, comp., *Selected Works of Ida B. Wells-Barnett*. New York: Oxford University Press, 1991.

———. "Ivy Lee and the Rockefellers' Response to the 1913–1914 Colorado Coal Strike," *Journal of PR Research* 14 (2002): 264–314.

———. "Seven Models of Framing: Implications for Public Relations," *Journal of Public Relations Research* 11.3 (1999): 205–42.

———. "W. L. Mackenzie King: Rockefeller's 'Other' Public Relations Counselor in Colorado," *Public Relations Review* 29.4 (2003): 401–14.

Heath, Robert L. and Toth, Elizabeth. *Rhetorical and Critical Approaches to Public Relations*, second edition. Thousand Oaks, CA: Lawrence Erlbaum Associates, 2009.

Heibert, Ray Eldon. *Courtier to the Crowd: The Story of Ivy Lee and the Development of Public Relations*. Ames: Iowa State University Press, 1966.

Iiousis, Spiro. *Political Public Relations: Principles and Applications*. New York: Routledge, 2011.

Karcher, Carolyn L. "Ida B. Wells and Her Allies against Lynching: A Transnational Perspective," *Comparative American Studies* 3.2 (2005): 131–51.

Kendall, Robert. *Public Relations Campaign Strategies*, second edition. New York: Addison Wesley Longman, 1996.

Ledingham, John A. and Bruning, Stephen D. eds. *Public Relations Management: A Relational Approach to the Study of Public Relations*. Mahwah, NJ: Routledge, 2000.

McMurry, Linda O. *To Keep the Waters Troubled: The Life of Ida B. Wells*. New York: Oxford University Press, 1988.

Miller, Karen S. *"Edward Bernays: Public Relations Pioneer,"* in Margaret A. Blanchard, ed., *History of the Mass Media in the United States: An Encyclopedia*. New York: Routledge, 1999.

Newsom, Doug, and Haynes, Jim. *Public Relations Writing: Form and Style*, tenth edition. Boston: Wadsworth Cengage Learning, 2011.

Newsom, Dean, Turk, Judy Vandyke, and Kruckeberg, Dean. *This Is PR: The Realities of Public Relations*. Independence, KY: Cengage Learning, 2013.

Perloff, Richard. *The Dynamics of Persuasion: Communication and Attitudes in the 21st Century*, fourth edition. New York: Routledge, 2010.

Pride, Armistead S., and Wilson, Clint C. *A History of the Black Press*. Washington, DC: Howard University Press, 1997.

Seiter, Robert and Glass, John S. *Persuasion, Social Influence, and Compliance Gaining*, fourth edition. Boston: Allyn and Bacon, 2010.

Senna, Carl. *The Black Press and the Struggle for Civil Rights*. Danbury, CT: Scholastic Library Publishing, 1994.

Shapiro, Herbert. *White Violence and Black Response: From Reconstruction to Montgomery*. Boston: University of Massachusetts Press, 1988.

Slater, Michael D. and Rouner, Donna. "How Message Evaluation and Source Attributes May Influence Credibility Assessment and Belief Change," *Journalism and Mass Communication Quarterly* 73.4 (1996): 974–91.

Sloan, Wm. David. *The Media in America: A History*, ninth edition. Northport, AL: Vision, 2014.

Streitmatter, Roger. *Raising Her Voice: African-American Women Journalists Who Changed History*. Lexington: The University of Kentucky Press, 1994.

Waldrop, Christopher, ed. *Lynching in America: A History in Documents*. New York: New York University Press, 2006.

Wells, Ida B. *Crusade for Justice: The Autobiography of Ida B. Wells*, edited by Alfreda M. Duster. Chicago: University of Chicago Press, 1970.

———. "Lynch Law in America," originally published in *Arena* (January 1900): 15–24.

———. *Mob Rule in New Orleans*. Chicago: Self, 1900.

Wilcox, Dennis L., Cameron, Glen T., Reber, Bryan H., and Shin, Jae-Hwa. *Think Public Relations*. Boston: Pearson, 2013.

Zangard, Robert L. *The NAACP Crusade against Lynching, 1909–1950*. Philadelphia: Temple University Press, 1980.

4

"The Modern Joan [of] Arc"

Press Coverage of Ida B. Wells-Barnett's Campaign for Woman's Suffrage

Lori Amber Roessner

In September 1914, ten-year-old Alfreda Wells—sporting a white taffeta and lace dress and braided pigtails—gazed into the camera with a serious expression from her perch atop an ornate end table. Her mother and her thirteen-year-old sister, Ida, Jr., flanked her, both donning frank expressions and their Sunday finest. The attire and countenance of Ida B. Wells-Barnett and her daughters signified their mother's commitment to abiding by the mores of middle-class respectability and her determination to struggle for equity and social justice for her children.[1] The trio celebrated the commencement of the second fall season of the Alpha Suffrage Club, the first such club for Black women in Chicago, which thanks to the antecedent public relations skills of Wells-Barnett, who founded the organization in January 1913, had enjoyed regular coverage in the *Chicago Defender*, one of the most prominent newspapers of the Black press.

Alfreda had worn a similar dress with an Alpha Suffrage streamer draped over her shoulder the prior summer as she marched down Michigan Avenue alongside her mother, who served as a section marshal of a parade celebrating the passage of the Municipal and Presidential Voting Act of 1913, which guaranteed women the right to vote in municipal and presidential elections.[2] The members of the Alpha Suffrage Club marching and motoring alongside other Chicago suffs, dressed in elaborate costumes and carrying yellow and white parasols, flags, banners, streamers, and emblems, had "made quite a gala appearance" in the suffrage parade that July 1st afternoon, and the popular antecedent public relations tactic had garnered national press coverage in the days that followed.[3]

Alfreda's mother had organized the Alpha Suffrage Club in January 1913 after learning that the Illinois General Assembly was considering additional enfranchisement measures for women, and in the coming years, Wells-Barnett would steadfastly encourage race women in the Second and Third Wards to take advantage of the vote.[4] This chapter considers the earlier involvement of Wells-Barnett in the woman's suffrage movement in the late nineteenth century, her establishment and participation in the Alpha Suffrage Club in the second decade of the twentieth century, and her subsequent activity in politics in the 1920s, the last full decade of her life. The chapter will focus particular attention on her engagement in the Alpha Suffrage Club and the press attention that the publicity-savvy social justice crusader garnered on behalf of the club.

Keeping in mind the work of historian Barbara J. Fields, who contended that race and gender are ideological constructs, which are "above all, historical product[s]," this chapter, through a combination of narrative and discourse analyses, involved the close examination of primary source documents housed at the University of Chicago and 140 articles published from 1894 to 1931 in prominent nationally circulating newspapers, including the *Chicago Defender*, the *Chicago Tribune*, and the *New York Times*.[5] In doing so, this manuscript answers the call of women's historian Julia Bush, who contended that historians should attempt to recover "the diversity of ideas and self-expression" of individuals involved in the women's rights movement and to put their voices into the intellectual, political, cultural, and social contexts of their day.[6]

When Ida B. Wells began her career as a journalist in the mid-1880s to crusade for racial equity and social justice in reaction to her experience teaching in an inequitable, segregated school system and the impeding of her civil rights aboard a Chesapeake, Ohio & Southwestern Railroad Company railcar, the woman's suffrage movement was still fractured into two national organizations—Susan B. Anthony and Elizabeth Cady Stanton's National Woman Suffrage Association and Lucy Stone and Julia Ward Howe's American Woman Suffrage Association. Both organizations favored competing strategies for how to win suffrage; however, neither the state-by-state strategy nor attempts at lobbying for an amendment to the Constitution were gaining much traction when Wells-Barnett took over as publisher of the *Memphis Free Speech and Headlight* in 1889.[7] Despite the paucity of significant legal or electoral victories that would have gained suffrage for a large body of women, the idea of women's rights was a continuing part of the era's political dialogue.

Although, as journalism historian Linda Lumsden suggests, castigating women's rights in the mainstream press was common, suffragists had gained more than a few advocates in some press quarters.[8] An editorial published in the *Boston Daily Globe* on November 28, 1890, for instance, reviewed with obvious delight the progress that suffragists had made during that year and concluded: "If the believers in woman suffrage couldn't eat their Thanksgiving turkeys with a good appetite yesterday after all these achievements, they must be hard to please."[9] *Woman's Journal* editor Lucy Stone also believed that suffragists had many accomplishments for which to be grateful that autumn; topping her list was the fact that the US House Judiciary Committee had reported in favor of an amendment to secure the political rights of women.

Wells would begin addressing women's rights in conjunction with her continental and international crusades for US anti-lynching legislation, in the wake of the horrific lynching of her friends, three Black, Memphis-area grocers, at the hands of a white lynch-mob in 1893. While on her second lecture circuit in Great Britain in 1894, Wells—now a reporter for Ferdinand Barnett's *Chicago Conservator*, the oldest Black newspaper in Chicago, and a paid correspondent for the *Chicago Daily Inter-Ocean*, the city's local Republican organ—faced significant opposition from Frances Willard, the prominent suffragist and president of the Women's Christian Temperance Union. Although both women were advocates of the burgeoning woman's suffrage movement, the two prominent public speakers were at odds with the other's strategic decisions. Wells, in particular, condemned Willard for perpetuating the myth of the Black male rapist in her campaigns against the wiles of drinking, and Willard became frustrated with Wells' public rebukes. Their dispute culminated in much controversy in the press, but as we have seen in earlier chapters, ended with Willard joining the London Anti-Lynching Committee.[10] Upon Wells' arrival back in the US, her friend, suffragist leader Susan B. Anthony, attempted to smooth over any hurt feelings over the incident by admitting that she too had been guilty of putting concerns of gender before racial equality.[11]

That same autumn, Wells' name also appeared in newspaper headlines for her role in the burgeoning women's rights movement. Mary Krout, the women's page editor at the *Chicago Inter-Ocean*, the newspaper that had carried Wells' accounts from her international lecture circuit, invited Wells to participate in a speaker's bureau on behalf of the election of a woman to the post of trustee for the University of Illinois.[12] The women of Illinois had acquired limited franchise rights a little more than three years prior, when the state legislature passed a bill entitling women to vote in the election of school officials.[13] Wells agreed to participate, and on October 11, 1894, she appeared with a number of influential women from Illinois at a gathering of the Women's Republican Campaign Committee at Central Music Hall in Chicago. Wells and other prominent area women's rights advocates spoke about the civic responsibility of voting in the State University Trustee election and provided attendees with information about three female candidates for the elected position at the event covered by the *Inter-Ocean*'s chief competitor, the *Chicago Tribune*, and other local news outlets. "There was no trace of political 'mud,'" at the meeting of "enthusiastic women," a *Chicago Tribune* reporter noted, "but instead the speakers wore beautiful gowns and made their addresses from a stage decorated with potted plants."[14] Influenced by the logic of the cult of true womanhood and the burgeoning women's housekeeping movement, the journalist indicated that the morally superior character of the ladies had not been sullied by participation in the political process.[15] Instead, after a musical intermission, leaders of the Women's Republican Committee encouraged the ladies to perform their political duties in a "womanly manner." Under the subhead "What a Colored Woman Said," a *Chicago Tribune* journalist reported that Wells argued that women would shirk their duties as mothers if they did not vote in the election of school board officials. Likewise, in the detached news account, the journalist noted Wells' assertion that, as naturalized citizens, women had possessed the right to vote since the passage of the Fifteenth Amendment.[16]

Although Wells contended that by the letter of the law women had possessed the right to vote for more than three decades, she—like other era women's rights advocates—was not convinced that the vote was the "panacea" for which they were looking.[17] It certainly had not yielded the equalizing power that Black men had sought. She told Anthony as much in a private conversation in autumn 1894. "Although I believe that it is right that they should have the vote," she said, "I do not believe that the exercise of the vote is going to change women's nature nor the political situation."[18] Despite these privately held beliefs, Wells, now working as the editor of the *Chicago Conservator*, joined the Illinois Woman Suffrage Association, and continued to participate in speaking engagements on behalf of the Women's State Central Committee, even after she married local attorney Ferdinand Barnett in 1895 and gave birth to their firstborn son, Charles, a year later.[19] Wells-Barnett disagreed with Anthony that her new roles as wife and mother would result in a "divided duty," and continued to be a staunch advocate of equal rights.[20] Even still, national press coverage of her commitment to the advancement of women's rights would be overshadowed by her campaign for racial equality over the next decade.

For her part, however, Wells-Barnett believed that enfranchisement was instrumental in her battle for social justice, and she told readers of *Original Rights Magazine*, a public-affairs magazine, as much in an article titled, "How Enfranchisement Stops Lynching," published in June 1910. "The flowering of the nineteenth century civilization for the American people was the abolition of slavery, and the enfranchisement of all manhood," she wrote. "The reproach and disgrace of the twentieth century is that the whole of the American people have permitted a part, to nullify this glorious achievement."[21] The only protection of citizenship, Wells-Barnett wrote, was gaining the vote and providing evidence of the correlation between disenfranchisement efforts and the steady rise of racial violence and lynchings. "With no sacredness of the ballot there can be no sacredness of human life itself," she contended, beseeching her brethren to fight for the enfranchisement of all mankind.[22]

Despite her pleas for enfranchisement, Wells-Barnett would not gain additional press attention for her role as a women's rights advocate until she spoke out on behalf of President William Howard Taft, the Republican incumbent, in October 1912. The 1912 presidential election cycle represented a unique shift in American politics. Wells-Barnett maintained her faith in the party of Lincoln and its continued commitment to education, social justice, and legislation to protect Black citizens, but other prominent national race leaders, most notably Booker T. Washington, lent their support to Progressive Party nominee Theodore Roosevelt.[23] In a speech delivered before the Women's Party of Cook County, Wells-Barnett provided a rationale for withholding her support from a Progressive Party that she believed did not have genuine interest in uplift for her sex or her race. "The suffrage cause would not be a vital issue with the Progressive leader were it not for the fact that the women of six states have the vote," Wells-Barnett had told those in attendance.[24] The *Chicago Inter-Ocean* and the *Chicago Defender* covered Wells-Barnett's formal comments at the event, and acknowledged the primacy of her role as a chief civil rights advocate with the *Defender* praising Wells-Barnett as the "'Old Roman' of racial endeavor and accomplishment within the range of femininity."[25] Suffrage, more so than issues of racial equality, was at the forefront of American politics in 1912. Women in six—mostly Western—states had secured the right to vote, and others were gaining limited enfranchisement.[26] In Illinois, for instance, the Municipal and Presidential Voting Act was being debated, a scenario that spurred Wells-Barnett and her white comrade Belle Squire to form the non-partisan Alpha Suffrage Club on January 30, 1913.[27]

The suffrage club met most Wednesday evenings at eight o'clock at 3005 State Street in Bronzeville, a Black neighborhood on the south side of Chicago, nearby the headquarters of the Negro Fellowship League (NFL), a social club that considered matters of race that Wells-Barnett had founded in the aftermath of the 1908 race riot in Springfield, Illinois.[28] Each week, guest speakers educated the two hundred members about politics and the civic duty attached to enfranchisement. Shortly after its establishment, the club's membership elected seven officers, including Ida B. Wells-Barnett as president, Mary Jackson as vice president, and K. J. Bills as editor, who cordially invited "all women interested in knowing how to become good citizens" to become members.[29] Wells-Barnett believed that the club might become a viable political force for the advancement of members of her race *and* her gender. She recalled her intentions for establishing the club in her autobiography:

> I had been a member of the Women's Suffrage Association all during my residence in Illinois, but somehow I had not been able to get very much interest among our club women. When I saw that we were likely to have restricted suffrage. . . . I made another effort to get our women interested. . . . I showed them that we could use our vote for the advantage of ourselves and our race.[30]

Shortly after establishing the organization, Wells-Barnett traveled to Washington, DC, to serve as the club's representative to the Illinois delegation at the inaugural Woman Suffrage Procession on March 8, 1913. Alice Paul and Lucy Burns, controversial leaders in the National American Woman Suffrage Association (NAWSA), organized the suffrage parade to coincide with incoming President Woodrow Wilson's arrival for his inauguration. "[The] march in the spirit of protest against the present political organization of society, from which women are excluded" was an antecedent public relations strategy designed to raise awareness of a national suffrage strategy.[31] Paul had become aware of such political strategies and publicity pseudo-events while in Britain several years prior from Emmeline and Christabel Pankhurst, the militant founders of the Women's Social and Political Union, and as chair of the NAWSA's Congressional Committee, Paul and Burns, vice-chair, recruited organizers and volunteers such as Crystal Eastman to plan and raise funds for the parade.[32]

After arriving in the nation's capital, Wells-Barnett encountered prejudice that she had not expected. Upon learning of the presence of a Black delegate, Southern participants had protested the inclusion of Black women in state delegations and Grace Wilbur Trout, former president of the Chicago Political Equality League and current president of the Illinois Equal Suffrage Association—both organizations of which Wells-Barnett was a longtime member— suggested that Wells-Barnett comply with the demands to avoid a Southern boycott. Anthony had been accurate a decade before: The movement often put gender before race. Wells-Barnett, however, rebuffed Trout's request, saying, "I shall not march unless I can march under the Illinois banner."[33] Two white delegates—Squire and Virginia Brooks—offered a compromise, agreeing to accompany Wells-Barnett in the colored section with delegations from the National Association of Colored Women and the Alpha Chapter of Delta Sigma Theta at Howard University; instead, at the appointed hour of the parade, it appeared as if Wells-Barnett had boycotted the affair, but to the chagrin of some organizers, she integrated the parade by stepping out of the crowd and joining the Illinois delegation.

Wells-Barnett's defiant act gained national media coverage. The *Chicago Tribune* described Wells-Barnett's initial reaction to the news that she could not accompany her Illinois contingent in a dramatic fashion. "Mrs. Barnett's voice trembled with emotion, and two large tears coursed their way down her cheek before she could raise her veil and wipe them away," the reporter wrote, before recounting her retort to Trout. "The southern women have tried to evade the question time and again by giving some excuse or other," Wells-Barnett said. "If the Illinois women do not take a stand now in this great democratic parade then the colored women are lost."[34] The crosstown rival, meanwhile, discarded objectivity in favor of heroic treatment. On March 8, 1913, an above-the-fold, page-one article in the *Chicago Defender* informed readers that "the Modern Joan [of] Arc," Mrs. Ida B. Wells-Barnett, had marched in the inaugural Woman Suffrage Parade in Washington despite the protests and the "scorn of her Southern sisters."[35] The news article celebrated Wells-Barnett as both the greatest "race . . . leader among the feminine sex," and an individual of the "highest type of womanhood."[36] "All praise to Mrs. Barnett for her firm stand against the bitter prejudice of the women of the South," the *Defender* correspondent wrote, acknowledging that woman's suffrage might not have the support of the federal government, but noting that it did have the respect and aid of the "average American, with his inborn deference to women."[37] Robert S. Abbott's *Chicago Defender* may have hailed Wells-Barnett as a conquering heroine, but in the immediate aftermath of the parade, other national newspapers made no reference to Wells-Barnett's brave stand against racial discrimination in the national woman's suffrage parade, and the incident became a footnote in the American imagination. Instead, other national newspapers focused on the violence of an unruly male mob and the police brutality that ultimately greeted hundreds of the thousands who marched alongside five mounted brigades, nine brass bands, twenty-six floats, and grand marshal Inez Milholland, the militant labor lawyer dressed theatrically in white and mounted atop a magnificent white steed.[38] The intriguing words and compelling photographs that accompanied the spectacle provided just the public symbols Paul had sought. She contended that they signified the systemic mistreatment of women in American culture, and used them as fodder in her struggle for women's rights.

In the aftermath of the inaugural national suffrage parade, members of the women's rights movement realized that Paul had chosen an effective publicity vehicle in the protest parade, and throughout the next year, as leaders sought to commemorate victories and maintain awareness about the issue, they planned both celebratory and protest parades. On July 1, 1913, for instance, suffragists in Chicago celebrated the passage of the Municipal and Presidential Voting Act of 1913 through the Illinois legislature with a festive automobile parade.[39]

Wells-Barnett's Alpha Suffrage Club participated in the day's events, hosting a "truly representative" reception at the NFL's Reading Room before joining the procession of the parade in five large touring cars.[40] The *Chicago Tribune* previewed "Women's Independence Day," announcing to its readers that the parade, featuring Mrs. Kenneth McClennan on a snow white horse as the grand marshal, hundreds of automobiles, and approximately 2,000 participants, would commence at the corner of Michigan Avenue and Peck Court at four o'clock.[41]

The bill, guaranteeing 1.5 million women of Illinois limited suffrage, had taken effect at 12:01 a.m. on July 1, and across the nation, its passage made newspaper headlines and sparked additional celebratory parades.[42] On July 2, the *Chicago Tribune* provided extensive coverage of the event on page three with reports of the peaceful spectacle, despite the attempts of one man to lead some automobiles off the parade course.[43] In its next Big Weekend Edition, the *Chicago Defender* included a front-page news brief about the suffrage celebration that involved more than 100 "gaily decorated automobiles," which "wended their way along Michigan avenue and Grand boulevard bound for Washington park."[44] "Conspicuous among them," the *Defender* correspondent wrote, "were five large touring cars bearing the members and friends of the Alpha Suffrage Club."[45]

The *New York Times*, the *New York Tribune*, the *San Francisco Chronicle*, the *Baltimore Sun*, the *Indianapolis Star*, and the *Christian Science Monitor*, among others, also carried news of the celebratory suffrage parade.[46] "Women Celebrate Ballot Victory," a headline in the July 2 edition of the *Indianapolis Star* informed readers.[47] The *New York Times*, meanwhile, told readers of additional spectacles that the Illinois victory had sparked. At 2 p.m. on July 1, members of the Woman Suffrage Party, marched alongside a symbolic Independence wagon constructed in 1776, distributed leaflets describing the history of woman's suffrage in Illinois at a series of street meetings, and celebrated with an auto parade of the city's shopping districts in hope that they might "awaken and bring the East up to the standard of the West," *Times* readers learned.[48]

Several days later, many of these same newspapers carried headlines and news of plans by the NAWSA to descend upon Capitol Hill on July 30 to demand that Congress pass a constitutional amendment granting women the right to vote.[49] The women had determined that the "'attack' on the national legislature would be marked by a monster automobile parade," the *Atlanta Constitution* told its readers on July 8.[50] Suffragists were beginning to learn the symbolic value of parades and other forms of pageants, and the symbolism was not lost on social commentators of the day. The July issue of *Current Opinion*, a popular literary magazine of the era, described the value of the pageant as a form of propaganda and provided examples of how the artistic form was being utilized by suffragists and labor leaders alike.[51]

Although they recognized the value of such symbolic spectacles, the women of Illinois were determined to organize. On the day of the parade, a segment had petitioned Judge John E. Owens to appoint women as election officials and judges, and shortly thereafter, behind the leadership of Trout, the president of the Illinois Equal Suffrage Association, Illinois suffragists began organizing every precinct in the state. "While the state association will wield a lot of power," Trout had told a reporter for the *Tribune*, "it will work on issues and not on men. The women will be taught to see the issues."[52]

Wells-Barnett may not have seen eye-to-eye with Trout on the day of the Woman Suffrage Procession in Washington, DC, earlier in the year, but they did agree on the next steps after securing limited enfranchisement. They must organize individual precincts and teach women voters about relevant political issues and how to exercise their civic duty. To that end, the Alpha Suffrage Club, under the helm of Wells-Barnett, convened weekly, attempting to orchestrate block-voting efforts to ensure the political advancement of local reform efforts. In advance of the spring 1914 election, Wells-Barnett also sought to secure five hundred Alpha Suffrage Club members, who would study politics and the issues so that they might come to wield a significant amount of power in the outcome of local elections.[53]

From the outset, Wells-Barnett had promoted the Alpha Suffrage Club as a site of advancement through united womanhood. Taking a cue from Jane Cunningham Croly, the founder of the national woman's club movement and the foremost proponent of united womanhood, Wells-Barnett consistently emphasized the one common key to the advancement of her race and gender—"sticking together."[54] To entice new members, she stressed the educational and entertainment components of the club. The renowned journalist understood the value of publicity, and taking a cue from the "father of public relations," Ivy Ledbetter Lee, she began submitting notices of upcoming events to Abbott's *Chicago Defender*. When prominent coverage was not initially forthcoming, she enlisted Alpha Suffrage Club officer K. J. Bills, who recently had been named as the editor for the club's fledgling newsletter the *Alpha Suffrage Record*, to draft promotional notices and meeting briefs.

Bills' first promotional piece appeared in the *Chicago Defender* on August 23, 1913. She reported on the club's educational initiatives. "The women are studying politics, getting all the necessary points on voting," Bills wrote. "Every week someone gives instructive talks." In addition to providing basic information about the club's make-up, its leadership, and the meeting location, dates, and times, Bills stressed the central tenet of the Alpha Suffrage Club: "Women as well as men must stand together as one if we hope to be successful."[55] To that end, Bills reported, as "the only woman suffrage club of the race in the Second ward," the club hoped to "become strong enough to help elect some conscientious race man as alderman."[56] Bills ended the notice with a warning of sorts: "If the colored women do not take advantage of the franchise, they may only blame themselves when they are left out of everything."[57] Bills' piece stressed the club's function as a site of united womanhood, empowering her gender by educating women about their potential as political actors, and as a site of resistance, acknowledging the organization's role in demanding recognition for Black women and ensuring the welfare of their local community.

By September 1913, Bills' notices became a regular feature of the *Chicago Defender*'s Clubs & Societies column, and they continued to receive favorable placement throughout Wells-Barnett's tenure as president. Due to the efforts of Wells-Barnett and her club's editor, the *Chicago Defender* provided regular coverage of Alpha Suffrage Club meetings and promoted the organization both as a site of united womanhood and as a site of resistance and empowerment over the next five years. The promotional notices written by the Alpha Suffrage Club editor, on occasion, sparked additional positive news coverage. On November 22, 1913, for instance, the *Chicago Defender* included a two-column article about the Alpha Suffrage Club's inaugural annual dinner. A reporter from the *Defender* described the event, which included "vocal and instrumental music of high order . . . readings from original manuscripts" enjoyed by the fifty members present and praised Wells-Barnett, who had "devoted her life to the uplift of her race and has been instrumental in securing justice and fair play for many who were unable to help themselves."[58] A prominent element of Wells-Barnett's plan for racial uplift included education, and to that end, after the entertainment, the women enjoyed a demonstration of the use of voting machines.

The club's "good showing" of united womanhood in a suffrage parade held the following May made headlines in the *Chicago Defender*.[59] The *Defender* carried the news brief written by Viola E. Hill, the first vice president of the Alpha Suffrage Club, on its front page. Wells-Barnett, "the only Afro-American commandant in the parade," Hill wrote, was a special guest speaker at the Hotel La Salle immediately following the parade.[60] At the event, the Alpha Suffrage Club received compliments from prominent Chicagoans, prompting Hill to write that "all Chicago should be proud of the impression that they made, and the significance of their unity in the parade."[61]

Although undoubtedly pleased with the promotional bravado, Wells-Barnett remained focused on her primary objective, the upcoming elections. To that end, she organized "one of the finest programs" in the club's history at the end of May 1914.[62] Miss Mary Bartelme, Chicago's first female judge, offered a lesson in municipal housekeeping, telling the women how they might help "remedy the awful conditions which have brought 600 girls" through the halls of Juvenile Court.[63] As the first Black individual appointed as probation officer [by Chicago's Municipal Court Chief Justice Judge Harry Olson], Wells-Barnett had come into frequent contact with Bartelme, and would invite her to speak to the club on several occasions in the coming years.[64] That summer, Wells-Barnett would organize addresses from other prominent political-minded women in the community, such as Miss Marion Drake, who had run for alderman in the First Ward the prior spring.[65]

That fall, Wells-Barnett also offered her membership their first glance at several state, district, and county candidates, who spoke at the club's fall reception and thereafter at their weekly meetings. Throughout the month of October, the *Defender* published the club's notices of an upcoming County Commissioners' Evening at

Bethel Church on October 12, which was to feature addresses from candidates to the County Commissioner's Board.[66] On October 17, the *Defender* published the club's notice of the successful event, which included speeches from Miss Mary McDowell and Miss Harriet Vittum, two candidates for County Commissioner, and an entreaty for all women to register so that they might vote for them and for the Black candidates on the County Commissioner's Board.[67] The Alpha Suffrage Club followed this event with a "Municipal Judges Night" and addresses from mayoral and aldermanic candidates such as William H. Thompson in advance of the spring 1915 elections.[68] As the *Defender* noted, these educational meetings were beneficial to "women young in the suffrage cause."[69] Although the club was witnessing "splendid results in teaching the women their duties in affairs of the government, . . . the women [were] studying all phases of politics in order to be up on all questions that might arise in the spring campaign."[70]

Wells-Barnett strongly believed that "all women should be connected with some suffrage club in order to thoroughly acquaint themselves in civics," but she ardently strived to increase the membership of the Alpha Suffrage Club, "the mother suffrage club," which not only taught "the principle of politics but [encouraged members] to unite their strength for their own advancement."[71] She encouraged new membership, reminding the women of the Second and Third Wards of the strength of the organization. The Alpha Suffrage Club was the only club "to secure any political appointments for its members so far."[72]

Local political candidates were beginning to learn of the influence of the Alpha Suffrage Club in 1915. All three Black aldermanic candidates presented their platforms in February 1915, and after some debate, the group voted to support Oscar DePriest.[73] They followed their endorsement with a vote to host a public reception in honor of Congressman Martin B. Madden "for his splendid defense of Negro womanhood."[74] At the reception held at Quinn Chapel on March 18, the Alpha Suffrage Club flaunted its newfound political muscle. Madden recently had spoken out against racial discrimination and the criminalization of interracial marriage, and at the event, the leadership of the Alpha Suffrage Club announced a resolution to celebrate Madden as a champion for the race, and to formally announce their decision to endorse DePriest and Republican mayoral candidate William H. Thompson, pledging to "leave no stone unturned to secure their election on April 6."[75] Their efforts to register and secure voters for the two candidates, despite some heckling from onlookers and castigation by the local press, paid off. On April 6, they helped elect Thompson as mayor and DePriest as Chicago's first Black alderman.[76] In the aftermath of the victory, DePriest attributed his victory to the vote of Black women, and Wells-Barnett and her suffrage club boasted of having the first opportunity to host a reception in DePriest's honor in mid-April, where the alderman-elect "pledged himself to work for the interests of the race."[77] It appeared as if the political agitation of the club was beginning to pay off.

Wells-Barnett's celebration, however, would be short-lived. She had made a political misstep during the 1915 campaign season, initially campaigning on behalf of Thompson, who promised his allegiance to the Black community based on the

Alpha Suffrage Club's endorsement, before switching allegiances mid-campaign to Chicago's Municipal Court Chief Justice Judge Harry Olson, who had appointed Wells-Barnett to her position as a detention officer in 1914. In the end, Thompson won in a landslide based in part on the early support of the Alpha Suffrage Club, but, as Wells-Barnett recalled in her autobiography, once in office, he "proceeded to ignore those of us who had helped make it possible for him to realize his ambition."[78] Within six months of his election, Wells-Barnett was forced to relinquish her position in the adult probation office.

In the aftermath of the spring election, Wells-Barnett and the Alpha Suffrage Club would find that the political climate of Chicago was growing increasingly hostile toward Black citizens. Without her salary from her role as a probation officer, Wells-Barnett struggled to fund the NFL, which included a settlement house that aided Black newcomers to the Chicago area. Her efforts were undercut further when the state of Illinois opened an unemployment office near the site of the NFL's headquarters.[79]

Despite these affronts in the summer of 1915, Wells-Barnett entreated the Alpha Suffrage Club to assist the NFL with addressing the emerging "Colored Boy Problem."[80] Cloaking her requests in rhetoric inspired by the cult of true womanhood, the undergirding logic of the woman's club movement and the accompanying women's housekeeping movement, Wells-Barnett promoted a series of "mothers' meetings" at the Alpha Suffrage Club, which informed women of children's welfare and other reform issues.[81] On June 15, the *Chicago Defender* published a club brief about the content of the most recent Alpha Suffrage Club meeting, which addressed the "Thomas case."[82] Wells-Barnett described the details of the Thomas case in her autobiography. George Thomas had migrated from Georgia in search of gainful employment, but upon arriving in Chicago, struggled to find adequate housing and as a result was detained in the juvenile justice system for vagrancy, loitering, and trespassing. Wells-Barnett had become aware of these issues in her role as the director of the NFL, and she noted that this was the plight of many Black male migrants, who were turned away from the whites-only YMCA.[83]

Later that summer, on July 3, 1915, the *Chicago Defender* published a club brief that recounted a recent Alpha Suffrage Club meeting that had educated members in attendance about how to take full advantage of pension laws, which would better assist single mothers in caring for their young. The brief included a quotation from Wells-Barnett, which stated that "the reason colored people fared so badly in the distribution of city and county patronage is because they have not one strong central organization representing the colored people."[84] Under the cloak of united womanhood, Wells-Barnett sought to make the Alpha Suffrage Club a site of resistance and empowerment for racial uplift. To that end, Wells-Barnett encouraged the Alpha Suffrage Club to send two delegates to a special "race conference" called on behalf of the NFL "to see what can be done about the alarming increase of race prejudice" in the Chicago area.[85]

Despite the increasingly hostile political climate, Wells-Barnett and her Alpha Suffrage Club remained active in the woman's suffrage movement. In February 1916, they listened to reports from delegates to the Illinois Equal Suffrage League, detailing NAWSA president Carrie Chapman Catt's strategies for a national suffrage amendment; in March, they made plans to attend the latest iteration of a national suffrage parade to be held in Chicago; in June, they celebrated the success of the "great march"; in July, they elected delegates to the upcoming National Suffrage Association meeting in Atlantic City.[86]

Under Wells-Barnett's leadership, the Alpha Suffrage Club had fostered notions of united womanhood and resistance to oppression, while gaining a powerful political voice in local politics and making great strides toward a national suffrage amendment, but Wells-Barnett increasingly found that her efforts as the director of the NFL were claiming the bulk of her time and energy. Thus, she informed club members of the "impossibility" of accepting another term as president of the Alpha Suffrage Club in mid-January 1917. She recommended Dr. Fannie Emanuel as her replacement and promised to remain in a leadership role as the chairman of the executive committee. In her last act as president, Wells-Barnett had secured two life memberships for club members in the Illinois State Suffrage Association and had overseen the election of new officers, including her recommended replacement, Emanuel.[87] Under Emanuel's leadership, club meetings dwindled to a fortnight affair and coverage in the *Defender* diminished with only three additional club notices appearing in 1917 and only nine in 1918.[88] Wells-Barnett, ever the savvy publicist, had understood the powerful role of the press in raising awareness of issues in a local community. Beginning in 1910, Wells-Barnett had begun contributing intermittent articles to Abbott's *Defender*, and after the inception of the Alpha Suffrage Club, she had served as the organization's de facto media liaison.[89] In this role, she had ensured consistent coverage of the club's activities.

The sustained efforts of women such as Ida B. Wells-Barnett and organizations such as the Alpha Suffrage Club would result in the passage of the Nineteenth Amendment in 1920.

Women such as Wells-Barnett, however, found that enfranchisement was not the "panacea" for which they were searching.[90] Without a central unifying cause, the women's rights movement fractured, and women continued to suffer from gender discrimination at the hands of a patriarchal society throughout the twentieth century. Furthermore, as the Alpha Suffrage Club discovered, block-voting initiatives promoted under the banner of united womanhood often resulted in tenuous political circumstances. After realizing their greatest victory with the election of DePriest and Thompson, the Alpha Suffrage Club and Chicago's Black community endured continued oppression. Once in office, Thompson did little to help the influx of Black migrants to gain employment and housing opportunities. These tensions contributed to the outbreak of the Chicago Race Riot of 1919, which ended in dozens of deaths and hundreds of injuries.[91]

As we will see in a later chapter, despite these cultural challenges and personal setbacks, Wells-Barnett continued her crusade for social justice. In 1925, Wells-Barnett established the Women's Forum, a group focused on social justice that had great success in advocating for the unionization of Chicago's Pullman Company employees into the Brotherhood of Sleeping Car Porters.[92] Two years later, Wells-Barnett formed the Third-Ward Women's Club to encourage Black women to pursue careers in politics under the motto: "For Women, of Women, by Women." Through the organization, she promoted many of the central tenets of the Alpha Suffrage Club, united womanhood and the club as a site of resistance to oppression. In January 1930, she took up the central mantle of the Third-Ward Women's Club, announcing her candidacy for a state senate seat.[93] Her bid ended in defeat, but her efforts toward advancing both her race and her gender were successful.

Although her attempt to gain a seat in political office was ineffective, Wells-Barnett enjoyed a fruitful career as a social justice crusader, and in the final years of her life, she sought to preserve that legacy, beginning an autobiography that would help Black children understand why she had once been called the "Modern Joan [of] Arc."[94] In the last instance, her efforts to preserve her legacy were mixed.[95] Once a footnote in American history, the anti-lynching campaign and journalistic career of Wells-Barnett now merits treatment in American history books. Even still, her career as a leader in the women's rights movement—a role that Wells-Barnett believed was critical to achieving social justice—remains a little-known facet of her life.

NOTES

1. The digitized photograph can be viewed at the University of Chicago Online Archives of the Ida B. Wells Papers 1884–1976 at https://www.lib.uchicago.edu/ead/pdf/ibwells-0010-001-09.pdf. See, Wells, Ida B. Papers. [Box 10, Folder 1, Photo 9], Special Collections Research Center, University of Chicago Library.

2. Ida B. Wells, *The Memphis Diary of Ida B. Wells*, ed. Miriam DeCosta-Willis (New York: Beacon Press, 1997), 197.

3. "The Alpha Suffrage Club," *Chicago Defender*, July 5, 1913, 1. See also, "Ballot Winners to Parade Today," *Chicago Tribune*, July 1, 1913, 1; "Suffragists Have Parade of Many Autos in Chicago," *Christian Science Monitor*, July 1, 1913, 1; "First Train Runs in Loop Subway," *New York Times*, July 1, 1913, 6; "Part of Suffrage Parade and Group of Prominent Leaders," *Chicago Tribune*, July 2, 1913, 3; "Banners Greet Suffrage Parade," *Chicago Tribune*, July 2, 1913, 3; "Chicago Women Celebrate Ballot," *Hartford Courant*, July 2, 1913, 16; Women Celebrate Ballot Victory," *Indianapolis Star*, July 2, 1913, 9; "Women More Attractive," *New York Tribune*, July 2, 1913, 1; "Women Celebrate Suffrage Victory," *San Francisco Chronicle*, July 2, 1913, 2.

4. Ida B. Wells, *Crusade for Justice: The Autobiography of Ida B. Wells*, edited by Alfreda M. Duster (Chicago: University of Chicago Press, 1970), xxix; See also, Patricia Ann Schechter, *Ida B. Wells-Barnett and American Reform, 1880–1930* (Chapel Hill: University of North Carolina Press, 2003), 198–202; Kristina DuRocher, *Ida B. Wells: Social Activist and Reformer* (New York: Routledge, 2016),122–66.

5. See Barbara J. Fields, "Ideology and Race in American History," In *Region, Race, and Reconstruction: Essays in Honor of C. Vann Woodward*. Ed. J. Morgan Kousser and James M. McPherson (New York: Oxford University Press, 1982), 143–77. This study involved the analysis of 140 articles identified through ProQuest Historical Newspapers Online. An initial advanced search of the following terms—"Ida B. Wells-Barnett," "Alpha Suffrage Club,"

"Vote," "Women's Forum," "Third Ward Suffrage Club," and "Women's Rights" yielded 243 results. After all unrelated articles were omitted, a final sample of 140 articles spanning Wells-Barnett's career as a social justice advocate was examined using a combination of narrative analysis, which studies the structure of text, and discourse analysis, which studies the text in relation to its cultural and political context. Following the steps outlined by cultural studies scholar Stuart Hall in his introduction to *Paper Voices*, the analysis involved a "long preliminary soak" in the text, which allowed the scholar to select representative examples, followed by a close reading of the text, the identification of discursive themes, and the interpretation of coverage surrounding Wells-Barnett's role as a women's rights advocate within the framework of a larger discussion of the role of the mainstream press in the late-nineteenth and early-twentieth centuries women's rights movement. See also, Stuart Hall, *Paper Voices: The Popular Press and Social Change, 1935–1965* (London: Chatto and Windus, 1975), 15.

6. Julia Bush, *Women against the Vote: Anti-Suffragism in Britain* (New York: Oxford University Press, 2007), 9.

7. Ellen Carol DuBois, *Feminism and Suffrage: The Emergence of an Independent Women's Movement in America, 1848–1869* (Ithaca: Cornell University Press, 1978), 40–41.

8. Linda J. Lumsden, *Rampant Women: Suffragists and the Right of Assembly* (Knoxville: University of Tennessee Press, 1997), xxvii.

9. "Progress of Woman Suffrage," *Boston Daily Globe*, November 28, 1890, 4.

10. Linda McMurry, *To Keep the Waters Troubled: The Life of Ida B. Wells* (Oxford University Press, 2000), 247.

11. Wells, *Crusade for Justice*, 228–31.

12. "Women out in Force," *Chicago Tribune*, October 12, 1894, 5.

13. Steven M. Buechler, *The Transformation of the Woman Suffrage Movement: The Case of Chicago, 1850–1920* (Boston: Rutgers University Press, 1986), 150.

14. "Women out in Force," *Chicago Tribune*, October 12, 1894, 5.

15. Barbara Welter, "The Cult of True Womanhood: 1820–1860," *American Quarterly* 18.2 (1966): 151; Agnes H. Gottlieb, *Women Journalists and the Municipal Housekeeping Movement, 1868–1914* (Lewiston, NY: Edwin Mellen Press, 2001).

16. "Women Out in Force," *Chicago Tribune*, October 12, 1894, 5.

17. See, for instance, the views of contemporary journalist Jane Cunningham Croly. Mrs. Croly, "Two Sides to a Question," *Godey's Lady's Book and Magazine*, January 1888, 3–5.

18. Wells, *Crusade for Justice*, 230.

19. Mia Bay, *To Tell the Truth Freely: The Life of Ida B. Wells* (New York: Macmillan, 2010), 217.

20. Wells, *Crusade for Justice,* 255.

21. The digitized article can be viewed at the University of Chicago Online Archives of the Ida B. Wells Papers 1884–1976 at https://www.lib.uchicago.edu/ead/pdf/ibwells-0008-008-05.pdf. See Wells, Ida B. Papers. (Box 8, Folder 8), Special Collections Research Center, University of Chicago Library.

22. Ibid.

23. DuRocher, *Ida B. Wells*, 122–66.

24. "Shooting of Roosevelt," *The Chicago Defender*, October 19, 1912, 8.

25. Ibid.

26. The states included California, Washington, Idaho, Utah, Colorado, and Wyoming.

27. Information about the establishment of the Alpha Suffrage Club can be found in the *Alpha Suffrage Record* newsletter and can be viewed at the University of Chicago Online Archives of the Ida B. Wells Papers 1884–1976 at https://www.lib.uchicago.edu/ead/pdf/

ibwells-0008-009-07.pdf. See Wells, Ida B. Papers. (Box 8, Folder 9), Special Collections Research Center, University of Chicago Library.

28. DuRocher, *Ida B. Wells*, 122–66.

29. "Alpha Suffrage Club," *Chicago Defender*, July 5, 1913, 1.

30. Wells, *Crusade for Justice*, 345.

31. Lumsden, *Rampant Women*, 78.

32. Christine Lunardini, *Alice Paul: Equality for Women* (New York: Westview Press, 2013), 31; Jim Stovall, *Seeing Suffrage: The 1913 Washington Suffrage Parade, Its Pictures, and Its Effect on the American Landscape* (Knoxville, University of Tennessee Press), 1–133.

33. Cited in McMurry, *To Keep the Waters Troubled*, 305; Mary Walton, *A Woman's Crusade: Alice Paul and the Battle for the Ballot* (New York: St. Martin's Press, 2010), 77.

34. Cited in McMurry, *To Keep the Waters Troubled*, 305.

35. "Marches in Parade Despite Protests," *Chicago Defender*, March 8, 1913, 1.

36. Ibid.

37. Ibid.

38. Stovall, *Seeing Suffrage*, 1–10.

39. "Ballot Winners to Parade Today," *Chicago Tribune*, July 1, 1913, 1.

40. "The Alpha Suffrage Club," *Chicago Defender*, July 5, 1913, 1.

41. "Ballot Winners to Parade Today," *Chicago Tribune*, July 1, 1913, 1.

42. "The Alpha Suffrage Club," *Chicago Defender*, July 5, 1913, 1. See also, "Ballot Winners to Parade Today," *Chicago Tribune*, July 1, 1913, 1; "Suffragists Have Parade of Many Autos in Chicago," *Christian Science Monitor*, July 1, 1913, 1; "First Train Runs in Loop Subway," *New York Times*, July 1, 1913, 6; "Part of Suffrage Parade and Group of Prominent Leaders," *Chicago Tribune*, July 2, 1913, 3; "Banners Greet Suffrage Parade," *Chicago Tribune*, July 2, 1913, 3; "Chicago Women Celebrate Ballot," *Hartford Courant*, July 2, 1913, 16; Women Celebrate Ballot Victory," *Indianapolis Star*, July 2, 1913, 9; "Women More Attractive," *New York Tribune*, July 2, 1913, 1; "Women Celebrate Suffrage Victory," *San Francisco Chronicle*, July 2, 1913, 2.

43. "Banners Greet Suffrage Parade," *Chicago Tribune*, July 2, 1913, 3.

44. "The Alpha Suffrage Club," *Chicago Defender*, July 5, 1913, 1.

45. Ibid.

46. "The Alpha Suffrage Club," *Chicago Defender*, July 5, 1913, 1. See also, "Ballot Winners to Parade Today," *Chicago Tribune*, July 1, 1913, 1; "Suffragists Have Parade of Many Autos in Chicago," *Christian Science Monitor*, July 1, 1913, 1; "First Train Runs in Loop Subway," *New York Times*, July 1, 1913, 6; "Part of Suffrage Parade and Group of Prominent Leaders," *Chicago Tribune*, July 2, 1913, 3; "Banners Greet Suffrage Parade," *Chicago Tribune*, July 2, 1913, 3; "Chicago Women Celebrate Ballot," *Hartford Courant*, July 2, 1913, 16; Women Celebrate Ballot Victory," *Indianapolis Star*, July 2, 1913, 9; "Women More Attractive," *New York Tribune*, July 2, 1913, 1; "Women Celebrate Suffrage Victory," *San Francisco Chronicle*, July 2, 1913, 2.

47. "Women Celebrate Ballot Victory," *Indianapolis Star*, July 2, 1913, 9.

48. "First Train Runs in Loop Subway," *New York Times*, July 1, 1913, 6.

49. See, for example, "Women Plan Descent on National Capital," *Atlanta Constitution*, July 8, 1913, 2; "Women to March on Congress," *The Sun*, July 8, 1913, 1.

50. "Women Plan Descent on National Capital," *Atlanta Constitution*, July 8, 1913, 2.

51. "The Pageant as a Form of Propaganda," *Current Opinion* 55.1 (1913): 32.

52. "Part of Suffrage Parade and Group of Prominent Leaders," *Chicago Tribune*, July 2, 1913, 3; "Banners Greet Suffrage Parade," *Chicago Tribune*, July 2, 1913, 3.

53. Information about the establishment of the Alpha Suffrage Club can be found in the Alpha Suffrage Record newsletter and can be viewed at the University of Chicago Online Archives of the Ida B. Wells Papers 1884–1976 at https://www.lib.uchicago.edu/ead/pdf/ibwells-0008-009-07.pdf. See, Wells, Ida B. Papers. [Box 8, Folder 9], Special Collections Research Center, University of Chicago Library.

54. "Alpha Suffrage Club Banquet," *Chicago Defender*, November 22, 1913, 4.

55. Mrs. K. J. Bills, "Clubs and Societies," *Chicago Defender*, August 23, 1913, 2.

56. Ibid.

57. Ibid.

58. "Alpha Suffrage Club Banquet," *Chicago Defender*, November 22, 1913, 4.

59. "Race Women Make Good Showing in Suffrage Parade," *Chicago Defender*, May 9, 1914, 1.

60. Ibid.

61. Ibid.

62. "Alpha Suffrage Club," *Chicago Defender*, May 30, 1914, 5.

63. Ibid.

64. See, fore example, "Alpha Suffrage Club," *Chicago Defender*, May 29, 1915, 6; "Alpha Suffrage Club," *Chicago Defender*, June 5, 1915, 7.

65. See, for example, "Alpha Suffrage Club," *Chicago Defender*, June 27, 1914, 5.

66. See, for example, "Alpha Suffrage Club," *Chicago Defender*, October 3, 1914, 5; "Alpha Suffrage Club," *Chicago Defender*, October 10, 1914, 3; "Clubs and Societies," *Chicago Defender*, October 17, 1914, 3.

67. "Clubs and Societies," *Chicago Defender*, October 17, 1914, 3.

68. "Clubs and Societies," *Chicago Defender*, October 24, 1914, 6; "Clubs and Societies," *Chicago Defender*, November 21, 1914, 3.

69. "Alpha Suffrage Club," *Chicago Defender*, July 5, 1913, 1.

70. "Clubs and Societies," *Chicago Defender*, November 21, 1914, 3.

71. "Alpha Suffrage Club," *Chicago Defender*, December 5, 1914, 2; "Clubs and Societies," *Chicago Defender*, December 26, 1914.

72. "Clubs and Societies," *Chicago Defender*, December 26, 1914, 2.

73. "The Alpha Suffrage Club," *Chicago Defender*, February 6, 1915, 3; "The Alpha Suffrage Club," *Chicago Defender*, February 13, 1915, 3.

74. "The Alpha Suffrage Club," *Chicago Defender*, March 13, 1915, 3.

75. "The Alpha Suffrage Club," *Chicago Defender*, March 20, 1915, 3.

76. Wells, *Crusade for Justice,* 346–8.

77. "Alpha Suffrage Club," *Chicago Defender*, April 17, 1915, 3.

78. Wells, *Crusade for Justice,* 350.

79. DuRocher, *Ida B. Wells,* 12–66.

80. "Alpha Suffrage Club," *Chicago Defender*, June 15, 1915, 6.

81. "Alpha Suffrage Club," *Chicago Defender*, May 29, 1915, 6; "Alpha Suffrage Club," *Chicago Defender*, June 5, 1915, 7; "Alpha Suffrage Club," *Chicago Defender*, June 12, 1915, 6; "Alpha Suffrage Club," *Chicago Defender*, July 3, 1915, 6.

82. "Alpha Suffrage Club," *Chicago Defender*, June 15, 1915, 6.

83. Wells, *Crusade for Justice,* 279–307.

84. "Alpha Suffrage Club," *Chicago Defender*, July 3, 1915, 6.

85. "Negro Fellowship League," *Chicago Defender*, June 26, 1915, 6.

86. Ida B. Wells-Barnett, "The Alpha Suffrage Club," *Chicago Defender*, February 19, 1916, 4; "The Alpha Suffrage Club," *Chicago Defender*, March 4, 1916, 4; "Clubs and

Societies," *Chicago Defender*, June 17, 1916, 8; "Clubs and Societies," *Chicago Defender*, July 29, 1916, 6.

87. "Clubs and Societies," *Chicago Defender*, January 27, 1915, 5.

88. See, for example, "Clubs and Societies," *Chicago Defender*, February 17, 1917, 8; "Clubs and Societies," *Chicago Defender*, March 3, 1917, 4; "Clubs and Societies," *Chicago Defender*, March 17, 1917, 6; "Clubs and Societies," *Chicago Defender*, March 16, 1918, 13; "Clubs and Societies," *Chicago Defender*, March 30, 1918, 12; "Clubs and Societies," *Chicago Defender*, April 27, 1918, 7; "Clubs and Societies," *Chicago Defender*, May 4, 1918, 12; "Clubs and Societies," *Chicago Defender*, May 11, 1918, 12; "Clubs and Societies," *Chicago Defender*, June 1, 1918, 12; "Clubs and Societies," *Chicago Defender*, June 15, 1918, 6; "Clubs and Societies," *Chicago Defender*, July 27, 1918, 12; "Clubs and Societies," *Chicago Defender*, November 2, 1918, 12.

89. Wells, *Crusade for Justice,* 350–52.

90. Barbara Ryan, *Feminism and the Women's Rights Movement: Dynamics of Change in Social Movement, Ideology, and Activism* (New York: Psychology Press, 1992), 34.

91. Gary Krist, *City of Scoundrels: The Twelve Days of Disaster That Gave Birth to Modern Chicago* (New York: Crown Publisher, 2012), 231.

92. Schechter, *Ida B. Wells-Barnett and American Reform*, 315.

93. DuRocher, *Ida B. Wells*, 167–213.

94. "Marches in Parade Despite Protests," *Chicago Defender*, March 8, 1913, 1; See also, DuRocher, *Ida B. Wells*, 167–213; Schechter, *Ida B. Wells-Barnett and American Reform*, 32–35.

95. DuRocher, *Ida B. Wells*, 206–13.

BIBLIOGRAPHY

Bay, Mia. *To Tell the Truth Freely: The Life of Ida B. Wells*. New York: Hill and Wang, 2009.

Buechler, Steven M. *The Transformation of the Woman Suffrage Movement: The Case of Chicago, 1850–1920*. Boston: Rutgers University Press, 1986.

Bush, Julia. *Women against the Vote: Anti-Suffragism in Britain*. New York: Oxford University Press, 2007.

DuBois, Ellen Carol. *Feminism and Suffrage: The Emergence of an Independent Women's Movement in America, 1848–1869*. Ithaca: Cornell University Press, 1978.

DuRocher, Kristina. *Ida B. Wells: Social Activist and Reformer*. New York: Routledge, 2016.

Fields, Barbara J. "Ideology and Race in American History," In *Region, Race, and Reconstruction: Essays in Honor of C. Vann Woodward*, edited by J. Morgan Kousser and James M. McPherson. New York: Oxford University Press, 1982.

Gottlieb, Agnes H. *Women Journalists and the Municipal Housekeeping Movement, 1868–1914*. Lewiston, NY: Edwin Mellen Press, 2001.

Hall, Stuart. *Paper Voices: The Popular Press and Social Change, 1935–1965*. London: Chatto and Windus, 1975.

Krist, Gary. *City of Scoundrels: The Twelve Days of Disaster That Gave Birth to Modern Chicago*. New York: Crown Publisher, 2012.

Lumsden, Linda J. *Rampant Women: Suffragists and the Right of Assembly*. Knoxville: University of Tennessee Press, 1997.

Lunardini, Christine. *Alice Paul: Equality for Women*. New York: Westview Press, 2013.

McMurry, Linda O. *To Keep the Waters Troubled: The Life of Ida B. Wells.* New York: Oxford University Press, 1998.

Ryan, Barbara. *Feminism and the Women's Rights Movement: Dynamics of Change in Social Movement, Ideology, and Activism.* New York: Psychology Press, 1992.

Schechter, Patricia A. *Ida B. Wells-Barnett and American Reform, 1880–1930.* Chapel Hill: University of North Carolina Press, 2001.

Stovall, Jim. *Seeing Suffrage: The 1913 Washington Suffrage Parade, Its Pictures, and Its Effect on the American Landscape.* Knoxville: University of Tennessee Press, 2013.

Walton, Mary. *A Woman's Crusade: Alice Paul and the Battle for the Ballot.* New York: St. Martin's Press, 2010.

Welter, Barbara. "The Cult of True Womanhood: 1820–1860," *American Quarterly* 18.2 (1966): 151–74.

Wells, Ida B. *Crusade for Justice: The Autobiography of Ida B. Wells,* edited by Alfreda M. Duster. Chicago: University of Chicago Press, 1970.

———. *The Memphis Diary of Ida B. Wells: An Intimate Portrait of the Activist as a Young Woman,* edited by Miriam Decosta-Willis. Boston: Beacon Press, 1995.

5

The Life of a Political Agitator

Ida B. Wells-Barnett's Transition from a National Activist to a Local Reformer

Kris DuRocher

At the 1924 National Association of Colored Women (NACW) meeting, Ida B. Wells-Barnett announced her candidacy for the presidency of the organization. Wells-Barnett had not actively participated in the association since 1910, while her opponent, Mary McLeod Bethune, had just completed a term as vice president.[1] As historian Paula Giddings remarked, "What was she thinking? Certainly it wasn't the prospect that she could actually win."[2] Indeed, her candidacy after more than a decade of estrangement from the group appears confusing, if not considered within the scope of her larger activism. Although Wells-Barnett possessed little chance of prevailing, her run for NACW presidency was not out of character. Wells-Barnett preferred action as a method for inciting change, and by nominating herself as a candidate for not just for any office, but the highest position, she gained a platform for her ideas about transforming the focus of the NACW. She felt the women remained too concerned about portraying an image of Black female respectability and that the strategies they employed, similar to those of the National Association for the Advancement of Colored People (NAACP) of lobbying for political change, were slow, compromising, and largely ineffectual.[3]

Wells-Barnett's bid for the NACW presidency in 1924 may have been an attempt to regain a role in a national organization, but Wells-Barnett likely knew she could not win against Bethune, and the presidency may not have been her goal. Although her press coverage rivaled that of Frederick Douglass during the 1890s, her contemporaries steadily pushed her out of the national spotlight during the twentieth century, eventually writing her efforts out the historical narrative.[4] Most current historical studies of her life end around 1909, despite the fact that during the following decades Wells-Barnett created the Alpha Suffrage Club to advocate for Black women's right to vote and established the Negro Fellowship League (NFL) to support urban Black men and fight issues of poverty in Chicago.[5] She spearheaded several legal battles for the fair treatment of Black individuals, advocated for the unionization of Pullman Porters, and became the first Black female probation officer in Chicago, applying her salary to support these undertakings. After the ratification of the Nineteenth Amendment, which granted universal woman's suffrage, Wells-Barnett enlisted Black women to participate in local and regional politics during the 1920s, culminating in 1930, when she ran for an Illinois state senate seat and lost. Her commitment to social justice was a lifelong endeavor, whether her efforts focused on the national or local level.

As we will see in this chapter, Wells-Barnett's transition toward local reform after 1909 resulted from several factors, including a shift in reform leadership at the national level and her previous successes with advocacy journalism and grassroots tactics to mobilize clubwomen. After whites and Black males within national associations stymied Wells-Barnett's attempts to advance in their organizations, she focused on her place of residence, Chicago, where as a Black female she could assemble and lead her own organizations. Even if she could have risen through the ranks of the NAACP or another national reform association, Wells-Barnett likely would have been frustrated. She accomplished her best work when she could direct her own efforts and concentrate on what she felt were the most pressing issues without following a chain of command or getting approval from a committee. Although she continually sought to influence change on a national level, her previous experience as a leader and her personality made local activism an appealing site to focus her energy.

At the 1909 initial meeting of what would become the NAACP, the two organizers, Mary White Ovington, a prominent white social worker, and Oswald Garrison Villard, a white journalist and the grandson of abolitionist William Lloyd Garrison, sought to keep the leadership in white hands. At the 1909 convention, the attendees determined that "a committee of forty should be appointed to spend a year in devising ways and means for the establishment of an organization."[6] Although supposedly secret, Wells-Barnett saw the finalized list of forty and felt relief in reading her name on the list.[7] This advanced notice only made her shock greater the next day when W.E.B. Du Bois, the only Black individual on the nominating committee, did not call her name. Du Bois himself had removed her from the NAACP's list of forty organizers. His actions may have been in response to pressure from Villard and Ovington, as both proffered paternalistic rationales for keeping control of the association in white hands, with Villard admitting that he "naturally" had "rigged" the list to assist "these poor people who have been tricked so often by white men."[8] Du Bois also may have believed that educated male leadership should be at the helm, which made him amenable to dropping Wells-Barnett, a female without a college degree, from the list.

Wells-Barnett and Du Bois previously had stood together as allies against Booker T. Washington, as both criticized Washington's beliefs that Black individuals should seek only an industrial education in order to provide the South with a viable workforce. The two shared the same ideas about restoring rights for the race through political, economic, and social reform. Du Bois, a professor with a Harvard PhD, and the author of several sociological books, and Wells-Barnett, who advocated for education as part of the path to racial equality, believed Washington's approach limited access to higher education for southern Blacks and harmed the progress of the race. Du Bois' dismissal of her from the formation of the NAACP wounded Wells-Barnett.[9] Despite her treatment from Du Bois, Ovington, and Villard at the initial meeting of the NAACP, Wells-Barnett attempted to participate in the organization while also directing her own efforts from Chicago.

Du Bois' feelings about leadership clearly emerged in 1906, when he created a new Black organization, the Niagara Movement, which identified itself as working with "determined and aggressive action on the part of *men* [emphasis added] who believe in Negro freedom and growth."[10] Although the group eventually allowed women, it is clear Du Bois considered racial uplift to be the primary purview of men, and he was not alone in that belief. The shifting sands of reform leadership contributed to the promotion of college-educated men, guided by intellectually grounded philosophies for change, at the helm of major organizations, and this new guidance began to minimize grassroots organizers and women's opportunities within national associations.[11] Wells-Barnett previously an ally of Frederick Douglass, opened herself to criticism when she voiced her opinions and failed to act deferential to whites or Black men in leadership roles.[12]

Wells-Barnett soon became estranged from another national Black organization when she attended the 1910 NACW meeting in Louisville, Kentucky. There, she recommended the election of a new editor for the official periodical of the NACW, the *National Notes*, currently under the purview of Booker T. Washington's wife, Margaret Murray Washington. Many members felt Wells-Barnett's motion was a veiled attempt by her to assume the editorship, and Wells-Barnett recognized this, noting in her autobiography, "Mrs. Washington's friends had construed my activity to mean that I wanted the paper to be taken away from her, and to be elected editor myself."[13] Before the proposal went to a vote, the president of the NACW, Elizabeth Carter, interceded and ruled Wells-Barnett's motion as out of order.[14] During the ensuing discussion, the women in the audience hissed at Wells-Barnett so loudly that she left the stage. Such a response to Wells-Barnett, a previously celebrated leader of the anti-lynching movement whose publications and passionate speeches had given her national recognition, seemed surprising, yet her fervor and outspokenness increasingly became a liability within national organizations as leadership became professionalized.

Wells-Barnett examined the limited roles of Black women in her April 1910 essay, "The Northern Negro Woman's Social and Moral Condition," published in the inaugural issue of *Original Rights Magazine*, a monthly public-affairs magazine. Wells-Barnett criticized reformers who ignored the impact Black women had on their communities and race. She noted how northern Black women's influence in social movements was "not wanted" by those in charge, who limited their roles within organizations to "menial" positions.[15] Yet Black women, she noted, were responsible for social and racial uplift. She credited their work and communal outreach with why so few Black men were in the "bread lines" or at "charity bureaus."[16]

In shining light on the contributions of Black women, Wells-Barnett drew attention to the lack of recognition Black women received and how, despite the lack of leadership opportunities for Black women in reform movements, they continued to work to better their race.

The elections of 1912 placed the issue of woman's suffrage at the forefront of politics.[17] Six states—California, Washington, Idaho, Utah, Colorado, and Wyoming—allowed women to vote. In California, the largest of these states, female voters directly affected the Electoral College and thus the presidential campaign. In 1913, the woman's suffrage movement made progress in Illinois with the passing of the Municipal and Presidential Voting Act, which allowed women to vote in local government and presidential elections, the only political contests not explicitly referred to in the state constitution as chosen by a majority of male voters.[18]

As discussed in an earlier chapter, in response Wells-Barnett, along with her white associate Belle Squire, formed the Alpha Suffrage Club, the first Black women's voting rights group in Chicago.[19] Wells-Barnett insisted that members of the non-partisan Alpha Suffrage Club align themselves with the candidate they felt best represented the needs of their race, rather than blindly voting along party lines.[20] The Alpha Suffrage Club, as visualized by Wells-Barnett, would alleviate the lack of information Black women had about voting and demonstrate to themselves and others the power they could wield with the ballot. Wells-Barnett's message built upon the motto of the NACW, "Lifting as We Climb," in that the female members sought to better the Black race, not themselves.[21] To that end, Fannie Barrier Williams, a fellow Black activist, joined the Alpha Suffrage Club in an attempt to end "prejudice and discrimination of all kinds."[22] The dynamics of their community, where Black women in the Second and Third Wards of Chicago were the racial majority, helped the organization succeed.

As we learned in the last chapter, in the 1915 election for the Alderman of the Second Ward, the Alpha Suffrage Club decided to support a single candidate so as not to divide the Black vote and chose Oscar DePriest. To support their candidate, members of the Alpha Suffrage Club began registering voters.[23] After a day of canvassing the neighborhood, women of the Alpha Suffrage Club reported to Wells-Barnett how "men jeered at them and told them they ought to be at home taking care of babies. Others insisted the women were trying to take the place of men and wear the trousers."[24] Wells-Barnett told her fellow women to respond to these criticisms by telling hecklers the women did this "so that they could help put a colored man in the city council."[25] In having the women answer in this way, Wells-Barnett reassured the community that Alpha Suffrage Club members sought the vote to support male political ambitions, likely because women did not have universal suffrage, limiting their options for political representation.

In addition to the face-to-face dismissals the women faced, they also experienced mockery in the press. Registering to vote required each woman to record her age, but since they only needed to be twenty-one-years-old to cast a ballot, many Black women tended to underestimate their years on the forms. The *Chicago Defender* re-printed several of the women's reported ages alongside with what the paper calculated as their real ages, intending to induce "a fit of laughter" in readers.[26] The fifty-one-year-old Wells-Barnett was not exempt from this conceit, as the article listed her reported age as thirty-two.[27] Despite these attempts to dismiss them, the women of the Alpha Suffrage Club proved their importance when their candidate won, and beyond that, DePriest directly credited Black women with his victory, a precedent that would require future candidates to gain the support of Black women in order to win local elections.[28]

In addition to mobilizing Black women, Wells-Barnett became determined to expand the NFL, an organization she established in the aftermath of the 1908 race riot in Springfield, Illinois, which met weekly to discuss matters affecting Black individuals.[29] Wells-Barnett found a supporter for her vision of developing the NFL into a full social service center for Black men molded after the Hull House at a 1910 Congregational Union dinner. During the event, Dr. J.G.K. McClure, the head of the Chicago Theological Seminary, spoke on the "White Man's Burden," arguing that the Black population had the highest rate of criminality in the nation. Wells-Barnett abandoned her prepared speech to contradict McClure's statements, openly resenting his implication that Black individuals possessed a racial disposition toward committing crime. She further noted that the Black race was "the most neglected group. All the other races in the city are welcomed into the settlements, YWCA's, gymnasiums and every other movement for uplift."[30] To help the Black race succeed, she argued, they deserved access to the same social services offered to other races, such as the neighborhood-based settlement houses for immigrants.[31]

In the audience, Jessie Lawson, a white woman whose husband was a major contributor to the YMCA, expressed surprise by the YMCA's racial policy of exclusion, and her husband Victor Lawson offered to fund Wells-Barnett's plan for the NFL.[32] With Lawson's financial support, Wells-Barnett transformed the NFL into the "Negro Fellowship League Reading Room and Social Center for men and boys." Similar to a settlement house, the NFL now offered employment services, a reading room, educational events, lodging, and food vouchers. Wells-Barnett located a property at 2830 State Street and considered the NFL to be a "lighthouse" in the middle of the Black south side of Chicago.[33]

After the expansion of the NFL, Wells-Barnett returned to journalism, one of her earliest mediums for activism. She founded the *Fellowship Herald* newspaper in May 1911 and served as its editor, aiming her pen at local issues affecting Black individuals. The paper, reaching five hundred subscribers, allowed Wells-Barnett to critique everything from legislation to local businessmen who failed to work toward the benefit of her race.[34] Her return to the press also offered her a method for defending herself from various criticisms leveled at her, as a woman, heading the NFL. She noted in one piece that she would "retire" when a "leader among men who will look after the race's affairs" emerged.[35] Returning to the newspaper business earned her criticism from her financial supporter Lawson, who felt her work at the *Fellowship Herald* was a distraction from the NFL.[36] Yet, Wells-Barnett, even while using the rhetoric of racial uplift for men, continued to support Black women reformers.

She included space at the NFL for other women to join her efforts, advertising "Ladies' Day" events and "mother's meetings" in addition to programs for men.[37] She also published a special women's edition of the *Fellowship Herald*. By 1914, her work at the *Fellowship Herald* won acclaim, with a fellow editor noting of her publication, "It is ably and brilliantly edited" and another praising it as "no doubt, the best paper the Negro has here in Chicago."[38]

Although Wells-Barnett threw herself into helping Black men at the local level, she continued her involvement with national Black organizations in the hope of aligning their focus on reform with hers. Wells-Barnett's initial exclusion from the NAACP remained temporary; she was added later, as Mary Ovington noted, "quite illegally," to the list of founding forty.[39] She had little voice in the association; however, and the executive committee proceeded to act upon her ideas without her participation. She suggested the NAACP develop its own publication to spread news about their work in combatting lynching. Her recommendation to issue a national journal was probably not entirely altruistic; Wells-Barnett likely assumed she would be the logical editorial choice based on her decades of journalistic experience and expertise on lynchings. The committee instead chose W.E.B. Du Bois to head the initiative. The situation further devolved when the NAACP's leadership began using this publication to minimize her contributions to the anti-lynching cause. Du Bois began leaving Wells-Barnett's activities out of his reports in the NAACP's new publication, *The Crisis: A Record of the Darker Races.*[40]

In the fall of 1910, Wells-Barnett's involvement in the Steve Green legal case increased tensions between her and the NAACP. Green, a sharecropper in Jericho, Arkansas, decided to leave his landowner, Will Seidle, for a more favorable situation. Angered, Seidle found Green and, according to Green, said, "Green, didn't I tell you that if you didn't work on my farm that there was no room enough in Crittenden County for you and me to live?" and drew his revolver.[41] Wounded in the neck, left arm, and right leg, Green grabbed his gun and returned fire, killing Seidle in self-defense.[42] Knowing that the consequence for slaying a white man would be the lynch mob, Green went into hiding and fled north. Just outside of Chicago, authorities arrested Green and arranged to return him to Arkansas. While in custody, Green tried to commit suicide by eating broken glass.[43] His attempt to take his own life made the news, alerting Wells-Barnett to his plight, and she mobilized to save Green from the waiting lynch mob.[44] While Green rode on a train back to Arkansas, she utilized the legal expertise of her husband to obtain a writ of *habeas corpus*. The request for the writ required the court to determine the legality and authority by which Arkansas law enforcement held Green in custody. Since Barnett filed in Chicago, Green returned to Illinois for the hearing. While lawyers sorted out his legal situation, Green stayed at the NFL.[45]

Green's case gained the attention of one of the wealthy white founders of the NAACP, Joel Spingarn, who donated one hundred dollars to his cause. When the treasurer of the NAACP asked Wells-Barnett if she needed Spingarn's donation to support Green's case, she asked him whether the donor "wishes the money to be used for Steve Green's personal expenses, or whether it is to be used as a contingent fund for the lawyers?"[46] Villard, in relaying the message, suggested to Spingarn that he not fund the legal defense, as Black lawyers "usually take advantage of philanthropic interest of this kind to make money for themselves."[47] Spingarn did not care for this response, and he and Wells-Barnett became allies. Although Villard's own words pushed Spingarn to support Wells-Barnett, he blamed her for appropriating a wealthy sponsor of the NAACP, and this further alienated her from the organization's leadership. Once the court settled the extradition issue, Wells-Barnett used her funds to send Green to Canada. The *Chicago Defender* praised Wells-Barnett for helping draw attention to Green's situation, with her actions likely saving his life, concluding that she served as the "watchdog of human life and liberty."[48] In contrast, the NAACP's report in *The Crisis* failed to mention Wells-Barnett's name, instead reporting, "the colored people of Chicago had heard of the story and got out [*sic*] a writ of habeas corpus," and "friends have engaged lawyers and are fighting his case for him."[49] Her old ally Du Bois omitted her actions out of the story she nearly single-handedly generated.[50]

Correspondence between Spingarn and Wells-Barnett reveal that such oversight was both intentional and related to Wells-Barnett's approach to reform. In 1911, while Wells-Barnett was traveling, Villard created a branch of the NAACP in Chicago, housed in Hull House. When her attempts to join failed, Wells-Barnett wrote to Spingarn noting that some members of the NAACP, among them Villard and Du Bois, "have the idea . . . that the organization should be kept in the hands of the exclusive 'academic few.'" Well-Barnett admitted that she did not "look with equanimity upon their patronizing assumptions."[51] The NAACP leadership, however, continued to minimize her current and past contributions. Ovington, in her history of the NAACP, published about lynchings in depth but mentioned Wells-Barnett only in regard to her presence at the inaugural meeting briefly, noting, "Mrs. Ida Wells Barnett and Dr. W.E.B. Du Bois detailed to the assembled people some of the difficulties under which Negroes labor," and failing to mention her decades of anti-lynching work.[52]

Recognizing her inability to penetrate national organizations, Wells-Barnett continued to focus on the NFL and uplifting Black men, but after 1913, Wells-Barnett's efforts with the organization began to suffer due to limited funds. She could no longer afford the rent at 2380 State Street, and moved the League to a "much smaller and very cramped" place down the street.[53] During this downsizing, municipal court chief justice Harry Olson, a supporter of her husband, appointed Wells-Barnett as the first Black female probation officer in his juvenile court, a position that paid one hundred and fifty dollars a month.[54] She used this salary to continue supporting the NFL, but in 1915 after she campaigned for Olson during his failed mayoral run, she lost her appointment. The profits from the employment service remained the only income supporting the organization. By 1919, the NFL was, as Wells-Barnett wrote in her autobiography, a "burden" growing "heavier each day."[55] After the state opened a free employment office nearby, even that meager income dropped, and "there was not always enough left to pay the rent."[56] In November 1919, a week before Thanksgiving, Wells-Barnett arrived at the NFL to find an empty building, everything confiscated by the landlord to cover unpaid rent.[57]

During 1920, Wells-Barnett clearly struggled to find her place in society. The NFL had closed, she remained unwelcomed at the NACW, and ignored by the NAACP. On December 15, 1920, Provident Hospital admitted Wells-Barnett for gallstones, but complications kept her in the hospital for five weeks.[58] After her release, she remained bedridden at home until March.[59] In her autobiography, Wells-Barnett admitted that her recovery took the better part of a year, during which the fifty-seven-year-old promised herself she would "make some preparation of a personal nature for the future."[60]

Just before she became ill in 1920, three-quarters of the states ratified the Nineteenth Amendment, granting all women the right to vote and presenting Wells-Barnett with a new focus for her reform efforts. Since 1883, when a conductor ejected Wells-Barnett from a train and she filed a lawsuit against the Chesapeake, Ohio, & Southwestern Railroad Company, she viewed the legal system as a way to fight discriminatory practices. She fought against lynching because whites used it as a social control mechanism that circumvented the legal process. Wells-Barnett created the NFL and the Alpha Suffrage Club specifically to uplift her race by helping Black men, as they were the only ones with access to political power. With the ratification of the Nineteenth Amendment, Wells-Barnett now no longer needed to work with interracial groups or male leaders to enact legal change. When she returned to the public sphere in 1922, her focus became gaining political power for Black women, culminating in her own run for political office.

Wells-Barnett, full of ideas for social change but lacking an organization through which to implement them, attempted to incite new momentum at the 1924 NACW meeting when she announced her candidacy for president. Wells-Barnett had little patience for policies that echoed Washington's accommodationist approach, and rather than asking for whites' help, she felt her race needed to demand change. Now that women could vote, she saw the NACW as having the potential to engage Black women in political issues. Her surprising candidacy against the popular Bethune failed to garner much support; Wells-Barnett received only forty-two votes to Bethune's six hundred and fifty-eight.[61] Upon hearing the results, Wells-Barnett motioned to make the vote for Bethune unanimous, which passed.[62] Due to her gracious action, she received positive media attention. The *Chicago Defender* reported, "No greater scene was enacted" at the conference, than when "Mrs. Ida B. Wells-Barnett walked to the center of the platform and put her arms around Mrs. Bethune."[63] Her presidential run and graceful deference to Bethune brought Wells-Barnett's name back into circulation among Black women.[64]

Two southern Black women, Mary Booze and Mamie Williams, both of whom had attended the recent NACW convention and witnessed Wells-Barnett's diplomacy, approached her about working with the Chicago chapter of the National League of Republican Colored Women (NLRCW). The NLRCW sought to mobilize Black women to vote for Republican candidates. Such work was needed, for as historian Catherine E. Rymph noted, in the decade after receiving the vote, many Black women "remained skeptical" about the act of voting, and clubs such as the NLRCW sought to educate them about how political change could alleviate social issues.[65] In addition to coordinating Black women, the association sought to educate them about their rights and ensure that they voted in their own best interests, not those of the Black men or the whites surrounding them.[66] Ready to engage Black women politically through an organization, Wells-Barnett agreed.

Further exercising this desire, in 1926, Wells-Barnett organized the Women's Forum, a local group focused on weekly social programs that introduced Black women to social injustices beyond racial violence, as Wells-Barnett recognized the interconnectedness of race, gender, and class in preventing social change. Most notably the women advocated for the unionization of Chicago's Pullman Company employees into the Brotherhood of Sleeping Car Porters (BSCP).[67] The Pullman Company, headquartered in Chicago, was the largest employer of Black individuals in the US, with most working as porters and maids.[68] Although they consistently underpaid their Black workers, the motivation to unionize stemmed in part from the dehumanizing working conditions. The company instructed all passengers to call the male Black porters "George," after George Pullman, the founder of the railroad company, who openly discussed his decision to hire Black men exclusively as porters in order to keep the idea of slavery alive for his white passengers.[69] As the wages for skilled Black laborers continued to rise and railroad salaries remained stagnant, the porters attempted to unionize.[70]

Chicago's Black clubwomen, led by Wells-Barnett, became the first advocates for the Black porters. Wells-Barnett invited the head of the BSCP, A. Phillip Randolph, to speak in her home and to offer his perspective. After she heard his account, Wells-Barnett brought Randolph to address the Women's Forum, and after his speech, the members endorsed unionization.[71] Wells-Barnett's efforts to garner public support included writing about the porters' objectives in the *Chicago Defender*. Her activities resulted in a network of assistance for The Brotherhood that led one historian to identify Wells-Barnett as "the most important figure in assisting the union."[72] These measures succeeded so well that the Pullman Company spent thousands of dollars to influence the Black press and Black ministers to renounce unionization.[73] In 1927, the Pullman Company discontinued the policy of addressing porters as "George," and in light of this progress, more Black individuals desired to join the BSCP.[74] This concession, however, remained the high point of the struggle for many years, as the Great Depression would delay progress, and BSCP union would not succeed until 1935.

In 1927, likely in preparation for the 1928 elections, Wells-Barnett intensified her efforts to mobilize Black women voters and founded the Third Ward Women's Political Club.[75] Her vision, unique among all previous political clubs, was not just to educate and encourage Black women to vote, but rather to train them to run for office.[76] In her address at the club's founding, Wells-Barnett spoke about enacting change through "women uniting politically and supporting women for office."[77] The motto "For Women, of Women, by Women" demonstrated the female-centered focus.[78]

In creating an organization solely for Black women, Wells-Barnett's activism returned to its roots and her original supporters. After her 1892 exile from the South for her "Eight Negroes lynched since last issue of the *Free Speech*" article, Black women formed the Ida B. Wells Testimonial Reception Committee, rallying around her. The following year, during The World's Fair, she spoke to Black women at the Tourgée Club and urged her audience to consider establishing a group of their own.[79] In September 1893, the Black women of Chicago started the Ida B. Wells Club, naming their organization after the driving force behind their formation.[80] Wells-Barnett's actions during the 1920s mirrored her earlier experiences with social reform. She returned to the tactics, ideas, and approaches of Black women from the clubwoman movement decades earlier to encourage newly enfranchised Black women to unify against the inequities uniquely affecting them.

The 1928 elections continued the migration of political ideologies within each party, and for the first time Black Democratic voters made a substantial showing, a result of both opposition to prohibition and mounting frustration with the Republican Party regarding their poor record on Black civil rights. This evolving political spectrum challenged Black women such as Wells-Barnett, who had spent the eight years since receiving the vote organizing for the Republicans. Notwithstanding Wells-Barnett's earlier determination to remain non-partisan, she threw herself into campaigning for the Republican presidential nominee, Herbert Hoover.[81] Wells-Barnett's decision to support the Republicans stemmed from her fear that if the Democrats successfully repealed the prohibition amendment, it could set a precedent for annulling other amendments, notably those that granted civil rights to Black Americans. In an October 1928 letter, Wells-Barnett wrote, "Al Smith cannot carry out his pledge to modify or annul the Volstead Law; and that if he could do so, it would open the door for the Democratic Party to try to repeal or modify other amendments to the Constitution—amendments which vitally affect the Negro more than any other group of our citizens, the 14th & 15th amendments which gave our race liberty and citizenship."[82] Her rationale explains why organizations such as the NACW remained focused on campaigning for Republican candidates despite their poor record on racial issues. Even worse, Republicans failed to repay the hard work done by Black women on their behalf. Clubwoman Ora Brown Stokes recalled receiving "No help from the white Republicans," and having to finance the cost of printing her own supporting literature for the Republican Party.[83]

In 1928, Wells-Barnett became a national organizer for the Colored Women of Illinois and traveled all over the state to campaign for Hoover on behalf of the Illinois Republican National Committee. She sent out mass mailings, planned rallies, and gave speeches. She wrote her own pamphlet, "Why I Am for Hoover," explaining that she felt the candidate would solve "racial problems with justice for all."[84] She credited her efforts with raising the number of Illinois Black women registered to vote by "nearly 50 percent."[85] In October, she summarized her activities in a letter to the Publicity Director, noting that she had founded Hoover-Curtis clubs in ten counties.[86] Despite her apparent success, the leadership refused to reimburse her for her expenses, including the cost of printing copies of her speeches and pledge cards, and her name did not appear on the organization's list of "outstanding women."[87] Records from private meetings suggest the administration viewed Wells-Barnett and her tactics with disdain, with one member dismissively commenting on an issue, "You know how Mrs. Barnett would act."[88] The leaders also chose not to forward a letter Wells-Barnett wrote to Hoover, noting, "Thank heavens he may never see it."[89] These responses insinuated that while Wells-Barnett remained useful to the organization's leadership, the upper levels of management found her undiplomatic. Although Wells-Barnett's energies on his behalf paid off when Hoover won the presidential election, he disappointed her early in his term when he refused to push the South to end segregation or confront issues of racial inequality.[90]

Wells-Barnett's work with the Third Ward and organizing for the Republican Party kept her name in circulation in regional efforts, yet she remained out of the national spotlight and with her earlier contributions largely forgotten. By 1922, the exclusion of Wells-Barnett in the NAACP narrative was complete. In the fall, NAACP officer James Weldon Johnson attended the annual NACW meeting to rally support for the re-introduction of the Dyer Bill.[91] With Wells-Barnett in the audience, Addie Waites Hunton, who also worked with the NAACP, introduced Johnson, and both speakers proceeded to disregard the fact that Wells-Barnett had created the national conversation about lynching in the first place, which directly led to the establishment of a national organization devoted to ending the practice.[92] Hunton did not possess an obvious reason for leaving Wells-Barnett out of her speech. Her only motive for doing so would be her acceptance of the NAACP's own narrative about the history of the anti-lynching movement, which failed to include the former "Princess of the Press."[93] Although Wells-Barnett joined the NAACP's efforts to pass the Dyer Bill, the leadership continued to dismiss her contributions.[94]

A 1927 conversation with a young woman provoked Wells-Barnett to fight her exclusion from the historical narrative. Wells-Barnett recalled, "a young woman recently asked me to tell her of my connection with the lynching agitation which was started in 1892."[95] The young lady explained how she, "the only colored girl" at a YWCA vesper service, offered Wells-Barnett's name when asked for someone who the youth knew that "had traits of character resembling" Joan of Arc.[96] The girl admitted she gave Wells-Barnett's name in response, but could not say why "she thought I deserved such mention," confessing "I have heard you mentioned so often by that name, so I gave it. I was dreadfully embarrassed. Won't you please tell me what it was you did, so the next time I am asked such a question I can give an intelligent answer?"[97] Wells-Barnett resignedly noted that at twenty-five-years-old, "the happenings about which she inquired took place before she was born" and "there was no record" for her generation to learn about "how the agitation against the lynching evil began."[98] With those in power at the national level reframing the movement for social progress on their own terms, this conversation spurred Wells-Barnett to "for the first time in my life" write about herself, and in 1928 she began her autobiography.[99] Wells-Barnett recognized that most members of the race lacked any knowledge "of authentic race history" and believed that her story would teach a new generation about the struggles of the past.[100]

In June 1929, the Third Ward Women's Political Club announced they would offer a "Race woman candidate" and ultimately endorsed Mary C. Clark for Senate.[101] Soon another Black woman joined the race, lawyer Georgia Jones-Ellis.[102] For several months, the two women canvassed for votes against two Black male candidates, lawyer Warren B. Douglas and incumbent Adelbert H. Roberts, who in 1925 had become the first Black man elected to the state legislature.[103] In January 1930, with an April primary looming, Wells-Barnett announced she also would run for the seat as an independent, but she did not mail her application to Springfield, Illinois, until February 12, 1930, less than two months before the primary.[104]

Wells-Barnett kept a daybook during 1930, which contained jottings about her daily life, budget, and social calendar.[105] She described the efforts of her campaign in matter-of-fact prose, mentioning going to an Urban League annual meeting for an endorsement on January 30, 1930, and later noting that she had secured signatures for her petition from several church members. Despite her late entrance to the race, she discussed several supporters of her candidacy, noting how "Lee Harlan leader of 2nd ward independent group" championed her and that "he called in a man named Cross who accepted my campaign with enthusiasm. He introduced me at Lincoln Center meeting got Fred Morris to endorse me and the fight was on."[106] Despite this, Wells-Barnett commented in her daybook, "Few women responded as I had hoped," and noted that she spent time "urging women voters to do their Christian duty & vote for race women on Primary Day April 8th."[107] She also discussed how she "made a deal" to receive $150 worth of printing for $75, resulting in 10,000 cards, 10,000 letters, and 600 window cards for her candidacy.[108] These efforts, ultimately consisting of little more than a paid announcement in the paper and handout materials, were rather meager and hampered by the short timeline in which to publicize her campaign.

Why Wells-Barnett chose to run is unclear. She believed Black women should be in politics, and likely felt that the possibility for success existed in light of the recent political achievements of white women and Black men. Yet her decision to campaign against two other Black women at the last minute seems incompatible with her desire for Black female representation, especially since the candidates could split the vote, with none of them succeeding.[109] Even more confusing was her decision when the campaign placed a significant financial burden on her family. The 1929 stock market crash hurt the economy, and the Barnett's financial status mirrored that of the country. Wells-Barnett did not currently work for a salary, and with only Ida, Jr., living at home, she and her husband sold their large house on State Street and moved to a smaller apartment.[110] Wells-Barnett's accounting of expenses in her daybook reveal her fear that she would be unable to afford a winter coat for Ida, Jr.[111] Yet, Wells-Barnett's run for Senate also is reflective of her approach to social issues. She likely assumed, in the wake of Ruth McCormick's success, a white woman who had challenged six Republican candidates to win a seat in the US House of Representatives, that if voters supported a white woman politician at the national level, then Black women could aspire to the state legislature.[112] She was sadly incorrect, for Wells-Barnett received only 752 of the ten thousand votes cast.

Additionally, constituents failed to elect a Black woman; instead, Roberts edged out Douglas.[113]

Regardless of the results, Wells-Barnett seemed at peace with the outcome of the election, perhaps because, similar to her candidacy for the NACW presidency in 1924, the campaign was more about the journey than a victory. She most likely wanted to show that Black women, who she had worked to organize for the past decade, could offer a variety of viable candidates. Wells-Barnett's run also may have reflected some personal desire, possibly prompted by the writing of her own life's story, to regain recognition for herself. Wells-Barnett did not appear to consider her defeat a failure; indeed, she seemed to take the loss in stride. She looked toward the future and to meeting with supporters so that Black women could "profit by the lessons of the campaign."[114] This optimism may have been misplaced; Illinois voters would not elect any woman to the State Senate for another twenty years.[115]

While she worked on her autobiography, the history of the anti-lynching movement continued to omit Wells-Barnett's actions. After the NAACP leadership of Ovington and Du Bois minimized her work, many others continued the practice of writing her out of the historical narrative. Wells-Barnett noted in the daybook that she read the new book from Carter G. Woodson for the January 13, 1930, "meeting of the local Negro History club."[116] Known as the father of Black history, Woodson's history of her race contained "no mention of [her] anti-lynching contribution."[117] Others followed Woodson's example. Walter White did not mention her in his book on lynching, *Rope & Faggot: A Biography of Judge Lynch* (1929), and neither did Arthur Raper in his 1933 examination of racial violence, *The Tragedy of Lynching*.[118] By contrast, her peers, including W.E.B. Du Bois, Booker T. Washington, James Addams, and Mary Church Terrell, received detailed mentions. Wells-Barnett's social position as a Black female lacking in education and focused on passionate social change enabled elite reformers of both races to push her aside, alienate her from national reform organizations, and diminish her previous accomplishments.

As a Black, middle-class female, Wells-Barnett, despite her accomplished career as a journalist, lacked the social capital to create her own legacy, yet those whose lives she directly affected recognized her impact. In 1927, the local clubwomen celebrated Wells-Barnett at a testimonial dinner hosted by the Ida B. Wells Club, where committee members discussed her role as the mother of the clubwoman movement and her influence on "all those from every walk of life" who benefited from her actions "in civic and social service."[119] To these women, Wells-Barnett, who had worn many hats in her life, represented the will to effect change every day against injustice, whether at the national or local level.

NOTES

1. Joyce Ann Hanson, *Mary McLeod Bethune and Black Women's Political Activism* (Columbia: University of Missouri Press, 2003), 105–6.

2. Paula Giddings, *Ida: A Sword among Lions, Ida B. Wells and the Campaign Against Lynching* (New York: HarperCollins Publishers, 2008), 632.

3. Mia Bay, *To Tell the Truth Freely: The Life of Ida B. Wells* (New York: Hill and Wang, 2009), 319.

4. Linda O. McMurry, *To Keep the Waters Troubled: The Life of Ida B. Wells* (New York: Oxford University Press, 1998), xiv.

5. Most studies of Wells-Barnett's life focus on her anti-lynching efforts. Jacqueline Jones Royster's edited short volume examines Wells' writings during an eight-year period highlighting her anti-lynching efforts during the height of her popularity. Jacqueline Jones Royster and Ida B.Wells-Barnett, *Southern Horrors and Other Writings: The Anti-Lynching Campaign of Ida B. Wells, 1892–1900* (Boston: Bedford Books, 1997). James West Davidson's *"They Say": Ida B. Wells and the Reconstruction of Race* (2007) focuses on Wells' early experiences during Reconstruction in the South and ends in 1892, before her anti-lynching crusade. James West Davidson, *"They Say": Ida B. Wells and the Reconstruction of Race* (New York: Oxford University Press, 2007). Linda O. McMurry's, *To Keep the Waters Troubled* (1998), spends only six pages on Wells-Barnett's life after the closure of the NFL in 1919. Patricia A. Schechter, in *Ida B. Wells-Barnett and American Reform, 1880–1930* (2001), devotes one chapter to the final decades of her life. In the work of Mia Bay, *To Tell the Truth Freely,* two chapters are devoted to Well-Barnett's life after 1920 while Paula Giddings' book, *Ida: A Sword among Lions,* spends 66 pages of 659 on Wells-Barnett after 1919.

6. Ida B. Wells, *Crusade for Justice: The Autobiography of Ida B. Wells,* edited Alfreda M. Duster (Chicago: The University of Chicago Press, 1970), 323–24.

7. Bay, *To Tell the Truth Freely,* 265.

8. Wells-Barnett claimed she could not help but notice Mary Ovington with "an air of triumph and a very pleased look on her face." Wells, *Crusade for Justice,* 324–25. Historian Paula Giddings doubted Du Bois acted alone and proposed Ovington behind the suggestion of removing Wells-Barnett. Giddings, *Ida,* 477–78. Ovington agreed with Villard's worldview; she kept "forgetting that the Negroes aren't poor people for whom I must kindly do something" but rather have "forceful opinions of their own." She also dismissed Black women reformers, claiming "they are ambitious for power, often jealous, very sensitive." Villard quoted in McMurry, *To Keep the Waters Troubled,* 281; Ovington in Schechter, *Ida B. Wells-Barnett and American Reform,* 142.

9. Wells, *Crusade for Justice,* 326. She wrote in her autobiography that his exclusion of her from the committee was a "deliberate" move intended to "ignore me and my work."

10. Bay, *To Tell the Truth Freely,* 258.

11. The standardization of education, created by an increasingly homogenous curriculum in most universities, professionalized many vocations. One result of this was the emerging perception that reform work was a career, and as such required a college education. Magali Sarfatti Larson, *The Rise of Professionalism: A Sociological Analysis* (Berkley: University of California Press, 1977), 152–53. This development often resulted in well-educated males replacing female reformers and their moral justifications. In 1892, Wells-Barnett drew on her feminine moral authority to validate her work as a reformer, directly addressing the reader in the preface of *Southern Horrors: Lynch Law in All Its Phases.* She began the work by explaining her motives, noting, "It is with no pleasure I have dipped my hands in the corruption here exposed" but "somebody must show that the Afro-American race is more sinned against than sinning." Ida B. Wells, *Southern Horrors: Lynch Law in All Its Phases* (CreateSpace Independent Publishing Platform, 1892), 2. By opening the pamphlet with these remarks, Wells situated herself as a reluctant participant compelled by her ethics into action and justified her authority as a Black

woman to enter the public sphere as consistent with her feminine virtue. Caroline C. Nichols, "The 'Adventuress' Becomes a 'Lady': Ida B. Wells' British Tours," *Modern Language Studies* 38.2 (2009): 56.

12. McMurry, *To Keep the Waters Troubled*, 289.

13. Wells, *Crusade for Justice*, 329.

14. Giddings, *Ida*, 493–4; McMurry, *To Keep the Waters Troubled*, 286.

15. Ida B. Wells, *The Light of Truth: Writings of an Anti-Lynching Crusader*. ed. Mia Bay (New York: Penguin Books, 2014), 432–33.

16. Wells, *The Light of Truth*, 436.

17. The Republicans after the Civil War had focused on issues of expansion, education, social justice, and laws protecting Black citizens, reflecting their conviction that the government existed to protect and serve its citizens. Yet by the 1930s, they began advocating for less governmental intervention, and the Democratic Party became the primary supporter of these beliefs. Thus, as the parties' core philosophies evolved, they essentially switched, with Democrats as proponents of policies to assist citizens and Republicans desiring to restrict governmental interference in people's lives. Arthur Schlesinger, *The Crisis of the Old Order: 1919–1933* (*The Age of Roosevelt*, vol. 1) (Boston: Houghton Mifflin, 1957), 26–36.

18. Bay, *To Tell the Truth Freely*, 287.

19. Wells, *Crusade for Justice*, 345.

20. Wanda A. Hendricks, "'Vote for the Advantage of Ourselves and Our Race': The Election of the First Black Alderman in Chicago," *Illinois Historical Journal* 87.3 (1994): 176. Wells-Barnett envisioned her group as a local representative of national organizations such as the Illinois Equal Suffrage Association and the City Federation of Colored Women's Clubs. This desire for non-partisanship can be traced back to an 1885 article Wells wrote in a *Living Way* where she praised T. Thomas Fortune, the Black editor of the *New York Age*, for suggesting Black individuals stop blindly voting for Republicans and instead consider both candidates' policies. McMurry, *To Keep the Waters Troubled*, 90–91.

21. Hendricks, "'Vote for the Advantage of Ourselves and Our Race,'" 177.

22. Ibid., 175.

23. Ibid., 182–83.

24. Wells, *Crusade for Justice*, 345.

25. Giddings, *Ida*, 535.

26. Ibid., 536.

27. Ibid., 536.

28. Anne Meis Knupfer, "'Toward a Tenderer Humanity and a Nobler Womanhood': African-American Women's Clubs in Chicago, 1890 to 1920," *Journal of Women's History* 7.3 (1995): 69; McMurry, *To Keep the Waters Troubled*, 309.

29. Wells, *Crusade for Justice*, 300.

30. McMurry, *To Keep the Waters Troubled*, 294.

31. Wells-Barnett was correct, in that despite the lack of social support for the Black community, there were surprisingly few black criminals. McMurry, *To Keep the Waters Troubled*, 292.

32. Giddings, *Ida*, 488–89.

33. Bay, *To Tell the Truth Freely*, 282; 284.

34. Giddings, *Ida*, 538. She criticized boxer Jack Johnson in the pages of the *Fellowship Herald* for using his money to open a large enterainment club near the NFL. His resources, she felt, would have been better spent converting the building into a gymansim for Black boys and thus helping the youth of the ecommunity. Giddings, *Ida*, 520.

35. Quoted in Schechter, *Ida B. Wells-Barnett and American Reform,* 191.

36. Giddings, *Ida,* 506.

37. Schechter, *Ida B. Wells-Barnett and American Reform,* 191–92.

38. McMurry, *To Keep the Waters Troubled,* 296.

39. Ibid., 282.

40. Giddings, *Ida,* 501.

41. W.E.B. Du Bois, "The Case of Steve Green," *The Crisis: A Record of the Darker Races* 1.14 (1910): 14.

42. Patricia A Schechter, "Ida B. Wells-Barnett and the Carceral State," *Portland State University History Faculty Publications and Presentations* Paper 16 (2012), 4.

43. McMurry, *To Keep the Waters Troubled,* 287.

44. Bay, *To Tell the Truth Freely,* 284–85.

45. Giddings, *Ida,* 494–5.

46. McMurry, *To Keep the Waters Troubled,* 287.

47. Ibid., 287.

48. Quoted in McMurry, *To Keep the Waters Troubled,* 287, and Giddings, *Ida,* 496.

49. Du Bois, "The Case of Steve Green," 14.

50. Giddings, *Ida,* 496. Despite the NAACP's dismissal of her work, Wells-Barnett proudly recalled her efforts on Steve Green's behalf, "He is one Negro who lives to tell the tale that he was not burned alive according to program." Wells, *Crusade for Justice,* 337.

51. Quoted in Giddings, *Ida,* 497.

52. Mary White Ovington, "The National Association for the Advancement of Colored People," *The Journal of Negro History* 9.2 (1924): 111.

53. Wells, *Crusade for Justice,* 332.

54. Bay, *To Tell the Truth Freely,* 286.

55. Wells, *Crusade for Justice,* 408.

56. In addition, the growth of a similar organization, the Urban League, pulled supporters from the NFL. Founded in New York in 1911 by an interracial coalition, the Urban League sought to help the influx of Black individuals to northern cities by assisting newly transplanted residents in locating jobs and housing. Touré F. Reed, *Not Alms But Opportunity: The Urban League & the Politics of Racial Uplift, 1910–1950* (Chapel Hill: University of North Carolina Press, 2008), 11–2. Although the Urban League shared similar goals as the NFL, the fact it drew upon Booker T. Washington's idea of industrial education meant Wells-Barnett would never support it. In 1915, the well-funded Urban League expanded to Chicago, and as other local reformers, including Jane Addams, began supporting the organization, the NFL could not survive the direct competition. Wells, *Crusade for Justice,* 372–73.

57. Giddings, *Ida,* 620. Wells-Barnett recalled in her autobiography that the NFL fulfilled its goal of helping the black man "at the hour of his greatest need" and "the race would get the benefit of our action." Wells, *Crusade for Justice,* 333.

58. Giddings, *Ida,* 620.

59. The *Chicago Defender* reported that she remained too sick to receive visitors until Christmas day when the "Barnett family attended en masse." McMurry, *To Keep the Waters Troubled,* 329.

60. Wells, *Crusade for Justice,* 414.

61. Giddings, *Ida,* 632.

62. Ibid.

63. Schechter, *Ida B. Wells-Barnett and American Reform,* 232. Although the organization likely saw Bethune as a moderate candidate compared to Wells-Barnett, it soon became

apparent that the new president harbored a similar desire to shift NACW's prevailing ideology. Bethune suggested the organization change their slogan from "Lifting as We Climb" to "Not for Ourselves, but for Others," a motto focused on helping all members of society regardless of race, class, or gender. Hanson, *Mary McLeod Bethune and Black Women's Political Activism*, 105.

64. Wells, *Crusade for Justice*, xxix. She became active in several local organizations, including the American Rose Art Club, the Chicago Association of Club Women, the Cook County Federation of Club Women, and regained the presidency of the Ida B. Wells Club.

65. Catherine E. Rymph, *Republican Women: Feminism and Conservatism from Suffrage Through the Rise of the New Right* (Chapel Hill: University of North Carolina Press, 2006), 55.

66. Ibid., 52–53.

67. Schechter, *Ida B. Wells-Barnett and American Reform*, 315.

68. Beth Tompkins Bates, *Pullman Porters and the Rise of Protest Politics in Black America, 1925–1945* (Chapel Hill: University of North Carolina Press, 2001), 18. The company served over thirty-five million travelers each year.

69. On referring to Black male employees as George, see Giddings, *Ida*, 635. The discussion of hiring Black men is in Larry Tye, *Rising from the Rails: Pullman Porters and the Making of the Black Middle Class* (New York: Henry Holt & Company, Inc., 2004), 3. Considering Black individuals interchangeable reflected a stereotypical cultural portrayal of Black men. The Pullman Company played on the image of the "Uncle Tom," which stereotyped subservient Black men as "good" slaves who were "obedient," "loyal," and "non-complaining." David Pilgrim, "The Tom Caricature," *Ferris State University Jim Crow Museum of Racist Memorabilia*, 2012, http://www.ferris.edu/news/jimcrow/tom/.

70. Giddings, *Ida*, 635–36. In response, the Pullman Company utilized every resource available to prevent organization, even placing spies on trains to report on the activities of their employees in order to fire anyone with union sympathies.

71. Bates, *Pullman Porters and the Rise of Protest Politics in Black America*, 72.

72. Ibid., 66.

73. Beth Tompkins Bates, "A New Crowd Challenges the Agenda of the Old Guard in the NAACP, 1933–1941," *The American Historical Review* 102.2 (1997): 347.

74. Giddings, Ida, 641.

75. Ibid., 644–45.

76. Ibid., 644.

77. Schechter, *Ida B. Wells-Barnett and American Reform*, 239.

78. Ibid., 217.

79. Wells, *Crusade for Justice*, 121–22.

80. Ibid., 123–24.

81. Bay, *To Tell the Truth* Freely, 322. Wells-Barnett nominated herself as a candidate from the First Congressional District to attend the 1928 Republican National Convention. The only woman to run, Wells-Barnett declared herself an independent. She ran against Oscar DePriest, a former City Councilman, and Daniel Jackson, another Black politician. Wells-Barnett was unable to beat either of these well-known and well-funded candidates.

82. Quoted in Lisa G. Materson, "African American Women, Prohibition, and the 1928 Presidential Election," *Journal of Women's History* 21.1 (2009): 79.

83. Quoted in Materson, "African American Women, Prohibition, and the 1928 Presidential Election," 71.

84. Giddings, *Ida: A Sword Among Lions*, 649.

85. Schechter, *Ida B. Wells-Barnett and American Reform*, 239.

86. Materson, "African American Women, Prohibition, and the 1928 Presidential Election," 79.

87. McMurry, *To Keep the Waters Troubled*, 334–35.

88. Ibid., 334–35.

89. Schechter, *Ida B. Wells-Barnett and American Reform*, 239.

90. Bay, *To Tell the Truth Freely*, 322–23.

91. The NAACP's campaign to pass a federal anti-lynching bill, known as the Dyer Anti-Lynching Bill, sought to make lynching a federal offense with a five-year minimum jail sentence. Claudine L. Ferrell, *Nightmare and Dream: Antilynching in Congress, 1917–1922* (New York: Garland Publishing, Inc., 1986), 306. Despite the NAACP organizing public demonstrations, including pickets, the Senate did not pass the bill. George C. Rable, "The South and the Politics of Antilynching Legislation, 1920–1940," *The Journal of Southern History* 51.2 (1985): 203.

92. Hunton spoke instead of the impact of John Mitchell, Jr., giving him credit for spreading knowledge about lynchings. Mitchell, the editor of the *Richmond Planet*, did not seek to explain or end lynchings. In contrast, Wells-Barnett exposed the reality behind lynchings and received national attention for doing so. Joy Weatherley Williams, "John Mitchell, Jr., and the Richmond Planet," *The Library of Virginia*, n.d., http://www.lva.virginia.gov/exhibits/mitchell/lynch1.htm.

93. See Susan Chandler, "Addie Hunton and the Construction of an African American Female Peace Perspective," *Affilia* 20, Fall (2005): 270–83. Wells-Barnett later sarcastically clarified that Hunton "was gracious enough" to mention her once in an offhand remark as having "done some work against lynching." Giddings, *Ida*, 628.

94. Giddings, *Ida*, 626. These efforts to pass anti-lynching legislation proved fruitless, and over the next few years, the NAACP repeatedly attempted to reintroduce the regulation, but the 1922 effort remained the closest the measure ever came to passing.

95. Wells, *Crusade for Justice*, 3–4.

96. Ibid., 3–4.

97. Ibid.

98. Ibid.

99. Ibid.

100. Ibid., 4.

101. Schechter, *Ida B. Wells-Barnett and American Reform*, 242.

102. Ibid.

103. Erma Brooks Williams, *Political Empowerment of Illinois' African-American State Lawmakers from 1877 to 2005* (Lanham: University Press of America, 2008), 7–8.

104. Ida B. Wells, *The Memphis Diary of Ida B. Wells: An Intimate Portrait of the Activist as a Young Woman*, ed. Miriam Decosta-Willis (Boston: Beacon Press, 1995), 170–72.

105. The daybook can be viewed at the University of Chicago Online Archives of the Ida B. Wells Papers 1884–1976 at https://www.lib.uchicago.edu/e/scrc/findingaids/view.php?eadid=ICU.SPCL.IBWELLS#idp19747940. Described as "Ida B. Wells' pocket diary, 1930. Entries begin Christmas Day, 1929, and end May 14, 1930." The handwritten account was also transcribed and included in Miriam Decosta-Willis' edited work of her Memphis Diary. Wells, *The Memphis Diary of Ida B. Wells.*

106. Ibid.; Wells, *The Memphis Diary of Ida B. Wells*, 174.

107. Ibid.; Wells, *The Memphis Diary of Ida B. Wells*, 174.

108. Ibid.; Wells, *The Memphis Diary of Ida B. Wells*, 173. Her husband she noted, "helped me, and got out the New Deal Paper—20000 copies and distributed them at his own expense."

109. She did consider withdrawing after learning that her son Herman stole money to pay for his gambling debts, but determined that it was "too late to withdraw." Giddings, *Ida*, 653–54.

110. Wells, *Crusade for Justice*, xxx.

111. Bay, *To Tell the Truth Freely*, 324.

112. Kristie Miller, "Ruth Hanna McCormick and the Senatorial Election of 1930," *Illinois Historical Journal* 81.3 (1988): 193–94.

113. Giddings, *Ida*, 654.

114. Ibid.

115. Schechter, *Ida B. Wells-Barnett and American Reform*, 240.

116. The daybook can be viewed at the University of Chicago Online Archives of the Ida B. Wells Papers 1884–1976 at https://www.lib.uchicago.edu/e/scrc/findingaids/view.php?eadid=ICU.SPCL.IBWELLS#idp19747940. Described as "Ida B. Wells' pocket diary, 1930. Entries begin Christmas Day, 1929, and end May 14, 1930"; see also, Wells, *The Memphis Diary of Ida B. Wells*, 168.

117. The daybook can be viewed at the University of Chicago Online Archives of the Ida B. Wells Papers 1884–1976 at https://www.lib.uchicago.edu/e/scrc/findingaids/view.php?eadid=ICU.SPCL.IBWELLS#idp19747940. Described as "Ida B. Wells' pocket diary, 1930. Entries begin Christmas Day, 1929, and end May 14, 1930"; see also, Wells, *The Memphis Diary of Ida B. Wells*, 168.

118. Walter White, *Rope & Faggot: A Biography of Judge Lynch* (New York: Knopf, 1929); Arthur Franklin Raper, *The Tragedy of Lynching* (Baltimore: Black Classic Press, 1933).

119. Schechter, *Ida B. Wells-Barnett and American Reform*, 238.

BIBLIOGRAPHY

Bates, Beth Tompkins. *Pullman Porters and the Rise of Protest Politics in Black America, 1925–1945*. Chapel Hill: University of North Carolina Press, 2001.

———. "A New Crowd Challenges the Agenda of the Old Guard in the NAACP, 1933–1941." *The American Historical Review* 102.2 (1997): 340–77.

Bay, Mia. *To Tell the Truth Freely: The Life of Ida B. Wells*. New York: Hill and Wang, 2009.

Chandler, Susan. "Addie Hunton and the Construction of an African American Female Peace Perspective." *Affilia* 20.3 (2005): 270–83.

Davidson, James West. *"They Say": Ida B. Wells and the Reconstruction of Race*. New York: Oxford University Press, 2007.

Du Bois, W.E.B. "The Case of Steve Green." *The Crisis: A Record of the Darker Races* 1.14 (1910): 14.

Ferrell, Claudine L. *Nightmare and Dream: Antilynching in Congress, 1917–1922*. New York: Garland Publishing, Inc., 1986.

Giddings, Paula. *Ida: A Sword among Lions, Ida B. Wells and the Campaign against Lynching*. New York: HarperCollings Publishers, 2008.

Hanson, Joyce Ann. *Mary McLeod Bethune and Black Women's Political Activism*. Columbia: University of Missouri Press, 2003.

Hendricks, Wanda A. "'Vote for the Advantage of Ourselves and Our Race:' The Election of the First Black Alderman in Chicago." *Illinois Historical Journal* 87.3 (1994): 171–84.

Knupfer, Anne Meis. "'Toward a Tenderer Humanity and a Nobler Womanhood': African-American Women's Clubs in Chicago, 1890 to 1920." *Journal of Women's History* 7.3 (1995): 58–76.

Larson, Magali Sarfatti. *The Rise of Professionalism: A Sociological Analysis.* Berkley: University of California Press, 1977.

Materson, Lisa G. "African American Women, Prohibition, and the 1928 Presidential Election." *Journal of Women's History* 21.1 (2009): 63–86.

McMurry, Linda O. *To Keep the Waters Troubled: The Life of Ida B. Wells.* New York: Oxford University Press, 1998.

Miller, Kristie. "Ruth Hanna McCormick and the Senatorial Election of 1930." *Illinois Historical Journal* 81.3 (1988): 191–210.

Nichols, Caroline C. "The 'Adventuress' Becomes a 'Lady': Ida B. Wells' British Tours." *Modern Language Studies* 38.2 (2009): 46–63.

Ovington, Mary White. "The National Association for the Advancement of Colored People." *The Journal of Negro History* 9.2 (1924): 107–16.

Pilgrim, David. "The Tom Caricature." *Ferris State University Jim Crow Museum of Racist Memorabilia,* 2012. http://www.ferris.edu/jimcrow/tom/.

Rable, George C. "The South and the Politics of Antilynching Legislation, 1920–1940." *The Journal of Southern History* 51.2 (1985): 201–20.

Raper, Arthur Franklin. *The Tragedy of Lynching.* Baltimore: Black Classic Press, 1933.

Reed, Touré F. *Not Alms but Opportunity: The Urban League & the Politics of Racial Uplift, 1910–1950.* Chapel Hill: University of North Carolina Press, 2008.

Rymph, Catherine E. *Republican Women: Feminism and Conservatism from Suffrage through the Rise of the New Right.* Chapel Hill: University of North Carolina Press, 2006.

Schechter, Patricia A. *Ida B. Wells-Barnett and American Reform, 1880–1930.* Chapel Hill: The University of North Carolina Press, 2001.

———. "Ida B. Wells-Barnett and the Carceral State." *Portland State University History Faculty Publications and Presentations,* Paper 16 (2012). http://pdxscholar.library.pdx.edu/hist_fac/16.

Schlesinger, Arthur. *The Crisis of the Old Order: 1919–1933. The Age of Roosevelt,* vol. 1. Boston: Houghton Mifflin, 1957.

Tye, Larry. *Rising from the Rails: Pullman Porters and the Making of the Black Middle Class.* New York: Henry Holt & Company, Inc., 2004.

Wells, Ida B. *Crusade for Justice: The Autobiography of Ida B. Wells,* edited by Alfreda M. Duster. Chicago: The University of Chicago Press, 1970.

———. *The Light of Truth: Writings of an Anti-Lynching Crusader,* edited by Mia Bay. New York: Penguin Books, 2014.

———. *The Memphis Diary of Ida B. Wells: An Intimate Portrait of the Activist as a Young Woman,* edited by Miriam Decosta-Willis. Boston: Beacon Press, 1995.

———. *Southern Horrors: Lynch Law in All Its Phases.* CreateSpace Independent Publishing Platform, 1892. http://www.gutenberg.org/files/14975/14975-h/14975-h.htm.

Wells-Barnett, Ida B. and Jacqueline Jones Royster. *Southern Horrors and Other Writings: The Anti-Lynching Campaign of Ida B. Wells, 1892–1900.* Boston: Bedford Books, 1997.

White, Walter. *Rope & Faggot: A Biography of Judge Lynch.* New York: Knopf, 1929.

Williams, Erma Brooks. *Political Empowerment of Illinois' African-American State Lawmakers from 1877 to 2005.* Lanham: University Press of America, 2008.

Williams, Joy Weatherley. "John Mitchell, Jr., and the Richmond Planet." *The Library of Virginia,* n.d. http://www.lva.virginia.gov/exhibits/mitchell/.

Figure 1.1 Ida B. Wells (standing left) with Betty Moss and her son, Tom Moss, Jr. (seated) the widow and son of Tom Moss, one of the three victims of a barbaric lynching in Memphis on March 9, 1892. This incident launched Wells' anti-lynching crusade. Photo Credit: Special Collections Research Center, University of Chicago Library.

Figure 1.2 This illustration by J. Garland Penn appeared in the Black Press circa 1895 at the height of Wells-Barnett's national fame. Photo Credit: Special Collections Research Center, University of Chicago Library.

Figure 1.3 Ida B. Wells-Barnett (standing right) appears here with thirteen-year-old Ida, Jr. (standing left), and ten-year-old Alfreda (seated) in September 1914, a year after the launch of the Alpha Suffrage Club, the first such club for Black women in Chicago. Photo Credit: Special Collections Research Center, University of Chicago Library.

Figure 1.4 Ida B. Wells-Barnett, circa 1920, continued her local reform efforts in Chicago throughout the final decade of her life, but she also sought to regain a role in the national freedom struggle, to encourage the political activism of women, and to safeguard the collective memory of her social justice crusade. Photo Credit: Special Collections Research Center, University of Chicago Library.

II

MIGHTIER THAN THE SWORD: DISCOURSE ON THE LIFE & LEGACY OF IDA B. WELLS-BARNETT

6

Constructing Monuments to the Memory of Ida B. Wells-Barnett

Institutionalization of Reputation, Memory Distortion, and Cultural Amnesia

Lori Amber Roessner

On January 15, 1938, nearly twenty-five years after Ida B. Wells-Barnett co-founded the Alpha Suffrage Club, a non-partisan organization devoted to raising awareness about women's rights, Rebecca Stiles Taylor, one of the only female columnists for the *Chicago Defender* and a social activist deeply committed to women's and civil rights, reviewed the lives of "three magnificent women."[1] "It is not given to all men and women to build material, tangible monuments which can be seen by the natural eye," Taylor wrote, referring to the barriers preventing Black Americans from constructing monuments to leaders of the race. "We must recognize and stress the importance of intangible, abstract, moral and spiritual monuments that are far more necessary than those of wood, brick, and stone."[2] In the absence of a stone monument commemorating the life of Ida B. Wells-Barnett, Taylor constructed a journalistic tribute, an "intangible, abstract monument" created with the raw material of printed words for the moral sake of preserving the legacy of Wells-Barnett and the spiritual cause of regeneration of leadership in her community.[3]

In the piece, Taylor engaged not only in memory work, but also in an effort to correct the historical record. As we saw in the last chapter, the anti-lynching efforts of Wells-Barnett had been written out of the first official version of Black history when political tensions among the anti-lynching crusader, W.E.B. Du Bois, and other leaders of the NAACP resulted in the omission of the militant social activist from the earliest narratives of the anti-lynching movement, but Taylor sought to correct the historical narrative, writing that "if the anti-lynching bill is ever passed by the Federal government, if lynching is ever eliminated in these United States: no person or group of persons will be more responsible for the success of the movement than the late Ida B. Wells-Barnett, for as martyr, editor, lecturer, organizer, and public worker, she pioneered the movement and traveled the world in its behalf."[4]

In what remains to be one of the most inclusive, incisive accounts of Wells-Barnett in American memory, Taylor offers a holistic portrait of Wells-Barnett by quoting one of the first historians of the Black woman's club movement, Elizabeth Lindsay Davis: "Teacher, writer, editor, lecturer, club woman, church and social worker, Ida B. Wells-Barnett was a woman of strong character, forceful personality, and unflinching courage. Her clarion voice and ready pen were always waged vigorously in agitating and protesting against any force of segregation and discrimination affecting the oppressed."[5] Davis, and by extension Taylor, omitted only one descriptor that most modern-day historians evoke—suffragist. Taylor acknowledged that the accomplishments of the "pioneer" had been devalued during her lifetime because she had been deemed as "radical," but she looked forward to the day when "the women of Mississippi, Tennessee and Illinois will join hands and together with those of the rest of the country and build to the memory of Ida B. Wells-Barnett some form of monument commensurate with the heroic service rendered by her."[6] Such efforts were underway in Taylor's time, but as we will see in this chapter, in many respects, these efforts remain incomplete—an unfinished project, an ongoing effort.[7]

This chapter will consider both the "intangible, abstract monuments" that have been built by individuals and communities of journalists, scholars, documentarians, and grassroots organizations over the last eight decades alongside the tangible tributes and memorials housed in disparate spaces across the nation.[8] As we will see, these monuments to the memory of Ida B. Wells-Barnett were constructed in distinct phases to chronicle, commemorate, or otherwise honor the legacy of the social justice crusader—the first version of Wells-Barnett's life narrative primarily was told by journalists of the Black press, such as Taylor, in the decades after Wells-Barnett's death in 1931; after her daughter Alfreda Duster's critical intervention as memory protector in 1970, historians, biographers, and documentarians reclaimed Wells-Barnett's story from the footnotes of African-American history; and in the most recent years, a relatively monochromatic narrative of the historical legacy and public memory of Wells-Barnett has been reprinted and institutionalized in digital spaces and museums. The majority of these remembrances have taken place outside of mainstream media outlets, where narratives of Wells-Barnett largely have been omitted and subjected to cultural amnesia by a white Western culture that has struggled to come to terms with its colonializing impulses and its dark history of racial violence and discrimination.[9] By closely exploring these stages in the memorialization of Wells-Barnett, we can gain insight not only into how Americans have remembered and forgotten Iola, the princess of the press, and what this reveals about American culture, but also into how collective memories operate in various sites of public memory, which is to say, we can offer insight into how individual and group memories are negotiated in these public spaces.

French sociologist Maurice Halbwachs first theorized the concepts of social and collective memory in the first half of the twentieth century. Social memory, for Halbwachs, involved how group ideologies inform individual memories whereas the study of collective memory encompassed examining how memories are shared and passed down by individuals and groups.[10] The study of collective—or public memory—was revitalized in the 1980s when a new generation of historians and sociologists, such as French historian Pierre Nora, extended the work of Halbwachs, considering, among other topics, the operation of memory in the evolution of national identity, sites of memory, and the relationship between memory and history. More recently, scholarship of public memory, defined by one scholar as "a purposeful engagement of the past, forged symbolically, profoundly constitutive of identity, community, and moral vision, inherently consequential in its ideological implications, and very often the fodder of political conflagration," has become a popular niche of interdisciplinary study among sociologists, historians, media studies scholars, and even psychologists who have considered the conceptual clarity of the terms collective, public, and social memory; the function of collective memory as an indicator of present attitudes; the process of remembering and forgetting; the operation of individuals or groups as preservers of reputation and legacy; and the phenomenon of memory distortion.[11] This longitudinal case study will extend that prior scholarship by considering the shift in the reputation and legacy of Wells-Barnett over time; the role of memory protectors in buttressing Wells-Barnett's legacy; the process of remembering and forgetting in various sites of collective memory; and the phenomenon of memory distortion. For heuristic purposes, the chapter will rely heavily on media studies scholar Michael Schudson's catalogue of memory distortion, which involves processes of distanciation, institutionalization, instrumentalization, and conventionalization, and historians Vered Vinitzky-Seroussi and Chana Teeger's typology of overt and covert silences in acts of remembering and forgetting.[12]

As we have seen in the chapters of this edited volume, since the publication of Ida B. Wells' autobiography in 1970, biographers, historians, and mass communication scholars have lifted the social activist's story from the footnotes of American history[13]; nonetheless, little research exists on the negotiation of Wells-Barnett's legacy and reputation in American memory.[14] Thus, the purpose of this chapter is to consider how public remembrances of Wells-Barnett have been "crystalize[d] and secrete[d]" in what memory scholar Pierre Nora called "les lieux de memoire," or sites of collective memory, and how her legacy has been negotiated in these cultural spaces[15]; to that end, the historian engaged in narrative and discourse analyses of hundreds of media texts—newspaper articles, editorials, and letters to the editor published in the Black and mainstream press; magazine features that appeared in the Black and mainstream press; documentaries; and several digital sites and physical spaces of collective memory.[16] The historian also traced the patterns and trajectories of remembrance across various mediums—dissertations and theses, historical and modern newspapers, historical and modern magazines, scholarly journals, books, trade journals, audio and video works, and conference papers and proceedings—from Ida B. Wells-Barnett's death on March 25, 1931, to the present moment in American history.[17] Since her death, the name Ida B. Wells has surfaced more than 7,000 times in the US media texts listed above, and tracing the patterns of remembrance and examining a sample of these media texts allowed the scholar to gain insight into how we struggled over the memory and legacy of Wells-Barnett throughout the course of the twentieth and twenty-first centuries; likewise, radically contextualizing these texts, permitted the author to explore why we have remembered Wells-Barnett in certain ways at certain times, why we largely have omitted her narrative from mainstream American culture, and what this cultural amnesia says about our nation at this present moment in time.

WRITING THE FIRST ACCOUNT OF THE PRINCESS OF THE PRESS' LEGACY INTO BLACK HISTORY, 1927–1970

A conversation with a young Black woman, who could not explain to her YWCA vespers' class why she had cited Ida B. Wells-Barnett's name as an individual with character resembling Joan of Arc, spurred the 65-year-old "Princess of the Press" to begin writing her autobiography in 1927.[18] Over the course of her life, Wells-Barnett had kept several diaries of her life; these life narratives served multiple purposes—as we witnessed in an earlier chapter, they helped a young Wells-Barnett hone her craft, they preserved personal memories of Wells-Barnett, and they served as a record of life for Wells-Barnett, her kin, and a potential extended audience.[19] Self-presentation likely contributed to Wells-Barnett's representation of self in these early accounts, and it definitely figured into her thought process when constructing her autobiography, which she intended to bolster her reputation and preserve her legacy among future readers, such as the young Black woman she had encountered in 1927.

Wells-Barnett's appreciation of history had originated with her parents' desire for her education.[20] It was a passion that she sought to instill in others first in her role as a schoolteacher, then in her role as an advocacy journalist, and finally in her role as a local reformer and social activist. In July 1912, for instance, she invited Dr. Carter Woodson, one of the nation's first Black historians, to speak at the Negro Fellowship League. On that occasion, Woodson recounted anecdotes about prominent members of the Black race and encouraged the youth present to "pay respect to Negro heroes."[21] At least one young man, Lucius C. Harper, took Woodson's directive at the event organized by Wells-Barnett to heart. "From that day on," he wrote in 1946, "I began to study and collect books on the subject which now total a sizeable library."[22] After Wells-Barnett's death in March 1931, the journalist would become one of the champions of Wells-Barnett's legacy—and a consummate protector of African-American memory—at the *Chicago Defender* in his column, "Dustin' Off the News." Within the space, he acknowledged Wells-Barnett's role as an advocacy journalist, but he also preserved her legacy as a local reform activist.[23] Harper's work counteracted the efforts of the NAACP to write the controversial militant figure out of the history of anti-lynching reform, or what Vinitzky-Seroussi and Teeger referred to as engaging in overt silence in the domain of forgetting.[24]

As we have already seen in this chapter, Black journalists of the *Chicago Defender*, such as Taylor and Harper, were some of the staunchest protectors of Wells-Barnett's legacy, but they also were the earliest curators of her story. Immediately following Wells-Barnett's death on March 25, 1931, the *Defender* published Wells-Barnett's obituary and several tributes to the famous anti-lynching crusader. These first-edition life narratives in many respects were anomalous for their holistic account of Wells-Barnett's life. On March 28, 1931, for instance, the *Chicago Defender* described Wells-Barnett's upbringing in Mississippi; her career as an educator who demanded equity; the public speaking and journalistic efforts involved in her anti-lynching crusade; her activism in politics as a suffragist and a local reformer; and her role as wife and mother.[25] As public memory scholar Janice Hume asserted, obituaries are instructive not only for what they reveal about the collective remembrances of an individual, but also for what they indicate about a culture.[26] In this case, it is worth noting that in a moment when most women were celebrated for their gentle, tender, and obedient natures, the *Defender* offered a tribute to Wells-Barnett, who was "internationally known for two generations for her agitation and leadership of women and public thought."[27] In the coming years, as Wells-Barnett's legacy was institutionalized in the Black press, her status as a militant leader would be de-emphasized as the Black press, most notably the *Defender*, engaged in what Vinitzky-Seroussi and Teeger referred to as covert silence in the domain of remembering, or a form of simplification in an act of commemoration designed to make Wells-Barnett's story more palatable to a wider audience.[28]

In the hiatus, the *Defender* followed the initial death announcement with an article that described the last rites of Wells-Barnett. Rev. Joseph M. Evans, pastor of the People's Community Church, told those in mourning "in simple words of her struggles, one after another, for the betterment of those with whom she had come in contact."[29] The service had involved "no fanfare of trumpets, no undue shouting, no flowery oratory," the *Defender* reported on April 4, and was conducted "with simple dignity and solemnity befitting the occasion of the passing of a great woman."[30] Additional memorial services and tributes would follow as the local Chicago community mourned the death of one of their greatest citizens. One such tribute, a sonnet, came from Wallace Webb Scott of 714 S. Dakota St., in Butte, Montana, an individual who had once known Wells-Barnett while living in Chicago. "Weeping for you is lost—worthless," he wrote. "Of [B]lack men. Yours is no death. For you are not dead, but yet with us in this realm ... where the glow of justice yet will go."[31]

In subsequent years, the *Defender* would remain one of the most steadfast keepers of Wells-Barnett's memory. Charles Abbott's newspaper regularly reported on the events surrounding the Ida B. Wells Club, including longer write-ups on the occasion of big events such as the fortieth anniversary of the club in December 1933, and the development of the Ida B. Wells Garden Homes, the Chicago Housing Authority's forty-seven-acre housing project. Over the next four decades, the *Defender* also would offer occasional profiles of Wells-Barnett.[32] In January 1938, for instance, a five-graph profile accompanied Taylor's column, but unlike the nuanced account offered in Wells-Barnett's obituary or Taylor's column, this profile focused only on Wells-Barnett's role as a "pioneer crusader against lynching," providing readers with an incomplete portrait of Wells-Barnett that included no mention of her suffrage or local reform efforts.[33] By the end of the decade, biographical accounts of

Wells-Barnett had dwindled to a handful of sentences in listings of prominent Black Americans that accompanied Negro History Week.[34] That remained largely the case until 1970, when Naomi Millender offered *Defender* readers with a more nuanced profile that accompanied the release of Wells-Barnett's autobiography by her daughter Alfreda Duster. Millender focused on Wells Barnett's anti-lynching crusade, but she also acknowledged that Wells-Barnett was the "mother of clubwomen," who worked with Jane Addams of the Hull House to "prevent the erection of segregated schools" and who "fought for women's suffrage, served as [Chicago's] first Negro adult probation officer, was instrumental in the founding of the Wabash YMCA and led the fight for Chicago's first [B]lack alderman."[35]

In the years prior to Duster's intervention, collective memories of Wells-Barnett also surfaced in other journalistic sites, most prominently in the Black press but also, on occasion, in the *Chicago Tribune*, a mainstream newspaper with a national circulation that covered the legacy of the prominent Black woman because of her status in the local community. As memory scholars have noted, communities—in this case, individuals in Bronzeville, the South Side Chicago neighborhood where the social justice crusader lived and worked, and the larger local, regional, and national communities—play a seminal role in the construction and negotiation of collective memory, and these stories, in turn, "are central to meaning making in a community that remembers its past."[36] The communal tributes in these newspapers, however, did not often follow a pattern that one might expect based upon anniversaries of key events in Wells-Barnett's life; instead, they surfaced more organically. For instance, in 1963, the one-hundredth anniversary of the Emancipation Proclamation and the fiftieth anniversary of Wells-Barnett's establishment of the Alpha Suffrage Club, the *Chicago Tribune* published one piece that mentioned Wells-Barnett in name only in an article about an upcoming "tea to mark Negro history."[37] The *Defender* also carried notice of the event designed to preserve Wells-Barnett's legacy and to institutionalize Negro history.[38] Other organs of the Black press, most notably the Memphis *Tri-State Defender*, carried stories of Wells-Barnett that year, but they did not focus on prominent anniversary milestones; instead, they offered profiles and briefs on Wells-Barnett's role as a pioneer civil rights leader, a journalist, a women's rights activist, an educator, and a mother of reform, and news of the efforts of Wells-Barnett's kin to research the life of the social justice crusader.[39] Although many of the articles referenced various aspects of Wells-Barnett's life, most still focused overwhelming attention on the social activist's anti-lynching crusade. As memory scholar Carolyn Kitch reminds us:

> The articulation of the past [in the Black Press] . . . is a dual process of documentation and disputation, of telling truth and challenging truth at the same time. These magazines [and other alternative mediums] invoke memory so that past successes and outrages are not forgotten. They also create "new" memory, showing us [B]lack faces in what we thought were historically white places and eras, gathering and connecting fragments of historical evidence, and asking readers to use the past in order to question the politics of the present.[40]

Wells-Barnett's role as a fearless anti-lynching crusader would remain at the forefront of her legacy until Duster rescued a more holistic account of her life from the footnotes of history with the release of her autobiography in 1970.

UP FROM THE FOOTNOTES: POPULAR REACTION TO SCHOLARSHIP ON IDA B. WELLS-BARNETT, 1970–2000

After Wells-Barnett's death in 1931, the Black press, and in particular the *Chicago Defender*, served as the champion of Wells-Barnett's legacy as a fearless anti-lynching advocate and crusader for justice, but by the 1960s, these journalists were joined by Wells-Barnett's daughter, Alfreda Duster, in preserving the memory of the social justice activist. Prior memory scholars have acknowledged the role that family members and friends in a community can play in bolstering the reputation and legacy of an individual, and during the 1960s, Duster engaged in such a role.[41] She remained involved in the local reform efforts that her mother had begun as a religious and civic reformer in the Chicago area, but she also made a resolution to finish the autobiographical work that her mother had commenced in the 1920s.[42] To that end, in summer 1963, she returned to Memphis and Holly Springs, her mother's birthplace, in an effort to research her mother's rise as a social justice crusader. She would complete the task that her mother had begun in 1927 by decade's end, and her efforts would be published by the University of Chicago Press in 1970.[43]

Within the autobiography's introduction, Duster offered her own account of the life, career, and legacy of the "fiery reformer, feminist, and race leader" alongside of her own personal memories of the "kind and loving parent, . . . who impressed upon her children . . . [the importance of] good conduct . . . education . . . [and] civic affairs" as a supplement to the memoir that Wells-Barnett crafted over the last four years of her life.[44] On those pages, Duster considered how her mother's memory had "been kept alive." Although she failed to recognize the efforts of the Black press and individual journalists, such as Taylor and Harper, she did acknowledge the efforts of women's clubs around the nation. "There are Ida B. Wells clubs in various parts of the country," she wrote. "The followers of this leader of women spearheaded the drive which secured for her the most significant recognition that she has yet received"— the distinction of the Ida B. Wells Garden Homes.[45] A few lines prior, Duster may have delivered her most sage piece of analysis. "Ida B. Wells will be remembered for her fight against the lynching of Negroes, and for her passionate demand for justice and fair play for them," she wrote. Nonetheless, she and Wells-Barnett's living kin remained committed to offering a nuanced portrait of the remarkable social justice crusader, and they shifted their efforts to the institutionalization of their mother's memory through the Ida B. Wells Museum in Holly Springs, Mississippi, which was established in 1970. These memory preservers offered a more comprehensive account of Wells-Barnett's life, but as we will see, efforts to widen the audience for Wells-Barnett's memory once again culminated in a homogenized version of Wells-Barnett's story.

The efforts of Wells-Barnett's kin as memory preservers coincided with attempts to institutionalize a national Black History Month and spurred a wave of interest from Black Americans that manifested itself in remembrances in popular culture, honors from professional organizations, and efforts by the first wave of women's historians, who sought to lift Wells-Barnett's story from the footnotes of American history. In July 1977, for example, novelist and activist Alice Walker published the short story, "Advancing Luna—and Ida B. Wells," in *Ms.* magazine, the alternative liberal feminist magazine co-founded by Gloria Steinem and Dorothy Pitman Hughes six years prior.[46] In the semi-autobiographical short story, Walker had an imaginary dialogue with Wells after her friend Luna, a white civil rights activist, told her that she had been raped by a Black man. In the piece, Walker's character wrestled over determining the veracity of Luna's story alongside of her understanding of the myth of Black male bestiality exposed by Wells. In Walker's account, Wells-Barnett once again was remembered for her anti-lynching efforts, and as her daughter suggested, this would remain largely the case in the coming years as Wells-Barnett's memory became institutionalized in Black culture.

In 1983, for instance, the National Association of Black Journalists established the Ida B. Wells Award to pay tribute to the efforts of Wells-Barnett to champion her race and to recognize distinguished leadership in increasing access and opportunities to people of color in journalism and to improving the coverage of communities of color in US media outlets.[47] Likewise, in February 1988, *Essence*, a monthly magazine established in 1970 to serve the neglected audience of Black women, paid tribute to the "woman warrior" as a part of its Black History Special. Editors enlisted the service of Paula Giddings, a Black activist, writer, and historian, who had recently completed *When and Where I Enter: The Impact of Black Women on Race and Sex in America*, to share the story of "Ida B. Wells, Crusader—Journalist." In the long-form profile, Giddings, who would go on to write a biography about Wells-Barnett, sketched out the details of Wells-Barnett's life, beginning with her first act of civil protest on the Chesapeake & Ohio railway in 1883 and concluding with her attempts to "retire" from public life in 1896 and 1904. Although Giddings aptly described Wells-Barnett as an individual "determined to fight for Black rights as an activist and crusading journalist," she echoed portraits from the past that largely ignored the social justice crusader's attempts to secure woman's suffrage and her local reform efforts.[48]

"Ida B. Wells: A Passion for Justice," the 1989 documentary produced and directed by William Greaves, marked the beginning of a point of departure from the monochromatic portrait of Wells-Barnett that had been offered in the past. The Emmy-award winning filmmaker sought to share the history of "one of the most dynamic figures in the Civil Rights Movement" with the American public.[49] "Though virtually forgotten today, Ida B. Wells-Barnett was a household name in Black America during much of her lifetime (1863–1931) and was considered the equal of her well-known African-American contemporaries such as Booker T. Washington and W.E.B. Du Bois," Greaves wrote of the cultural amnesia surrounding the social justice crusader within American culture, and in some segments of African-American culture, due to her omission from the first histories of anti-lynching. "Ida B. Wells: A Passion for Justice" documents the dramatic life and turbulent times of the pioneering African American journalist, activist, suffragist and anti-lynching crusader of the post-Reconstruction period."[50] Greaves had enlisted an all-star team to assist with the documentary, including Wells-Barnett's remaining kin; renowned historians such as Giddings, Catherine Clinton, and Eric Foner; narrator Al Freeman, Jr., an award-winning actor, director, and educator; and Nobel Prize-winning author Toni Morrison, who read selections from Wells-Barnett's memoirs and other writings, and through their efforts, the documentary offered a more nuanced, holistic account of Wells-Barnett's life than had been previously offered. "Wells had two battles to fight—racism and sexism," Freeman told his audience before helping to recount Wells-Barnett's efforts to secure woman's suffrage alongside the account of her latter-day local reform efforts.[51]

The winner of more than twenty film festival awards obtained a wide audience when it was broadcast on the Public Broadcasting System's "American Experience" and thus served as a potential antidote to the cultural amnesia surrounding Wells-Barnett. Our history "is buried in oblivion," Freeman chose to conclude his documentary with words that Wells-Barnett had written in her autobiography. "Our youth are entitled to the facts of race history, which only the participants can give, I am thus led to set forth the facts in this volume which I dedicate to them."[52] With the assistance of historians such as Giddings, Greaves had followed in the footsteps of journalists such as Taylor and organizations such as the *Chicago Defender*, who sought to preserve the legacy of Wells-Barnett and to lift her story up from the footnotes of history into the mainstream cultural narrative. The efforts of Greaves and others spurred a new round of scholarship on Wells-Barnett that offered a more holistic account of her life, but as we will see in the next section, the history and memory of Wells-Barnett has only begun to seep into mainstream American public memory, and when it does, Americans often are offered with monochromatic, institutionalized accounts of a "one woman crusade" as a result of what Vinitzky-Seroussi and Teeger referred to as covert silences in the domain of forgetting, or the act of incorporating difficult aspects of a story in ways that minimize their impact.[53]

INSTITUTIONALIZING THE MEMORY OF THE FEARLESS ANTI-LYNCHING CRUSADER, 2000–2016

In recent years, accounts of Wells-Barnett have materialized in mainstream American public memory in sites such as anniversary journalism; public honors, awards, and recognitions; commissioned portraits and exhibits in spaces at public universities and national museums; and in digital spaces such as the Google Doodle and standalone websites. In July 2002, for instance, in a site of anniversary journalism, popular historian Gail Collins recounted the seventy-two-year struggle for women's suffrage in the mainstream newspaper outlet, the *Washington Post*. "Those 72 years are rich with stories of superhuman persistence, low comedy, unexpected heroics and tragic betrayal," she wrote, continuing, "Some of the betraying was done by the women themselves, almost always on account of race. The great Alice Paul, who finally pushed what became known as the Susan B. Anthony Amendment through Congress with her White House picket lines and prison hunger strikes, tried to placate racist Southern suffragists by keeping [B]lack women out of her historic suffrage parade through Washington in 1913."[54] Collins then recounted Wells-Barnett's act of bravery against racial discrimination. "Ida B. Wells-Barnett, the head of the [B]lack Alpha Suffrage Club of Chicago, was far too smart and stubborn to accept exclusion. In the end, Paul reluctantly allowed [B]lack marchers to bring up the end of the procession. The Alpha Club was dispatched to the rear, but Wells-Barnett disappeared into the crowd. She then stepped back onto the street as the Illinois delegation passed, joining her white friends in the middle of the parade."[55] Such collective memories of Wells-Barnett in mainstream spaces, however, were anomalous, and most still tended to paint Wells-Barnett in two-dimensional, sepia tones.

Wells-Barnett's legacy also has begun to be institutionalized through mainstream public honors, awards, and recognitions. Since 1999, for instance, the Coordinating Council for Women in History has awarded an annual Ida B. Wells Graduate Student Fellow Award for historical dissertations that interrogate race and gender, and more recently, in 2016, the Investigative Fund, a non-profit organization dedicated to improving the scope and quality of investigative journalism, launched the Ida B. Wells Fellowship to promote diversity in journalism by bolstering the efforts of investigative reporters of color.[56] These awards, honors, and recognitions at mainstream entities follow in the tradition of long established honors, such as the National Association of Black Journalist's Ida B. Wells Award.[57] Once again, however, many of these honors focus only on one aspect of Wells-Barnett's life without conveying the nuance of the social activist's legacy.

A demand for commissioned portraits and exhibits in spaces at public universities and national museums coincided with the peak in the wave of scholarship about Wells-Barnett in the early twenty-first century. In 2006, for instance, Harvard's Kennedy School commissioned a portrait of Wells-Barnett for a celebration of the life of Wells-Barnett that featured prominent speakers such as Giddings and Greaves.[58] Likewise, in 2015, the Tennessee Press Association unveiled a redesign of its Tennessee Newspaper Hall of Fame, including a digital placard for 1985 inductee Ida B. Wells-Barnett, at the University of Tennessee in Knoxville.[59] The redesign followed the launch of the Ida Initiative, an interdisciplinary project to foster research about the life, the work, and the legacy of Ida B. Wells-Barnett and other like-minded social justice crusaders by scholars and students of communication and history in 2011, a digital site dedicated to preserving the life and legacy of Wells-Barnett in 2013, and a one-day Ida B. & Beyond conference at the University of Tennessee in spring 2015.[60] Many of these commissioned efforts were encouraged by the Ida B. Wells Memorial Foundation, an entity established by Wells-Barnett's grandchildren in 1988 to protect, preserve, and promote the legacy of Ida B. Wells.[61]

The Ida B. Wells Memorial Foundation has wielded a degree of control over Wells-Barnett's public memory, but it is not omnipotent, and although the foundation and

Wells-Barnett's descendants often have been consulted when museums curate an exhibit related to the social justice crusader, they do not always have final approval. The descendants of Wells-Barnett played a key role in the development of the Ida B. Wells-Barnett Museum in Holly Springs, Mississippi, after its establishment in 1970, and the hand of her kin can be observed in the nuanced interpretation of Wells-Barnett as a "passionate crusader against oppression; a teacher and acclaimed journalist; an articulate public speaker; a civil rights activist; an anti-lynching crusader; a woman's rights activist; and one of the founders of the NAACP."[62]

That nuance is lacking from more recent exhibits erected to Wells-Barnett at mainstream national museums such as the Newseum, the Grand Cathedral of the Fourth Estate erected in Washington, DC, in 2008 to pay tribute to the memory of American journalism, and the National Museum of African American History and Culture, the Smithsonian museum erected in Washington, DC, in 2016 to pay tribute to the "African American experience" in American culture.[63] Media historians Lori Amber Roessner and Carrie Teresa recently critiqued the interpretation of the life of Wells-Barnett offered in the Newseum's News Corporation News History Gallery for its lack of nuance and improper contextualization within the rest of the Newseum. "We must read the bias of institutional memory as a bias of history and communication," they wrote. "For the sake of parsimony, the curators—like the historians before them—disregarded nuanced details that might complicate their grand narrative. The result has been memory distortions and cultural amnesias that reveal much about our continuing cultural anxieties surrounding race in America."[64]

On the contrary, the interpretation of Wells-Barnett's life offered by the National Museum of African American History and Culture in Washington, DC, offers a more nuanced portrait of a Black woman "making a way in a hostile world."[65] "When you see Ida B. Wells, the turn-of-the-20th-century social justice warrior—a journalist who traveled the country writing about the brutality of lynching—honored with a beautiful portrait, part of her china collection and a first edition of her anti-lynching work alongside a display of some of her most poignant words, you feel that her cause, the cause, is being honored righteously," wrote Blair L. M. Kelley, an assistant professor of history at North Carolina State University, in the *Washington Post*.[66] The exhibit is juxtaposed with one of Wells-Barnett's most famous quotations—"The way to right wrongs is to turn the light of truth upon them"—located on the Founding Wall, which is meant to introduce visitors to the museum's most important themes—"freedom, democracy, and America's uphill journey to ensure both for all of its citizens."[67] The quotation embraces the fullness of Wells-Barnett's social justice crusade, but the exhibit still places its focus on the most well-remembered facet of Wells-Barnett's life, her anti-lynching crusade, failing to offer an account that captures the depth and scope of Wells-Barnett's activism.

Museums such as the Newseum and the National Museum of African American History and Culture in Washington, DC, have offered an important intervention inserting collective memories of Wells-Barnett into the nation's mainstream historical narrative, thereby battling the cultural amnesia surrounding Wells-Barnett's legacy, but by reproducing the dominant existing narrative about Wells-Barnett's legacy they have offered an incomplete account of the activist's life that fails to capture the nuance of her social justice crusade, and in some cases, have engaged in a covert silence in the domain of forgetting by including but downplaying difficult aspects of Wells-Barnett's life. Nonetheless, these efforts do move the nation closer to Taylor's vision of a stone monument "commensurate with the heroic service rendered by [Wells-Barnett]," a primary focus of the Ida B. Wells Foundation, which has worked in recent years to raise the funds necessary to construct a sculpture to Wells-Barnett in Bronzeville, the South Side Chicago neighborhood where the Ida B. Wells Garden Homes stood from 1939 to 2011.[68]

Taylor's vision of a stone monument spoke to a desire for a permanent site of remembrance constructed to Wells-Barnett, but as we have seen throughout this manuscript, the "intangible, abstract monuments," though less durable than monuments constructed of stone, have remained remarkably immutable as individual and collective keepsakes in collections across the country and as material or digitized artifacts available to the public or institutionalized in public spaces.

In recent years, collective remembrances of Wells-Barnett also have been preserved in digital spaces, such as the semi-permanent standalone websites of the Ida B. Wells Foundation, the Ida B. Wells Museum, and the Ida Initiative, among others, or in the more ephemeral anniversary sites such as the Google Doodle that accompanied Wells-Barnett's 153rd birthday, and it is within these spaces, often created by individuals with an interest in preserving the nuanced legacy of Wells-Barnett, that we find some of the most holistic portraits of Wells-Barnett. For instance, founders of the Ida Initiative, an interdisciplinary project to foster research about Wells-Barnett, designed a permanent website dedicated to preserving the memory of Wells-Barnett's life, career, and legacy in 2013.[69] The site offers individual pages that describe Wells-Barnett's role as an advocacy journalist with an investigative impulse, an educator, a civil rights activist, an anti-lynching crusader, a suffragist, and a local reformer. Likewise, the anniversary site constructed by Google Doodle to celebrate Wells-Barnett's 153rd birthday, described Wells-Barnett as a journalist and activist "who documented civil rights abuses and worked toward women's suffrage."[70] "We salute Ida B. Wells with a Doodle that commemorates her journalistic mettle and her unequivocal commitment to the advancement of civil liberties," Google explained.[71]

In many respects, these digital sites have offered the most nuanced portraits of Wells-Barnett as a social justice activist committed to the advancement of all marginalized people. As public memory scholars have suggested, these spaces have the potential to challenge "the dictatorial role of official institutions of memory," and as we have seen, in this case, several digital sites have challenged more simplistic accounts of Wells-Barnett, but these sites, despite their potential to offer a holistic, comprehensive account in unlimited space, in many respects are still governed by traditional logics of memory display and technical infrastructures that limit the depth of detail.[72] Thus, the bias of communication can determine the bias of memory, how stories are told and remembered.[73]

CONCLUSION

As memory scholar Janice Hume suggests, "when interpretations of historical fact change, those new meanings provide insight."[74] In the case of Wells-Barnett, as we have seen in this chapter, journalists primarily working for organs of the Black press wrote Ida B. Wells-Barnett into the historical narrative after her death in March 1931. During her lifetime, the accomplishments of Wells-Barnett had been written out of the history of anti-lynching by the NAACP in an act of overt silence in the domain of forgetting, and in the aftermath of her death, the storytellers of the Black Press mythologized the "Princess of the Press," constructing her as a pioneering advocate and investigative journalist and a heroic anti-lynching crusader.[75] As Roland Barthes taught us, cultural myths as "second-order signs" function not to "deny things," but to "talk about them; simply, it purifies them . . . it gives them the simplicity of essences."[76] In the case of Wells-Barnett, these early mythological accounts of the Black Press served to essentialize her, to paint her in monochromatic tones that eliminated the nuance of her social activism that straddled efforts for race, class, and gender equity. As other memory scholars have suggested, these acts of narrative simplification often occur during the process of instrumentalization in order to promote present interests, in this case, making the narrative of Wells-Barnett more palatable to a mainstream audience.[77] In the years that followed, these simplistic portraits on occasion were reprinted in local mainstream outlets with a national circulation such as the *Chicago Tribune*. More often than not, however, Wells-Barnett's story was omitted from mainstream American public memory; she was marginalized from the narrative as a woman of color. Nonetheless, Wells-Barnett's memory preservers, first members of the Black press and then her daughter Alfreda and other kin, used the tools at their disposal—journalism and modern public-relations techniques—to both preserve her legacy and to insert her story into the mainstream narrative.[78]

Only slowly, over time, has a more comprehensive portrait of Wells-Barnett emerged. By 1970, shortly before the release of Wells-Barnett's autobiography by her daughter Alfreda, Wells had begun to be portrayed as a "dynamic lady," who was "outspoken against injustice," but only gradually was her role as a suffragist and local reformer emphasized in popular culture.[79] In the years that followed, historians, biographers, and documentarians sought to offer an intervention into the existing narrative by moving Wells-Barnett's story up from the footnotes of Black history, and the mainstream popular press, on occasion, was receptive to their efforts. Newspapers with national circulations such as the *New York Times* and the *Washington Post* first reviewed scholarly works before inserting Wells-Barnett's narrative into mainstream commemorative journalism, such as Gail Collins' 2013 anniversary account of the National Woman's Suffrage Parade in March 1913.[80] The first wave of histories on Wells-Barnett focused on the facet of her life that she was best remembered for—her anti-lynching crusade, but subsequent scholarship offered a more complex portrait of Wells-Barnett as an educator, reformer, and activist who championed a social justice crusade; more often than not, however, this nuance remained absent from narratives that found their way into popular culture. Furthermore, as scholarship about Wells-Barnett appeared to peak at century's turn, a cultural amnesia surrounding Wells-Barnett settled in mainstream American culture, signaling the nation's struggle to come to terms with its colonializing impulses and the resistance of white Americans to confront its dark history of racial violence and discrimination.

In the most recent years, collective memories of Wells-Barnett have become institutionialized in disparate sites, public spaces such as the Newseum, the National Museum of African American History and Culture, and the Google Doodle. Scholars of "digital memory" have contended that digital landscapes, such as the Google Doodle, have the potential to challenge "the dictatorial role of official institutions of memory," but as we witnessed, both physical museums and digital spaces are determined by traditional logics of memory display and technical infrastructures.[81] Furthermore, they are limited by the mentalities of curators, who often imprint exhibits for the masses with simplistic narratives inspired by the most well-known or remembered facets of an individual's public memory, ones that have dominated accounts from popular culture. Once again, these sites often have offered monochromatic portraits of Wells-Barnett that lack the nuance encompassed by her life, or in some cases, they have engaged in covert silence in the domain of forgetting by incorporating difficult topics in ways that minimize impact in order to attract larger audiences but still remain above reproach.

In the final analysis, we still live in a place where stone monuments offering tribute to the lives of magnificent Black women remain the anomaly situated among monuments of Confederate generals; as memory scholar Janice Hume wrote, "some memory sites struggle to even exist," and thus, as is the case with Wells-Barnett, we are left with the "intangible, abstract monuments" that Taylor described in the *Chicago Defender* in January 1938.[82] Abstract monuments such as those of Duster, who wrote in 1970 words that still remain true today: "The most remarkable thing about Ida B. Wells-Barnett is not that she fought lynching and other forms of barbarianism. It is rather that she fought a lonely and almost single-handed fight, with a single-mindedness of a crusader, long before men or women of any race entered the arena; and the measure of success she achieved goes far beyond the credit she has been given in the history of the country."[83] Duster's words lend credence to those of memory scholar Barbies Zelizer, who wrote about the fragmentary and mutable nature of memory, contending that we can only truly understand our past by reading official versions of history against the grain.[84]

Our understanding of a past phenomenon is always limited; memory studies, like our histories themselves, are governed by a scholar's own subjectivities. As cultural historian Raymond Williams wrote, "We 'see' in certain ways—that is, we interpret sensory information according to certain rules—these rules and interpretations—are, as a whole, neither fixed or constant. We can learn new rules and new interpretations, as a result of which we shall literally see in new ways."[85] This study examined a sample of the "intangible, abstract monuments" that have been built to Wells-Barnett by communities of journalists, scholars, documentarians, and grassroots organizations over the last eight decades alongside the tangible tributes and memorials housed in disparate spaces across the nation.[86] The dataset gave the scholar insight into the patterns and trajectories of remembrance across various mediums as well as to close readings of texts of mass mediums, in their historical context, that have shaped our popular understandings of Wells-Barnett. Another subsample of the dataset may have yielded slightly different results. Future research might consider in greater depth phenomena of memory studies that we have encountered in this case study of Wells-Barnett—the negotiation of identity, reputation, and legacy in journalistic sites of memory; the role of memory preservers—close kin, journalists, and even scholars—in shaping reputation; and the institutionalization of memory in physical spaces such as museums and monuments and digital sites such as the Google Doodle or websites devoted to the legacy of an individual.[87]

Until then, it is fitting to recall the words of Bernice Powell Jackson, who wrote in 2003 of the importance of Wells-Barnett's legacy: "The truth is, Black History is every American's history and the sooner we recognize that, the sooner we will begin to understand African Americans have made significant contributions to the building of this nation and have every right to be here and to enjoy the same rights and privileges as other Americans."[88] Two recent memorials—Well-Barnett's tribute in the *New York Times'* overlooked obituary and the Memorial for Peace and Justice in Montgomery, Alabama—offer our nation hope for truth to combat cultural amnesia and future reconciliation.[89]

NOTES

1. See Rebecca Stiles Taylor, "A Review of the Lives of Three Magnificent Women," *Chicago Defender*, January 15, 1938, 17; on Rebecca Stiles Taylor, see Caryl Cooper, "Selling Negro Women to Negro Women and the World: Rebecca Stiles Taylor and the *Chicago Defender*, 1939–1945," *American Journalism* 39.2 (2014): 241–49; on the establishment of the Alpha Suffrage Club, see, the *Alpha Suffrage Record* newsletter and can be viewed at the University of Chicago Online Archives of the Ida B. Wells Papers 1884–1976 at https://www.lib.uchicago.edu/ead/pdf/ibwells-0008-009-07.pdf. See Wells, Ida B. Papers. [Box 8, Folder 9], Special Collections Research Center, University of Chicago Library; Ida B. Wells, *Crusade for Justice: The Autobiography of Ida B. Wells*, edited by Alfreda M. Duster (Chicago: University of Chicago Press, 1970), 345.

2. Taylor, "A Review of the Lives of Three Magnificent Women," *Chicago Defender*, January 15, 1938, 17.

3. Ibid.

4. Ibid.

5. Ibid.

6. Ibid.

7. See, for example, *Ida B. Wells Monument*, http://www.idabwellsmonument.org.

8. Taylor, "A Review of the Lives of Three Magnificent Women," 17.

9. Lisa Ann Tota, "Collective Memories at 'Work': The Public Remembering of Contested Pasts," *Comparative Social Research* 21.2 (2003): 63–85.

10. Janice Hume, "Memory Matters: The Evolution of Scholarship in Collective Memory and Mass Communication," *Review of Communication* 10.3 (2010): 181–196.

11. Ibid.; C.E. Morris, III, "My Old Kentucky Homo: Lincoln and the Politics of Queer Public Memory," In Kendall Phillips (Ed.), *Framing Public* Memory, (Tuscaloosa: University of Alabama Press, 2004), 90.

12. Michael Schudson, "Dynamics of Distortion in Collective Memory," In *Memory Distortion: How Minds, Brains, and Societies Reconstruct the Past*, edited by: Schacter, D. L. (Cambridge, MA: Harvard University Press, 1995), 346–64; Vered Vinitzky-Seroussi and Chana Teeger, "Unpacking the Unspoken: Silence in Collective Memory and Forgetting," *Social Forces* 88.3 (2010): 1103–22.

13. See, for example, Wells, *Crusade for Justice*; Linda O. McMurry, *To Keep the Waters Troubled: The Life of Ida B. Wells* (New York: Oxford University Press, 1998); Paula Giddings, *Ida: A Sword among Lions, Ida B. Wells and the Campaign against Lynching* (New York: HarperCollins Publishers, 2008); Mia Bay, *To Tell the Truth Freely: The Life of Ida B. Wells* (New York: Hill and Wang, 2009).

14. See, for example, Patricia Ann Schechter, *Ida B. Wells-Barnett and American Reform, 1880–1930* (Chapel Hill: University of North Carolina Press, 2001), 238.

15. Pierre Nora, "Between Memory and History: Les Lieux de Memoire," *Representations* 26.2 (1989): 7.

16. Narrative analysis involves a search for common thematic and structural choices that journalists make. It has become a common tool for analyzing journalistic content. See Steve M. Barkin, "The Journalist as Storyteller: An Interdisciplinary Perspective," *American Journalism* 1.2 (1984): 27–33, and S. Elizabeth Bird and Robert W. Dardenne, "Myth, Chronicle and Storytelling: Exploring the Narrative Qualities of News," In *Social Meanings of News,* ed. Daniel Allen Berkowitz (Thousand Oaks, CA: Sage, 1997), 333–50. Discourse analysis posits that word choice used within a text is ideologically based and is reflective of the social context within which it was created. It considers the symbolic nature of news narratives and "the ideational function of language," according to Norman Faircloth, *Media Discourse* (London: Arnold, 1995). See also Roger Fowler, *Language in the News: Discourse and Ideology in the Press* (New York: Routledge, 1991). All texts were gathered through ProQuest Databases using the search term "Ida B. Wells." In total, a sample of 257 articles, editorials, and letters to the editor published in local, regional, and national outlets of the Black and mainstream press isolated from a census of 3,390 newspaper texts culled through through ProQuest Historical Newspapers and ProQuest Newspapers were examined. The sample was gleaned by examining a census of 126 texts in ProQuest Historical Newspapers isolated through the search term "Ida B. Wells-Barnett" and a census of 131 texts isolated through the search term "Ida B. Wells" in milestone anniversary years (twenty-fifth, fiftieth, seventy-fifth, and one hundredth) of Wells-Barnett's co-founding of the NAACP in 1909 and the Alpha Suffrage Club in 1913. These newspaper articles were examined alongside 197 magazine features, one documentary, five digital sites, and three museums.

17. These patterns and trajectories of remembrances were explored by examining the bar graph representation by medium of 7,386 mentions of "Ida B. Wells" in approximately 50 ProQuest databases.

18. Wells, *Crusade for Justice*, 3–4.

19. See, for example, Ida B. Wells, *The Memphis Diary of Ida B. Wells: An Intimate Portrait of the Activist as a Young Woman*, ed. Miriam Decosta-Willis (Boston: Beacon Press, 1995); the daybook can be viewed at the University of Chicago Online Archives of the Ida B. Wells Papers 1884–1976 at https://www.lib.uchicago.edu/e/scrc/findingaids/view. php?eadid=ICU.SPCL.IBWELLS#idp19747940. Described as "Ida B. Wells' pocket diary, 1930. Entries begin Christmas Day, 1929, and end May 14, 1930." The handwritten account also was transcribed and included in Miriam Decosta-Willis' edited work of her Memphis

Diary. On the earlier use of diaries to share literary experiences, see Ronald and Mary Zboray, *Everyday Ideas: Socioliterary Ideas among Antebellum New Englanders* (Knoxville: University of Tennessee Press, 2006). Wells, *The Memphis Diary of Ida B. Wells*, 174.

20. Schechter, *Ida B. Wells-Barnett and American Reform*, 11–12.

21. Lucius C. Harper, "Dustin' Off the News," *Chicago Defender*, February 9, 1946. Woodson already had begun advocating for the study of Black history and established a national Negro History Week in 1927. His efforts would be expanded to Negro History Month in 1976. As we saw in the last chapter, however, Woodson did not include Wells-Barnett in his history of the race.

22. Ibid.

23. See, for example, Lucius C. Harper, "Dustin' Off the News," *Chicago Defender*, February 9, 1946; Lucius C. Harper, "Dustin' Off the News," *Chicago Defender*, April 15, 1950, 7.

24. Vinitzky-Seroussi and Teeger, "Unpacking the Unspoken: Silence in Collective Memory and Forgetting," 1103–22.

25. "Ida B. Wells-Barnett Passes Away," *Chicago Defender*, March 28, 1931, 1.

26. Janice Hume, *Obituaries in American Culture* (Oxford: University of Mississippi Press, 2000).

27. "Ida B. Wells-Barnett Passes Away," *Chicago Defender*, March 28, 1931, 1.

28. Vinitzky-Seroussi and Teeger, "Unpacking the Unspoken: Silence in Collective Memory and Forgetting," 1103–22. This act is similar to what Schudson refers to as the simplification involved in the process of instrumentialization. Schudson, "Dynamics of distortion in collective memory," 346–64.

29. "Hold Last Rites for Ida B. Wells-Barnett," *Chicago Defender*, April 4, 1931, 2.

30. Ibid.

31. Wallace Webb Scott, "A Tribute to Mrs. Barnett," *Chicago Defender*, April 18, 1931, 15.

32. See, for example, "Mrs. Ida B. Wells Barnett's Work Goes Forward: A Pioneer Crusader against Lynching," *Chicago Defender*, January 15, 1938, 17; "A Page from Our History," *Chicago Defender*, February 10, 1940, 12; Naomi Millender, "Ida B. Wells: Dynamic Lady," *Chicago Defender*, April 9, 1970, 17.

33. "Mrs. Ida B. Wells Barnett's Work Goes Forward: A Pioneer Crusader against Lynching," *Chicago Defender*, January 15, 1938, 17.

34. "A Page from Our History," *Chicago Defender*, February 10, 1940, 12.

35. Naomi Millender, "Ida B. Wells: Dynamic Lady," *Chicago Defender*, April 9, 1970, 17.

36. Hume, "Memory Matters," 184.

37. "Tea to Mark Negro History," *The Chicago Tribune*, March 3, 1963, A2.

38. "Southside Panel to Eye 'Negro History' at Tea," *The Chicago Defender*, February 9, 1963, 12. Memory scholar Michael Schudson describes the process through which collective memories are institutionalized in Michael Schudson, *Watergate in American Memory: How We Remember, Forget, and Reconstruct the Past* (New York: Basic Books, 1993); Schudson, "Dynamics of distortion in collective memory," 346–64.

39. See, for example, Nat D. Williams, "Dark Shadows," *Tri-State Defender*, January 12, 1963, 6; Lt. George W. Lee, "Graphic Story about City's First Negroes," *Tri-State Defender*, February 9, 1963, 13; Marjorie I. Ulen, "Merry Go-Round," *Tri-State Defender*, February 9, 1963, 5; "NAACP Demonstrates Against Double Shifts In Negro High Schools," *Tri-State Defender*, August 3, 1963, 1; "Daughter of Memphis Crusader Comes Here to Dig for Facts," *Tri-State Defender*, August 3, 1963, 1.

40. Carolyn Kitch, *Pages from the Past: History and Memory in American Magazines* (Chapel Hill: University of North Carolina Press, 2005), 107–8.

41. Hume, "Memory Matters," 181–96.

42. "Women's Day Slated At Metropolitan Church," *Chicago Defender*, May 25, 1963, 13; "Daughter of Memphis Crusader Comes Here to Dig for Facts," *Tri-State Defender*, August 3, 1963, 1.

43. Wells, *Crusade for Justice*.

44. Ibid., xiii, xxiii.

45. Ibid., xxxii.

46. Alice Walker, "Advancing Luna—and Ida B. Wells," *Ms. Magazine*, July 1977, 75–79.

47. See, for example, the *National Association of Black Journalists' Ida B. Wells Award*, http://www.nabj.org/?page=IdaBWells.

48. Paula Giddings, "Woman Warrior, Ida B. Wells: Crusader-Journalist," *Essence*, February 1988, 75–76, 142.

49. Major Robinson, "The Tattler," *New York Amsterdam News*, May 21, 1988, 16.

50. William Greaves, "Ida B. Wells: A Passion for Justice," *California Newsreels*, 1989, http://newsreel.org/video/ida-b-wells.

51. Ibid.

52. Wells, *Crusade for Justice*, 5.

53. Lori Amber Roessner and Carrie Teresa, "Always Already Hailed: Negotiating Memory and Identity at the Newseum." Presented at the Association for Education in Journalism and Mass Communication, Minneapolis, Minn., August 2016; see also, Vinitzky-Seroussi and Teeger, "Unpacking the Unspoken: Silence in Collective Memory and Forgetting," 1103–22.

54. Gail Collins, "Women's Suffrage," *Washington Post*, July 28, 2002, C12.

55. Ibid.

56. See *The Coordinating Council for Women in History's Ida B. Wells Graduate Student Fellow Award*, https://theccwh.org/ccwh-awards/wells-graduate-student-fellowship/, and the *Investigative Fund's Ida B. Wells Fellowship*, http://www.theinvestigativefund.org/about/2219/ida_b._wells_fellowship.

57. See, for example, the *National Association of Black Journalists' Ida B. Wells Award*, http://www.nabj.org/?page=IdaBWells.

58. See, for example, *A Celebration of Ida B. Wells*, http://iop.harvard.edu/forum/celebration-ida-b-wells.

59. See, for example, *Tennessee Newspaper Hall of Fame*, http://www.tnpress.com/halloff-ame.html.

60. See, for example, the Ida Initiative, September 16, 2013, https://theidainitiative.word-press.com; *Ida B. & Beyond*, http://jem.cci.utk.edu/colloquium15/ida-b.

61. See, for example, the *Ida B. Wells Foundation*, http://www.ibwfoundation.org.

62. See the *Ida B. Wells Museum*, http://www.idabwellsmuseum.org.

63. On the history of the Newseum, see, Ted Friedman, "Reading the Newseum: From Heroic Objectivity to the News Stream: The Newseum's Strategies for Relegitimizing Journalism in the Information Age," *Critical Studies in Mass* Communication 15.3 (1998): 325–35; Rachel Gans, "The Newseum and Collective Memory: Narrowed Choices, Limited Voices and Rhetoric of Freedom," *Journal of Communication Inquiry* 26.4 (2003): 370–90; Lori Amber Roessner & Carrie Teresa, "Always Already Hailed: Negotiating Memory and Identity at the Newseum." Presented at the Association for Education in Journalism and Mass Communication, Minneapolis, Minn., August 2016. On the grand opening of the National

Museum of African American History and Culture, see, for example, Maya Rhodan, Smithsonian Offers Sneak Peek of Museum of African-American History, *Time*, May 15, 2016, http://time.com/4329075/smithsonian-museum-african-american-history/.

64. Lori Amber Roessner and Carrie Teresa, "Always Already Hailed: Negotiating Memory and Identity at the Newseum." Presented at the Association for Education in Journalism and Mass Communication, Minneapolis, Minn., August 2016.

65. See *The Smithsonian's National Museum of African American History and Culture*, http://nmaahc.si.edu.

66. Blair L. M. Kelley, "You Can't Tell U.S. History Without Black History. Finally, a Museum Gets That." *Washington Post*, September 22, 2016, https://www.washingtonpost.com/opinions/you-cant-tell-us-history-without-black-history-finally-a-museum-gets-that/2016/09/22/95f5f784-8053-11e6-b002-307601806392_story.html?utm_term=.7a1ba7bd946f.

67. Ibid.

68. Taylor, "A Review of the Lives of Three Magnificent Women," 17; see also, *The Ida B. Wells Foundation*, http://www.ibwfoundation.org; *Ida B. Wells Monument*, http://www.idabwellsmonument.org.

69. See *The Ida Initiative*, September 16, 2013, https://theidainitiative.wordpress.com.

70. See Tessa Berenson, "Today's Google Doodle Celebrates Journalist Ida B. Wells' Birthday," *Time*, July 16, 2015, http://time.com/3960699/google-doodle-ida-b-wells/.

71. Ibid.

72. Ekaterina Haskins, "Between Archive and Participation: Public Memory in a Digital Age," *Rhetoric Society Quarterly* 37: 419.

73. Harold Innis, *The Bias of Communication* (Toronto: University of Toronto Press, 2008); Raymond Williams, *The Long Revolution* (New York: Chatto & Windus, 1961), 146.

74. Hume, "Memory Matters," 183.

75. On Wells-Barnett as "Princess of the Press," see, Giddings, *Ida: A Sword Among Lions*, 628; see also, Taylor, "A Review of the Lives of Three Magnificent Women," 17.

76. Roland Barthes, "Myth Today," in John Storey, *Cultural Theory and Popular Culture: A Reader* (Athens: University of Georgia Press, 2006), 293–303.

77. Michael Schudson, "Dynamics of distortion in collective memory," In *Memory Distortion: How Minds, Brains, and Societies Reconstruct the Past*, edited by: Schacter, D. L. (Cambridge, MA: Harvard University Press, 1995), 346–64; Vered Vinitzky-Seroussi and Chana Teeger, "Unpacking the Unspoken: Silence in Collective Memory and Forgetting," *Social Forces* 88.3 (2010): 1103–22.

78. See, for example, Wells, *Crusade for Justice*; on research into memory preservers see, Hume, "Memory Matters," 181–96.

79. Naomi Millender, "Ida B. Wells: Dynamic Lady," *Chicago Defender*, April 9, 1970, 17.

80. Collins, "Women's Suffrage," *Washington Post*, C12.

81. Haskins, "Between Archive and Participation," 419.

82. Hume, "Memory Matters," 185; Taylor, "A Review of the Lives of Three Magnificent Women," 17.

83. Wells, *Crusade for Justice*, xxxii.

84. Barbie Zelizer, "Reading the Past Against the Grain: The Shape of Memory Studies," *Critical Studies in Mass Communication* 12.2 (1995), 214–39.

85. Williams, *The Long Revolution*, 34.

86. Taylor, "A Review of the Lives of Three Magnificent Women," 17.

87. For additional areas of productive future research, see Hume, "Memory Matters," 193–96.

88. Bernice Powell Jackson, "Black History Is America's History," *People's World*, February 14, 2003, http://www.peoplesworld.org/article/black-history-is-america-s-history/.

89. Caitlin Dickerson, "Ida B. Wells," *Overlooked, New York Times*, March 8, 2018 https://www.nytimes.com/interactive/2018/obituaries/overlooked-ida-b-wells.html; Caleb Gayle, "No Reconciliation Without Truth," *New Republic*, April 23, 2018, https://new republic.com/article/148066/no-reconciliation-without-truth; For recent news on the fundraising for Ida B. Wells monument, see Maya Dukmasora, "Donations Pour in for Ida B. Wells Monument," *Chicago Reader*, April 14, 2018, https://www.chicagoreader.com/Bleader/archives/2018/04/14/an-online-fund-raising-push-may-finally-bring-a-monument-to-ida-b-wells-to-chicago.

BIBLIOGRAPHY

Barkin, Steve M. "The Journalist as Storyteller: An Interdisciplinary Perspective," *American Journalism* 1.2 (1984): 27–33.

Barthes, Roland. "Myth Today," in John Storey, *Cultural Theory and Popular Culture: A Reader*. Athens: University of Georgia Press, 2006.

Bay, Mia. *To Tell the Truth Freely: The Life of Ida B. Wells*. New York: Hill and Wang, 2009.

Bird, S. Elizabeth, and Robert W. Dardenne. "Myth, Chronicle and Storytelling: Exploring the Narrative Qualities of News," In *Social Meanings of News*, ed. Daniel Allen Berkowitz, Thousand Oaks, CA: Sage, 1997.

Cooper, Caryl. "Selling Negro Women to Negro Women and the World: Rebecca Stiles Taylor and the *Chicago Defender*, 1939–1945" *American Journalism* 39.4 (2014): 241–49.

Faircloth, Norman. *Media Discourse*. London: Arnold, 1995.

Fowler, Roger. *Language in the News: Discourse and Ideology in the Press*. New York: Routledge, 1991.

Friedman, Ted. "Reading the Newseum: From Heroic Objectivity to the News Stream: The Newseum's Strategies for Relegitimizing Journalism in the Information Age," *Critical Studies in Mass Communication* 15.3 (1998): 325–35.

Gans, Rachel. "The Newseum and Collective Memory: Narrowed Choices, Limited Voices and Rhetoric of Freedom," *Journal of Communication Inquiry* 26.4 (2002): 370–90.

Giddings, Paula. *Ida: A Sword among Lions, Ida B. Wells and the Campaign against Lynching*. New York: HarperCollings Publishers, 2008.

Haskins, Ekaterina. "Between Archive and Participation: Public Memory in a Digital Age," *Rhetoric Society Quarterly* 37.4 (2007): 419.

Hume, Janice. "Memory Matters: The Evolution of Scholarship in Collective Memory and Mass Communication," *Review of Communication* 10.3 (2010): 181–96.

———. *Obituaries in American Culture*. Oxford: University of Mississippi Press, 2000.

Innis, Harold. *The Bias of Communication*. University of Toronto Press, 2008.

McMurry, Linda O. *To Keep the Waters Troubled: The Life of Ida B. Wells*. New York: Oxford University Press, 1998.

Morris, C.E., III. "My old Kentucky homo: Lincoln and the politics of queer public memory," In Kendall Phillips. ed., *Framing Public Memory*. Tuscaloosa: University of Alabama Press, 2004.

Nora, Pierre. "Between Memory and History: Les Lieux de Memoire," *Representations* 26.2 (1989): 7.

Roessner, Lori Amber, and Teresa, Carrie. "Always Already Hailed: Negotiating Memory and Identity at the Newseum." Presented at the Association for Education in Journalism and Mass Communication, Minneapolis, MN, August 2016.

Schechter, Patricia A. *Ida B. Wells-Barnett and American Reform, 1880–1930.* Chapel Hill: University of North Carolina Press, 2001.

———. "Ida B. Wells-Barnett and the Carceral State." *Portland State University History Faculty Publications and Presentations* Paper 16 (2012).

Schudson, Michael. *Watergate in American Memory: How We Remember, Forget, and Reconstruct the Past.* New York: Basic Books, 1993.

———. "Dynamics of Distortion in Collective Memory," In *Memory Distortion: How Minds, Brains, and Societies Reconstruct the Past,* Edited by: Schacter, D. L. Cambridge, MA: Harvard University Press, 1995.

Tota, Lisa Ann. "Collective Memories at 'Work': The Public Remembering of Contested Pasts," *Comparative Social Research* 21.2 (2003): 63–85.

Wells, Ida B. *Crusade for Justice: The Autobiography of Ida B. Wells,* edited by Alfreda M. Duster. Chicago: University of Chicago Press, 1970.

———. *The Memphis Diary of Ida B. Wells: An Intimate Portrait of the Activist as a Young Woman,* edited by Miriam Decosta-Willis. Boston: Beacon Press, 1995.

Williams, Raymond. *The Long Revolution.* New York: Chatto & Windus, 1961.

Vinitzky-Seroussi, Vered, and Teeger, Chana. "Unpacking the Unspoken: Silence in Collective Memory and Forgetting," *Social Forces* 88.3 (2010): 1103–22.

Zelizer, Barbie. "Reading the Past against the Grain: The Shape of Memory Studies," *Critical Studies in Mass Communication* 12.2 (1995): 214–39.

Zboray, Ronald and Mary Zboray. *Everyday Ideas: Socioliterary Ideas among Antebellum New Englanders.* Knoxville: University of Tennessee Press, 2006.

7

Ida B. Wells-Barnett and the Carceral State

Patricia A. Schechter

I am truly humbled to be here with my distinguished colleagues and all of the people in this room. I would like to thank Cheryl Hicks very much for inviting me to participate in this session. I would also like to take a moment to acknowledge and recognize my beloved friend and co-author, Avel Louise Gordly, who is here with me today. Some of you met her at the author's signing last night. Ida B. Wells-Barnett (IBWB) ran for state senate in Illinois in 1930 and lost; Avel Gordly ran for state senate in Oregon and won and served in the legislature with distinction for a total of eighteen years. Since this is our first time at the Association for the Study of African American Life and History (ASALH), I want to thank everyone who has made us feel so welcome. It has also been a special pleasure to reconnect with Professor Paula Giddings. Twenty years ago, at a Berkshire conference in 1993 at Vassar College in New York State, I sat on a panel for the first time, and with her. What a delight that things have come full circle to new beginnings. I must also say a special word of thanks to Michelle Duster for her warm embrace this meeting. The generosity of your family to me over the years has been a precious gift. I will continue to work to honor and be worthy of that gift in all that I do with history.

My remarks today are titled "Ida B. Wells-Barnett and the Carceral State." I want to focus on the carceral state—that is, the government functions of "confining, surveillance and punishment"—in order to engage with some of the recent scholarship on race, policing, and imprisonment in the United States.[1] These are topics that Wells-Barnett had a great deal to say to us about a hundred years ago, especially, of course, as related to lynching. I'd like to suggest that her work's connection to prison reform, probation work, and advocacy for inmates back in the Progressive Era addresses the contemporary crisis around race and mass incarceration in important ways.

My book, *Ida B. Wells-Barnett and American Reform*, today over a decade old, did not set out to explain lynching, mobs, or the criminal justice system, per se. When I started that project around 1990, there were experts on lynching in and outside the academy, mostly in the sociology field. Instead, what I wanted to explain was . . . and I had to reread my preface to remind myself exactly . . . what happened to the "historical belief that women could be a unique force for racial healing in this county."[2] That is, I was interested in the connections between gendered activism and social justice, especially racial justice. But the thing is, I did not write that book, Crystal Feimster did, and I commend her scholarship to you most heartily. What I did write about—that is, where the evidence lead me—was how IBWB's analysis and ideas were selectively adopted within new social and political movements called "progressive era reform" and what that selectivity tells us about the distribution of power in our society. I argued that some of her more radical ideas were ignored—like her insight that a movement against the rape of Black women was necessary to an anti-lynching movement because sexualized violence against Black people was linked in this country. Some of her other key insights, however, were appropriated, especially the notion that lynching expressed outrage on the part of white men across class against Black men (and others) who asserted political, economic, and social equality in US society. This idea of IBWB's became a kind of "new truth" for activists even as she herself was nudged to the sidelines of the nationally coordinated efforts to redress racial injustice in both the National Association of Colored Women and, later, the National Association for the Advancement of Colored People (NAACP).

Today I'd like to shift focus again, to the carceral state, by retelling a story that Wells-Barnett told in her autobiography, *Crusade for Justice*, in order to revisit and maybe reweave some of these threads about racial violence, power, and the state. To do this retelling, I'm going to borrow the framework of an outstanding historian and scholar Khalil Gibran Muhammad, whose book, *The Condemnation of Blackness*, is a brilliant study of race, crime, and urban America in Wells-Barnett's time. Dr. Muhammad's argument is that during the 1920s, a young cohort of sociologists, many of whom were based in Chicago, critically reframed the so-called "Negro problem" of the day and its acute association with issues of criminality. In particular, they turned the tables on the statistics used to make this link and instead asserted that there was a "policing problem instead of a crime problem" where Black people were concerned in the US.[3] Dr. Muhammad acknowledges Wells-Barnett as an important antecedent to this new generation's efforts to call out the bias, discrimination, and often malicious intent in the policing and punishment of Black people. And his work opened my eyes more clearly to the radicalism of IBWB's thinking about the state and strategies for action and engagement.

The radicalness I want to reacquaint us with this evening is expressed in Wells-Barnett's decision in 1910 to get a Black man named Steve Green out of the country and into Canada in order to avoid the justice system altogether. This stance she never admitted to publicly at the time. Instead, she told Green's story some twenty years after the fact, in her autobiography, as a story about a racially biased prison system in order to help readers learn about how it worked and how to resist it. In addition to Wells-Barnett's autobiography, there exists documentation of some of the debate, even consternation, among activists about what to do about Steve Green. Most historians—including me—who have commented on the Green case assign its main significance to a larger "growing pains of the NAACP" story, rather than tie it back to any commentary on the racist functioning of carceral state itself.[4] Dr. Muhammad's work changed my mind about this by heightening my consciousness of what gets said, counted, and measured in instances of African Americans' contact with the justice system.

Steve Green was a sharecropper in Jericho, Arkansas, who, at harvest time in 1910, left the farm where he worked for better terms of labor within Crittenden County in the eastern part of the state.[5] Upon hearing of Green's plans to migrate, his landlord, a man named Seidle, threatened to kill Green should he leave the premises. Discovering Green at work on another farm, Seidle shot Green, who managed to run—with three bullet wounds in his body—to his cabin, grab his gun and return fire, killing his attacker. Green then fled Arkansas to Mississippi, where friends raised money to send him north. Back in Arkansas, officials got a lead on Green's destination and mobilized Chicago authorities, possibly by telephone. In the city, "an informant" tipped off local police, who picked Green up on a trumped up petty crime charge. At the central jail on Harrison Street in the downtown loop, abusive "third degree" tactics, including deprivation of food and water, were used on Green to extract confession of murder. Green knew he would be lynched if he returned south and when the extradition papers came through from Arkansas to Chicago, he attempted suicide. As the *Chicago Defender* put it, Green would face "uncertain trial, but certain death" back in Arkansas.[6]

Wells-Barnett learned from the newspapers that Steve Green had attempted to end his life in jail. Moved to intervene, she made some phone calls and learned that Green had been already sent back south by authorities. Nonetheless, she and local activists sprang into action. Attorney Edward H. Wright, a local Black lawyer and political associate of the Barnetts, investigated and found an irregularity in the extradition papers. In a highly publicized proceeding in circuit court, Wright and a colleague, William Anderson, persuaded Judge Richard Tuthill to issue a writ of habeas corpus on the notion that Green was being unjustly deprived of his liberty. The writ challenged Arkansas' custody of Green, news of which was conveyed along the rail lines to southern Illinois just before Green crossed the state line by train. According to the press, "every method known to modern ingenuity was put into effect to intercept the prisoner before crossing the line of the State" of Illinois, including "telegraph, telephone, and wireless telegraphy."[7] The person who responded to the telegraphy—and the reward incentive secured by Wright—owed the Barnetts and governor of Illinois, Charles S. Deneen, a favor: Sheriff Nellis of Cairo. Nellis had replaced another white law enforcement official who had been removed under the Illinois Anti-Mob Violence Act. This bill was passed in 1905 through the advocacy and political pressure of the Barnetts—and the Chicago Bar Association—and enforced by Barnetts in particular after a terrible downstate lynching in Cairo in 1909, just a year before Green's situation exploded.

Upon Green's return to Chicago, Wells-Barnett and her associates kept him, in her words, "hidden away," as they surmised that Arkansas officials would soon petition the Illinois governor again for extradition of Green. The excitement around the writ proceedings in Chicago was intense—*Broad Ax* said it "rival[ed] . . . the old underground [railroad] scenes of a half century past"—and journalists cheered the accomplishments of the defense committee, including Wells-Barnett and the attorneys.[8] Yet once Green made it back to Chicago, a cone of silence begins to descend on the case. In late September, Green gave personal testimony at Quinn Chapel African Methodist Episcopal church to raise money and support; but the event was reported quietly: no pictures, no direct testimony from Green, no details, no embellishments. And, Wells-Barnett's autobiography describes local activists huddled in a private meeting at home as they conferred on a strategy. "A collection was taken and placed in my hands," she wrote of this gathering, "and I was ordered to get Green out of town, since the governor would have no choice in honoring a properly presented requisition."[9]

Once Wells-Barnett and her colleagues decide to protect Green, most of the evidence of his whereabouts is in private correspondence rather than public documents. Green's situation was picked up by the Washington, DC, media and the news apparently stirred New York activists around the NAACP, barely a year old, to try and gain some traction on the case. In mid-October, Oswald Garrison Villard wrote to Joel Spingarn in New York and quoted a Wells-Barnett letter: "Steve Green was started to Canada a week ago today" (October 12, 1910).[10] She further stated to Spingarn that she could not "give . . . any detailed information as to the movements of Steve Green because our Committee has decided that there is danger in too much publicity."[11] The last media report on Green I have found is in *The Crisis* in November 1910, in which W.E.B. Du Bois makes no note of the legal question marks around the case in favor of testimony in Green's "own words." This narrative provides details of the events leading up to the confrontation with Seidle in Arkansas, the gun fire, the escape to Mississippi then to Illinois, the writ secured by Ed Wright in Chicago, and Green's near return south but for the intervention of Sherriff Nellis.[12] Wells-Barnett and Du Bois both noted that Steve Green was "illiterate." "He cannot read or write," Wells-Barnett wrote to Spingarn, "so we do not know for certain whether he has reached his destination and we are afraid to inquire."[13] Given the still relatively elite status of telephones, Green might not have been able to keep in contact that way, though this deserves further investigation. State legal documents also warrant exploration, as it is not clear Arkansas made a full attempt to recover Green, though Wells-Barnett tells us in *Crusade for Justice* that "the [Arkansas] sheriff gave [the search] up as a hopeless job."[14]

So what to make of the Steve Green story?

Wells-Barnett certainly drew her contemporaries' attention on paper to how New York activists tended to downplay the value of work in Chicago and her claim to leadership.[15] But what is she NOT saying? Where is Steve Green? What are the details of the Chicago activists' plans? Could it be that Steve Green was escaping everyone, and decided to roll the dice and run to Canada himself, without aid by reformers? These details are less accessible to historians in the archival record—at least as far as my research has gone. But maybe this, too, is purposeful. By keeping the Chicago deliberations out of the media, out of correspondence, and out of the autobiography, Wells-Barnett continued to shield Green. And in Du Bois' case, rather than ignoring or minimizing Wells-Barnett's leadership, maybe he bought her and Green some time. Perhaps even unwittingly, Du Bois gave her cover to try and save Green's life. Some seventeen years after the fact, Wells-Barnett wrapped the tale in a kind of parable: "The last I heard of him he was still here in Chicago," she wrote. "He is one Negro who lives to tell the tale that he was not burned alive according to program."[16] Indeed, maybe it was only his story to tell in the end.

Muhammad's work also opens up some further dimensions of the case in light of the workings of a racially biased carceral state.

First, Steve Green's landlord asserts control over his tenants to the extent of taking his life rather than countenance economic choice-making and mobility by his tenants/employees. This authoritarian control over Black workers has its roots in slavery and, as Muhammad's book points out, feeds the law enforcement patterns of convict lease, vagrancy, and "work or fight" statutes that compelled the labor and restricted the mobility of Black citizens according to white whims and needs. As Muhammad recently points out in an interview with Bill Moyers, these practices also form the precedent and the roots of "stop and frisk" protocols used by today's law enforcement.[17]

Second, self-defense is essentially unthinkable under white supremacist logic. This logic produces a perverse situation in which self-defense for an African-American protagonist is literally suicide, and, by a further tortured logic, suicide becomes the only way to reclaim one's body from that situation. The connections between race, mental health, and incarceration remain as urgent today as ever.[18]

Third, and here Muhammad's work is again key, Wells-Barnett describes the informal and shadowed dimensions of the carceral state's operation. The use of informants is a muted but important part of Green's story as is the use of the "citizen's arrest." In the dramatic scene at the Illinois state line, Wells-Barnett does not call out Nellis' identity—which is unusual for her as a seasoned politician, for whom knowing who was on her side of a particular dispute was absolutely essential. Instead, she renders the interception of Green on the train car more anonymously, as a "man" who approached Green on the train and announced: "I arrest this man in the name of the great state of Illinois."[19] Theoretically, any citizen can make a "citizen's arrest," yet who actually feels empowered to exercise this right and whose exercise of that right is enforceable has much to do with this society's status categories and designations, including "race."

My point here is that in Ida B. Wells-Barnett's story about Steve Green, her silences as much as her words tell us much about the delicate trip wires facing African Americans tangling with the carceral state. Twenty years after the Green case, Wells-Barnett was more characteristically blunt on the issue of policing. In the

Chicago *Daily News* in 1930, she declared that Chicago's "colored citizens" had witnessed several "object lessons of police 'incompetence or worse'" in shootings of at least four Black people, including a sixteen-year-old boy who was repeatedly shot by officers in his home. "These victims," she wrote, "murdered on the Chicago streets in broad daylight, were black and poor and with no organization behind them, and it seemingly was not worthwhile to hold the police department to account for outrages against them."[20] As my co-panelists' work has borne out in different ways and Dr. Muhammad's further underscores, Ida B. Wells-Barnett worked her entire life to change these conditions for the better.

So must we.

Thank you.

NOTES

1. Marie Gottschalk, "Hiding in Plain Sight: American Politics and the Carceral State," *Annual Review of Political Science* 11 (2008): 235–60; Vesla M. Weaver and Amy E. Lerman, "Political Consequences of the Carceral State," *American Political Science Review* 104.4 (2010): 817–33. See also Heather A. Thompson, "Why Mass Incarceration Matters: Rethinking Crisis, Decline, and Transformation in Postwar American History," *The Journal of African History* 97.3 (2010): 703–34.

2. Patricia Ann Schechter, *Ida B. Wells-Barnett and American Reform, 1880–1930* (Chapel Hill: University of North Carolina Press, 2003), xii.

3. Khalil Gibran Muhammad, *The Condemnation of Blackness: Race, Crime, and the Making of Modern Urban America* (Cambridge: Harvard University Press, 2010), 235. See also Shaun L. Gabbidon, Helen T. Greene, and Vernetta D. Young, *African American Classics in Criminology & Criminal Justice* (Sage, 2002), and Helen T. Green and Shaun L. Gabbidon, eds. *African American Criminological Thought* (Albany: State University of New York Press, 2000).

4. Although the Crisis does not give credit to her, it is clear that Mrs. Barnett managed the Steve Green case in Chicago Ida B. Wells, *Crusade for Justice: The Autobiography of Ida B. Wells*, edited by Alfredo M. Duster (Chicago: The University of Chicago Press, 1970), 335. "New York officials failed to contribute or publicly credit her effort to aid a black refugee from Arkansas named Steve Green, who had fled the country to avoid a lynch mob." Schechter, *Ida B. Wells and American Reform*, 142; See also Giddings, *A Sword among Lions*, 496 and Bay, *To Tell the Truth Freely*, 287.

5. Sources are inconsistent on this point.

6. "Steve Green Liberated," *Chicago Defender*, September 24, 1910, 1. See also Karlos Hill, "Resisting Lynching: Black Grassroots Responses to Lynching in the Mississippi and Arkansas Deltas, 1882–1938" (PhD diss., University of Illinois: Urbana Champagne, 2009).

7. "Attorneys William G. Anderson and Edward H. Wright Won One of the Greatest Legal Battles of their Lives," *Chicago Broad-Ax*, September 24, 1910. Leaving nothing to chance, Wright had persuaded the state's attorney's office to "offer a reward for the return" (Wells, *Crusade for Justice*, 335) of Green to Chicago and raised additional reward money himself from private contributions to "increase" it (Giddings, *A Sword among Lions*, 495).

8. *Broad Ax*, October 1, 1910.

9. Wells, *Crusade for Justice*, 337. By claiming that she was "ordered" by the ad hoc Green defense group in Chicago, Wells-Barnett mutes her own agency. Of course maybe she

was "ordered," though that cuts against her usual approach. Then again, perhaps only ret-rospectively was it important to blunt the radicalness of the act by suggesting that it was someone else's idea.

    10. Villard to Spingarn, October 19, 1910, Joel E. Spingarn Papers.

    11. Edward Wright to JES, October 17, 1910, JES Papers.

    12. "Steve Green's Story," *The Crisis*, November 1910, 14. This article mentions a Green's birth in Tennessee and his marriage to an Arkansas woman in the 1880s, which I believe I have confirmed. Ancestry.com. *Arkansas, County Marriages Index, 1837–1957* [database on-line]. Provo, UT, USA: Ancestry.com Operations, Inc., 2011. Accessed on September 13, 2012.

    13. Villard to Spingarn, October 19, 1910, Joel E. Spingarn Papers.

    14. My search of the finding aids of the Donaghey papers at State Archives and University of Arkansas yielded nothing, as did the Charles S. Deneen collection at the Abraham Lincoln Presidential Library in Springfield. See Wells, *Crusade for Justice*, 377.

    15. Schechter, *Ida B. Wells-Barnett and American Reform*, 142.

    16. Wells, *Crusade for Justice*, 337.

    17. "Confronting the Contradictions of America's Past," July 22, 2012, http://billmoyers.com/episode/full-show-confronting-the-contradictions-of-america%E2%80%99s-past/.

    18. See Avel L. Gordly, *Remembering the Power of Words: The Life of an Oregon Activist, Legislator and Community Leader* (Corvallis: Oregon State University Press, 2011) and Heather Ann Thompson, *Whose Detroit? Politics, Labor and Race in a Modern American City* (Ithaca: Cornell University Press, 2004).

    19. Wells, *Crusade for Justice*, 336.

    20. "Murder in Chicago," *The Crisis* (August 1930), 282.

BIBLIOGRAPHY

Bay, Mia. *To Tell the Truth Freely: The Life of Ida B. Wells.* New York: Hill and Wang. 2009.

Gabbidon, Shaun L., Greene, Helen T., and Young, Vernetta D. *African American Classics in Criminology & Criminal Justice.* New York: Sage, 2002.

Giddings, Paula. *Ida: A Sword among Lions, Ida B. Wells and the Campaign against Lynching.* New York: HarperCollings Publishers, 2008.

Gordly, Avel L. *Remembering the Power of Words: The Life of an Oregon Activist, Legislator and Community Leader.* Corvallis: Oregon State University Press, 2011.

Gottschalk, Marie. "Hiding in Plain Sight: American Politics and the Carceral State," *Annual Review of Political Science* 11 (2008): 235–60.

Green, Helen T., and Gabbidon, Shaun L. eds. *African American Criminological Thought.* Albany: State University of New York Press, 2000.

Hill, Karlos "Resisting Lynching: Black Grassroots Responses to Lynching in the Mississippi and Arkansas Deltas, 1882–1938." PhD diss., University of Illinois: Urbana Champagne, 2009.

Muhammad, Khalil Gibran. *The Condemnation of Blackness: Race, Crime, and the Making of Modern Urban America.* Cambridge: Harvard University Press, 2010.

Schechter, Patricia Ann. *Ida B. Wells-Barnett and American Reform, 1880–1930.* Chapel Hill: University of North Carolina Press, 2003.

Thompson, Heather Ann. *Whose Detroit? Politics, Labor and Race in a Modern American City.* Ithaca: Cornell University Press, 2004.

Thompson, Heather Ann. "Why Mass Incarceration Matters: Rethinking Crisis, Decline, and Transformation in Postwar American History," *The Journal of African History* 97.3 (2010): 703–34.

Weaver, Vesla M., and Lerman, Amy E. "Political Consequences of the Carceral State," *American Political Science Review* 104.4 (2010): 817–33.

Wells, Ida B. *Crusade for Justice: The Autobiography of Ida B. Wells*, edited by Alfreda M. Duster. Chicago: The University of Chicago Press, 1970.

8

Pioneering Advocacy Journalism

What Today's Journalists Can Learn from Ida B. Wells-Barnett's Methodology

R. J. Vogt

On September 15, 1883, a twenty-one-year-old schoolteacher sat in the ladies' car of a train operated by the Chesapeake, Ohio & Southwestern Railroad, traveling on her way to her teaching post in Woodstock, Tennessee, from her residence in Memphis. When a conductor instructed her to give up her bought-and-paid-for seat and move to the jam-packed smoking car—solely because she was Black—the indignant Ida B. Wells refused. Biographer Linda McMurry recounted the event in *To Keep the Waters Troubled: The Life of Ida B. Wells*: "When Wells refused . . . the conductor grabbed her by the arm to remove her forcibly. Instead of meekly submitting, Wells held on to the back of her seat, braced her feet on the seat in front of her, and sank her teeth into his hand."[1]

Conductors pushed the young teacher off the train at the next stop. She countered with a lawsuit against the railroad, winning her complaint in a local court before its eventual reversal by the Tennessee Supreme Court. Despite the legal setback, the biting passion with which Wells battled discrimination inspired her to write her first published article: an account of the incident in the Memphis *Living Way,* a Black newspaper.[2]

The career of an advocate journalist had begun, and over the ensuing decades Wells would make a name for herself as a pioneer, unafraid to expose injustice from a decidedly political—and personal—point of view. The deeply subjective aspect of her investigations lent them an activist tilt, one that represented an intentional deviation from the press of the day's shift toward objectivity. Whether advocating for a greater national and international response to the atrocities of lynching in the South, championing the cause of race before gender in the women's suffrage movement, or protesting the injudicious treatment of accused Black men in greater Chicago, Ida B. Wells established an effective methodology for producing an alternative strain of advocacy journalism.

In today's media world, her methodology is worth revisiting. Over one-hundred-and-twenty years after *New York Times* publisher Adolph S. Ochs first began employing the detached and "objective" treatment of news that would become the industry standard, new technologies are forcing the industry to re-examine itself. Online media, including internet blogs, news aggregation websites, and even "fake news" are proliferating and quickly eclipsing the twentieth-century model of news. In an era of abundance, the explosion in media providers has decreased each individual news agency's incentive to appeal to a wide and non-partisan demographic; instead, it is often more profitable for organizations to speak directly to a target audience.[3] Consequently, the ideology of modern media is deviating further and further from the objective principles that have long defined journalism's ethos.

The departure from objectivity has led to a resurgence of work known as advocacy journalism; defined by *Media Ethics Magazine,* advocacy journalism is a form of journalism that "endeavors to be fact-based, but does not separate editorial opinion from news coverage and often approaches the news from a specific viewpoint."[4] Furthermore, unlike writing a traditional editorial or commentary, writing in this style calls a journalist to shift from observer to activist.

In print, advocacy journalism has seeped into the pages of mainstream magazines such as *The Atlantic* and *Esquire.* In November 2014, for instance, *Esquire*'s feature, "How to Fix Congress Now," through fact-based reporting, addressed national politics from a perspective bent on changing them.[5] Likewise, online, environmental news agencies such as Mongabay also have adopted this style of journalism; Mongabay was founded "with the mission of raising interest in and appreciation of wild lands and wildlife."[6] Some content from these sources merely convey commentary, but content that seeks to enact change through the reportage of transparent facts qualifies as advocacy journalism.

With this in mind, the life and work of Ida B. Wells offers as a case study in effective and ethical advocacy journalism. First, Wells used raw, factual, and anecdotal evidence to demonstrate the problem at hand; second, she worked to inform diverse audiences about said problem; and third, she proposed or embodied solutions to the identified issues. By studying her method, the modern advocacy journalist might achieve similar success.

THE ANTI-LYNCHING CRUSADE

Publishing the account of her struggle on the rails inspired Wells to keep writing, and as we have observed in an earlier chapter, she went on to produce a series of articles about inequality in segregated schools based upon her own experiences in the classrooms. Although "she was eventually fired from her teaching job as a result," the end of her teaching career opened the door to a new one—that of a journalist.[7]

By 1892, eight years after her story on the railroad court case ran in Black papers throughout the country, Wells had become the well-established editor and co-owner of the *Free Speech,* another Black-owned, Memphis-based newspaper. As we have seen in an earlier chapter, the brutal and unjust Memphis lynchings of three Black grocers that year elicited an unprecedented response from the Black press. Religious and secular publications from around the country reflected upon the ramifications of the murders, with some calling for boycotts of white businesses in the area and others calling for a mass exodus to Oklahoma.[8] Wells spearheaded the national outcry, using the *Free Speech* to write a series of anti-lynching tirades that grew increasingly more pointed. The most poignant response from Wells was published on May 21, 1892. Wells exposed the efforts of white males to advance the myth of Black male bestiality in order to avoid confronting white female promiscuity:

> Nobody in this section of the country believes the old thread-bare lie that Negro men rape white women. If Southern white men are not careful, they will over-reach themselves and public sentiment will have a reaction; a conclusion will then be reached which will be very damaging to the moral reputation of their women.[9]

The words cast doubt over the claim that the so-called victims in many of the so-called rapes were forced into interracial sex against their will. Shortly after its publication, on May 27, a mob destroyed the *Free Speech* offices, and Wells became an exiled advocacy journalist, who relied upon her pen and her voice for her social justice crusade.[10]

As we have seen in earlier chapters, Wells made limited gains in her cause over the next year as she wrote for the *New York Age* and embarked on a national and transnational lecture circuit, but she would extend those gains in her second transnational effort. In cities such as Birmingham, London, and Liverpool, in 1894, Wells distributed pamphlets ahead of her lectures, hoping to incite prominent citizens to an outcry. When one such citizen asked what good her message could do in the land of her exile, she replied with an explanation: "Great Britain did much for the final overthrow of chattel slavery. They can in like manner pray, write, preach, talk and act against civil and industrial slavery; against the hanging, shooting and burning alive of a powerless race."[11] Her words had powerful effect, amplified as they were by the immense coverage Wells' travels garnered. On her second tour of Europe, she would deliver more than one hundred lectures and more than fifty accounts of her talks filled British press, mostly praising her and offering support. A review of one of her lectures, published by the *Birmingham Daily Post* on May 17, 1894, embodied the heightened global awareness of the atrocities of lynching that she had brought about:

> Since 1882 over a thousand [B]lack men and women and children had been lynched. Some of the charges made against the victims were of the vilest description, and often without any ground whatsoever. They were made with the object of shutting off the sympathy of the world, and as the papers and the telegraph were in the hands of the whites it was impossible to contradict these statements. One-third of the victims had been charged with assaults on white women, and the remainder with all sorts of crimes, ranging from murder to that on which a man was hung in Tennessee—namely, that he was "drunk and 'sassy' to white people."[12]

The method by which she garnered so much attention—that is, employing various mediums (lectures, editorials, essays, pamphlets, etc.)—is one modern-day advocacy journalists might consider. Diversifying her delivery platforms paid dividends.

Wells returned from England in the summer of 1894 to be greeted with coverage in the white and Black presses. This access to white audiences allowed her to emphasize a comparative rhetoric between American society and Victorian-era Britain. She stressed English social acceptance for Blacks—as opposed to America's institutionalized racism—and highlighted the corresponding scorn with which the Brits regarded the mob violence conducted by self-proclaimed civilized "Christians."[13] Such boldness elicited much criticism, as it had throughout her career, but Wells mastered the art of using attacks against her character to benefit her cause.

At the turn of the twentieth century, society frowned upon women who openly discussed sexuality, and Wells' willingness to buck the norm left her vulnerable to attacks on her chastity. As a defense against their accusations of untrustworthy ethos, she would frequently quote directly from the words of her attackers, a tactic that imbued legitimacy to her message.[14] The shock of hearing an unmarried young woman detail the brutality of her detractors might have even increased the impact of her campaign.

This raw presentation of those who opposed her mission reflected what would become a hallmark of Wells' anti-lynching journalism: detailed reporting of facts and well-researched storytelling. It is evidenced most clearly in the 1892 publication of *Southern Horrors: Lynch Law in All Its Phases* and the 1895 publication of her investigative pamphlet, *A Red Record: Tabulated Statistics and Alleged Causes of Lynchings in the United States, 1892-1893-1894. Respectfully Submitted to the Nineteenth Century Civilization in "The Land of the Free and the Home of the Brave."*

The first of these, released in response to the 1892 Memphis lynchings, represented Wells' initial attempt at compiling the factual stories and accounts of lynchings across the South, and served as lecture material for her European tour. In her follow-up, *A Red Record*, Wells, who recently had married Chicago lawyer Ferdinand Barnett, delved even deeper into lynching as a widespread horror. Its cheeky title page, as Angela Sims asserts, "implies that the information that she provides about the latter half of the last decade of the nineteenth century challenges ideas about justice in a society that self-identifies as civilized."[15] By blatantly countering the nation's pre-conceived notion of justice, Wells-Barnett created an exigency for hard data; without proof of her claims, opponents and detractors could de-legitimize her entire crusade.

So, in a departure from her traditional prose, Wells-Barnett devoted three entire chapters of the book to statistics—raw facts. In chapter 2, she presented the lynch records as published in the *Chicago Tribune*. The myth of rape fell away quickly, as only 39 of 149 lynchings punished rape in 1893. She noted that "the facts contended for will always appear manifest—that not one-third of the victims lynched were charged with rape, and further that the charges made embraced a range of offenses from murders to misdemeanors."[16] Wells-Barnett also tabulated the data from 1892, finding that of 160 Black lynchings, only 57 charged the victim with rape or attempted rape. Other categories included insulting women, race prejudice, and no offense. This last category identified two victims as simply "boy and girl," which she explained:

> In the case of the boy and girl above referred to, their father, named Hastings, was accused of the murder of a white man; his fourteen-year-old daughter and sixteen-year-old son were hanged and their bodies filled with bullets, then the father was also lynched. This was in November 1892, at Jonesville, Louisiana.[17]

Here, Wells-Barnett interspersed the data with a story, a tool she used to ground her research in human emotion.

Scattered throughout the pamphlet, these graphic accounts of lynching provided a shock factor to Wells-Barnett's diverse audience and granted authenticity to her journalism. One account demonstrated the hypocrisy of lynching:

> In Texarkana, Arkansas, Edward Coy was accused of assaulting a white woman. The press dispatches of February 18, 1892, told in detail how he was tied to a tree, the flesh cut from his body by men and boys, and after coal oil was poured over him, the woman he had assaulted gladly set fire to him, and 15,000 persons saw him burn to death. October 1st, the Chicago *Inter-Ocean* contained the following. . . . She [the woman] was publicly reported and generally known to have been criminally intimate with Coy for more than a year previous. She was compelled by threats, if not by violence, to make the charge against the victim. . . . A large majority of the "superior white men prominent in the affair are the reputed fathers of mulatto children."[18]

Wells-Barnett reported similar accounts again and again within the pamphlet's pages, cleverly juxtaposing the barbarism of lynching with Southern hospitality. The detailed accounts served to support her central thesis—that lynch law reflected an unfounded belief in the inherent bestiality of Black men. Hypocrisy became easier to prove with specific instances of unequal treatment, and her style of advocacy journalism became harder to dispute.

In the closing chapter of *The Red Record,* Wells-Barnett identified a potential remedy to the plague of lynching. Proposing a solution goes directly against the tenant of objectivity in traditional journalism because it imparts the author's point of view, but, Wells-Barnett was never interested in being a traditional journalist. Diversifying her audience gave her reporting more power and using facts/details lent it legitimacy, but it was the willingness to suggest solutions to the evil of lynching that made her work effective. In her book, *Voices for the Voiceless,* Jinx Coleman Broussard finds that Wells-Barnett's solutions were a mainstay in her work, concluding that "Wells-Barnett's writings did not merely provide statistics or graphic details of lynchings; instead, the journalist always proposed a remedy."[19]

Her solution focused on the system first, calling for fair trial by law for those accused and equal punishment by the law's enforcement. "No maudlin sympathy for criminals is solicited, but we do ask that the *law* shall punish all alike," she wrote.[20] This rhetoric expertly evaded putting opponents on the defensive by pushing an agenda any rational mind would recognize as fair.

She went on to address the actions individual citizens might take, offering more explicit instructions: disseminate facts; protest and condemn lynchings; and boycott. Above all, she said, tell everyone the truth, so as to inform the world of the anarchy in the South. In section 111, the last of the book, she wrote, "When the Christian world knows the alarming growth of outlawry in our land, some means will be found to stop it."[21] Essentially, she suggested change could be achieved if people reported the facts and details of lynching—applying sound journalistic techniques to advocate for a social issue could incite change.

In addition to her consideration of solutions available to individual citizens, Wells-Barnett's later work demonstrated a lifelong commitment to systemic reform. At the first meeting of the 1909 National Negro Conference, which was attended by both whites and Blacks, Wells-Barnett spoke on "Lynching: Our National Crime." She opened with three assertions: lynching is a color-line murder; crimes against women are not the causes but the excuses of lynching; and lynching is a national crime and requires a national remedy. She then proposed a remedy: "The only certain remedy is an appeal to the law. Lawbreakers must be made to know that human life is sacred and that every citizen of this country is first a citizen of the United States and secondly a citizen of the state in which he belongs."[22] Her argument remained logically sound, grounded in fact and spread across diverse audiences through various media. The boldness of her journalism entitled her to suggest such solutions, an act that only served to legitimize her advocacy more. But it also required her to suggest sound and valid arguments. In this instance, she appealed to a bi-racial sense of justice using the rhetoric of law. Through the lens of history, we can see that the period of her most active advocacy journalism against lynching—that is, from 1892 to 1909—coincided with a steep decline in lynching prevalence across the country. The epidemic peaked at 230 in 1892, the year she released *Southern Horrors;* by the time she spoke at the 1909 National Negro Conference (NNC), the number of Black lynchings had dropped to 82.[23] In her biography, McMurry notes that "the gradual demise of lynching was the result of many factors, but surely the first step had to be the public's awareness and rejection of the practice."[24] Wells-Barnett was a major factor in generating that awareness, providing evidence of the success of the methodology of advocacy journalism.

COLOR BEFORE GENDER IN THE WOMEN'S SUFFRAGE MOVEMENT

Though Wells-Barnett is most well-remembered for her anti-lynching campaign, the advocate journalist also participated in the women's suffrage movement of the early twentieth century. It was a movement divided along the color line—some leaders, such as Susan B. Anthony and Elizabeth Cady Stanton, supported equality between Black and white women. Their support, however, had a foil in a certain sect of politically minded leaders, who sought to appease a different audience: Southern white women.[25] Because the temperance movement was the main vehicle for garnering support for the female vote, suffragists depended in large part upon the support of the Bible Belt, a region of primarily Christian society that also encompassed the most entrenched social racism.

Women such as Frances E. Willard, the national president of the Woman's Christian Temperance Union, sacrificed the interests of Black women in their attempts to woo belles below the Mason-Dixon Line. In an interview with the *New York Voice*, Willard actually condemned Blacks along the lines of the very stereotypes Wells was attacking. "'Better whiskey and more of it' is the rallying cry of great, dark-faced mobs," Willard said in an 1890 interview with the *New York Voice*. "The safety of [white] women, of childhood, of the home, is menaced in a thousand localities." Willard had told the publication that the local tavern "is the Negro's center of power . . . the colored race multiplies like the locusts of Egypt."[26] Remarks such as these infuriated Wells because they undermined the legitimacy of her anti-lynching campaign while at the same time exiling Black women from the suffrage agenda. Willard was admired widely by the British public, and Wells prepared for questions about the suffragists' interview by bringing the inflammatory story with her during her second trip to England in 1894.

In keeping with the established methodology, Wells used only facts in her response, sending the verbatim article to British high society. She included the comment: "Here we have Miss Willard's words in full, condoning fraud, violence, murder at the ballot box, raping, shooting, hanging and burning."[27] This strategy elicited a defensive response from Willard, who scrambled to assure the public that she was united with the Black community against the taking of human life without due process. Wells responded, again applying the president's own words to paint Willard as someone selfishly concerned with her own image, more focused on her reputation than the inhumane deaths of hundreds. McMurry contended that Wells was "exceptionally adroit in using attacks against her character or credibility to further her cause."[28]

The dispute would wage on, eliciting editorials from American and British papers that supported Willard and condemned Wells on account of her character. Some Black papers even turned against her, but the majority of Black editors defended her. The British press eventually fell on the side of Wells, and at the close of her 1894 tour, she managed to form the Anti-Lynching Committee to raise money for the investigation and exposure of lynching. Notable members included P. W. Clayden, the editor of the *London Daily News*, and Sir John Gorst, Duke of Argyle and a member of Parliament. Most notable was the invitation extended to Willard, an olive branch that the temperance leader accepted. Wells reflected on the social victory in her autobiography, writing that the moment "was not only a boomerang to Miss Willard. It seemed to appeal to the British sense of fair play . . . joining hands in the effort to crush an insignificant colored woman who had neither money nor influence—nothing but the power of truth with which to fight her battles."[29]

Despite her successes in England, Wells encountered the ramifications of her highly publicized spat with Willard after her return to the US. In 1895, the Boston Woman's Club held a convention on behalf of the new Mrs. Ida B. Wells-Barnett.

At the convention, the women passed a resolution expressing their admiration for the "noble and truthful advocacy" of Wells-Barnett against the "lying charge of rape." However, the resolution was never published; a Missouri delegate—aware of her dispute with Willard—protested the statement.[30]

This dissidence within the suffrage community troubled Wells-Barnett. She bemoaned the exile in *The New York Age:*

> I am indeed placed in a peculiarly unenviable position; for trying to defend the good name of the manhood of my race my business was destroyed in Memphis, my life threatened, and three times since, my good name has been most wantonly assailed by the white people who are lynching the race and blasting its reputation.[31]

Nevertheless, Wells-Barnett continued to advocate for her cause by appealing to diverse audiences, looking beyond her own race. Just as her anti-lynching crusade relied on support from white newspaper editors, her battle for Black women's suffrage came to depend upon support from white suffragists. In a speech to the Chicago Political Equality League in early 1903, Wells-Barnett espoused biracial communication to diminish prejudice. A predominantly white audience listened as she proposed that Black women might "emancipate the white women of the country from the prejudice which fetters their noblest endeavors and renders inconsistent their most sacred professions."[32] The message inspired Celia Parker Wooley, a Unitarian minister, to start an interracial social club—it would become the Frederick Douglass Center—and though Wells would later fall out of favor with the group, its existence spoke to the value of diversifying one's audience. By advocating to the white suffrage leadership, Wells managed to highlight the injustice of excluding Black women from the movement and to inspire integration.

After moving to Chicago and starting a family with the prominent lawyer Ferdinand Barnett, Wells-Barnett remained involved with the national movement through local organizations in the early 1900s. She formed the Alpha Suffrage Club in 1913, Illinois' first suffrage organization for Black women. The club sent her as a delegate to a national suffrage parade in Washington, DC, but when Southern delegates objected to her presence, she was instructed to march in the colored delegation. Wells-Barnett objected, saying, "I shall not march at all unless I can march under the Illinois banner."[33] The journalist made good on her word and switched delegations during the parade, slipping out of the Black group and into procession alongside the Illinois representatives. The move increased her visibility; in the March 8, 1913, front-page account of the march, a *Chicago Defender* correspondent wrote that the "modern Joan [of] Arc" had marched in the parade despite the protests and "scorn of her Southern Sisters."[34] The article went on to celebrate Wells-Barnett as an individual of the "highest type of womanhood," suggesting her action was well-received. Wells-Barnett sensed an opportunity to amplify her message of racial equality within the battle for women's suffrage by making a public stand, and the rebellious subversion successfully integrated the suffrage march.

Wells-Barnett's actions during the parade reflected her personal philosophy on race and suffrage, a philosophy she proposed as a solution to strained relationships within the movement. If a woman deserved the right to vote because American democracy viewed all men and women as equals, she reasoned, then why would a Black woman not deserve the same right for the same reason? Women fighting for gender equality were morally obligated to support racial equality.

Her stance alienated her and limited her influence on the national suffrage movement, but in Illinois, Wells-Barnett emerged as a political force. After the state legislature enacted a limited suffrage law in 1913, she organized a door-to-door campaign to encourage women to vote. On the first day they were eligible to vote, more than 153,000 women cast a ballot. In her autobiography, Wells-Barnett recalled the response from the Black elected officials: "Our men politicians were surprised because not one of them, not even our ministers, had said one word to influence women to take advantage of the suffrage opportunity Illinois had given to her daughters."[35] Her triumphant tone illustrated the pride she felt for the success of her solution—by advocating directly to women and placing race interests ahead of gender interests, Wells-Barnett felt she had generated progress for both.

Wells-Barnett also managed to champion racial equality in general woman's clubs. After the Chicago Woman's Club denied a Black woman named Fannie Barrier Williams from joining for fourteen months, Wells-Barnett reported on their inaction.[36] Williams eventually became the club's first Black member, exemplifying the value of Wells-Barnett's solution—writing about suffrage gave her an audience, but practicing actual advocacy through the Alpha Suffrage Club legitimized her words and beliefs. Her philosophy of racial equality between women produced results.

National leadership followed the pattern established by white woman's clubs, and in 1915, Wells-Barnett met with President Woodrow Wilson to discuss segregation within governmental departments. She asked him to use his influence as president to help abolish discrimination based on the color line. Though Wilson never passed an anti-discrimination law, Wells-Barnett's petitions to his administration reveal her to be an activist who proposed a solution by actually practicing one.[37] The advocacy journalism she conducted for woman's suffrage did not explicitly recommend solutions—like her anti-lynching campaign did—but it did materialize into a solution by example, and when the Nineteenth Amendment was finally passed in 1920, it extended the right to vote to Black women, as well as white women.

DEFENDING THE RIGHTS OF THE BLACK ACCUSED

As part of her argument for enfranchisement, Wells-Barnett pointed out that Black political power might enable anti-lynching legislation. She would devote much of the latter half of her life to organizing support for Black officials, and even more so, working to defend the rights of those accused of lynching or similar crimes. As we have seen earlier in this book, Wells-Barnett employed the tactics of advocacy journalism in her activism related to the case of the lynched Black man William "Frog"

James, ultimately establishing the Negro Fellowship League (NFL), a community organization that advocated for equity and social justice for Black men, in the case's aftermath.

The justice Wells-Barnett achieved in Cairo represented a huge victory for interracial law enforcement, and six years later, she found similar success by preventing the unjust killing of another Black man in the case of Joseph "Chicken Joe" Campbell. In 1915, Campbell was accused of setting a fire in the Joliet Penitentiary and killing Odetta Allen, the warden's (white) wife. Having earned the status of "trusty" for good conduct after his imprisonment for murder, Campbell had been assigned to be Odetta's personal servant; he must have served her well, as she had promised to testify on his behalf when he went before the Board of Pardons and Parole. Though the Allens' physician, previously convicted for murdering his own wife, failed to make a thorough examination or analyze the body, he claimed Allen also had been strangled and sexually assaulted. Despite the lack of physical proof of rape, the authorities accused Campbell of trying to conceal the evidence by arson. He was arrested swiftly and assigned to solitary confinement. After living in a completely dark cell for forty hours—undergoing third-degree questioning and bread-and-water rationing—Campbell confessed to the crime.[38] At his testimony, he would retract the confession and insist on his innocence. Ferdinand Barnett took charge of the defense and said, "I feel confident he cannot be convicted."[39]

When Wells-Barnett read of the case, she reached out to James Keeley, the editor of a local white-owned Chicago newspaper, the *Chicago Record-Herald.* Claiming that other white papers no longer printed her letters on mobs, she asked Keeley if he would publish her letter. He agreed, placing her appeal prominently in the paper. It also ran in the *Chicago Defender,* the city's largest Black paper and one of her former employers:

> All shudder to think so terrible a crime could be committed within the prison walls, but I write to ask if one more terrible is not now taking place there in the name of justice. . . [Campbell was] sweated and tortured to make him confess to a crime he may not have committed. Is this justice? Is it humanity? Would we stand to see a dog treated in such a fashion without protest?[40]

By using a white newspaper to protest Campbell's treatment, Wells-Barnett once again managed to diversify the audience of her advocacy, reaching readers who might not otherwise know or care about the injustice she identified. Although Wells-Barnett would claim in her autobiography that the letter persuaded the Illinois governor to move Campbell from the penitentiary to the nearest county jail, she did not confine herself to the white audience.

More than biracial support, Wells-Barnett needed funding to cover the court costs and legal fees of defending Campbell. To pay them, she organized a campaign through the Alpha Suffrage Club, the NFL, and the *Chicago Defender.* In an article published November 6, 1915, the paper noted: "Up to the present time about $125.00 has been collected. The expenses will exceed $300.00, so that justice-loving people may contribute to help Campbell in his struggle for his life."[41] A successful effort, the campaign raised more than five hundred dollars for the case, and her husband served as Campbell's lawyer. The initial trial resulted in a guilty verdict and death sentence, but after haranguing influential Blacks to offer more support, Wells-Barnett and her husband raised additional money for appeals. Three years later, the Illinois governor granted clemency. "Although unable to get his release, the Barnetts and the NFL saved Campbell's life."[42] This case demonstrates how Wells-Barnett managed to tap into both white and Black audiences for different resources; she knew that white readers of the *Record-Herald* might have the power to aid Campbell's current condition, but that the Black readers of *Chicago Defender* might be moved to make monetary contributions for his defense.

A similar diligence to justice in the 1917 case of Leroy Bundy had equally victorious results. After economic competition erupted into race riots in East St. Louis, nearly one hundred Blacks were slaughtered on the morning of July 3. Wells-Barnett arrived two days later to hear the stories of Black women who fled the white mobs and were growing outraged at the criminal negligence and complicity of police and state militia. She particularly was concerned about Bundy; the Black dentist had been charged with the murder of two policeman during the riots, becoming an apparent scapegoat who faced a disproportionately longer sentence compared to those received by whites.[43]

Wells-Barnett interviewed Bundy in his jail cell, and convinced of his innocence, teamed up with her husband to fight the conviction in court. Working with the *Defender* and the NFL, Wells-Barnett focused on raising money for the cause; her husband stayed with the case through lost trials and appeals and eventually helped Bundy win his freedom. A key aspect of her fundraising was the publishing of the pamphlet *The East St. Louis Massacre, The Greatest Outrage of the Century*. In the account, she used her typical tactic of detailed victim narratives to tug the heart and purse strings of her readers. "Ida wrote briefly about their backgrounds, how long they had lived in the city, the material possessions they had lost . . . and their eyewitness accounts of seeing [B]lacks beaten and killed."[44] To help generate more national action, Wells-Barnett also wrote a letter to another Black Chicago newspaper, the *Broad Ax*. According to McMurry, the appeal "urged African Americans to raise money to have people observe the congressional hearings and the trials of riot participants to see that the truth was told and justice done."[45] In this instance, she diversified her audience, not by appealing to both white and Black readers, but by offering her appeals in more than one publication.

Throughout the legal battles she and her husband also fought for Black convicts, Wells-Barnett came to embody a solution to injustice in the legal system by working within it. In 1913, she took a full-time position as Chicago's first Black adult probation officer, a job closely intertwined with her efforts at the NFL. The center would become the office where she had meetings with Black probationers. She reported having two hundred men under her charge in 1914, but in December 1915, her contract was not renewed. Despite the slight, she continued working with accused criminals through the NFL, even helping many of them find jobs.[46] In a *Chicago Defender* article published on February 19, 1916, the author noted that a recent

NFL meeting attracted three hundred and one people and wrote that "a number of persons were given employment."[47] One such man was George Thomas, a teenager who had made his way alone from Georgia to Chicago but ended up in the court system. Wells-Barnett helped him through homelessness, unemployment, and police brutality, eventually seeing him become a citizen of Chicago in good standing with the law. Merely one of hundreds of probationers whom Wells-Barnett supported, Thomas' experience confirms the importance of advocate journalists who advocate beyond the page.[48]

This embodiment of advocacy journalism also is evidenced by the case of Steve Green, a tenant farmer from Arkansas who had killed his landlord in self-defense. Having fled to Chicago, Green was arrested on a dubious charge of petty larceny and kept without adequate nourishment for four days as authorities interrogated him. He attempted suicide and was hospitalized. The Chicago police chief put Green on a train back to Arkansas, but Wells-Barnett stepped in and contacted Edward Wright, a candidate for alderman. With his help, she raised a reward for Green's re-arrest along the route in hopes of returning him to Chicago. He was taken off the train in Cairo and returned to Chicago, where Wells-Barnett hid him in the NFL headquarters. In the vein of the Underground Railroad, she harbored Green until collecting enough money to sneak him out of the country into Canada.[49] A September 24, 1910, *Chicago Defender* account of the case labeled Wells-Barnett a "watchdog of human life and liberty" and a "humanitarian of the race."[50]

Her solution proposals, found in her pamphlets and letters about these cases and others, echoed those of her earlier anti-lynching work. Invariably, they called on Blacks to help fund her organizations as they fought for the rights of the poor and wrongfully accused community members; they also called on the criminal justice system to offer all defendants a fair trial. Her activism, however, illustrates a more powerful solution by providing her own example. She did not merely advocate in print, but rather through the undertakings of her own life. Whether within the NFL or as an adult probation officer, she dedicated herself to the cause of the criminally accused Black population.

CONCLUSION

In 1840, Scottish philosopher Thomas Carlyle noted that the three estates of government—in that time, the church, the nobility, and the townsmen—were balanced by a fourth estate: the press.[51] Though the first three branches of American government are known as the legislative, executive, and judicial branches, the process of governing still depends upon journalism to disseminate information; democracy relies upon informed citizens in order to function. In a representative democracy, the responsibilities of journalism grow into a feedback loop, making actions of the government known to the voters and equipping them with the knowledge they need to cast their votes.[52] Journalism becomes as much a record of events as it is a harbinger of change, one that serves communities by investigating and exposing injustice within government and/or society. Ideally, the stories a news reporter writes are those that he or she believes serve the public's best interest. In an online essay, media critic and blogger Jeff Jarvis links this fundamental core of journalism—to serve the public's best interest—to advocacy journalism:

> When an editor assigns reporters to expose a consumer scam or Wall Street fraud or misappropriation of government funds, that is advocacy. When a newspaper takes on the cause of the poor, the disadvantaged, the abused, the forgotten, or just the little guy against The Man, that is advocacy. When health reporters tell you how to avoid cancer or even lose weight, that is advocacy on your behalf. When an editor decides to cover a crime in this neighborhood but not that one, she is advocating for the allocation of attention to the first.[53]

The essential decision any journalist makes, then, is not how to present objectively the news; choosing any story rather than another requires that the journalist consider its importance and relevance to this audience, a sort of opinion that is inseparable from journalism's responsibility as the fourth estate.

With the onslaught of online media, opinionated journalism can shift from advocacy to dangerously unfounded reporting. Bloggers and web reporters can generate more traffic by posting about cats and celebrity trends than they can by posting about serious social issues, simply because the average web user has an attention span of eight seconds.[54] Jarvis notes that because this brand of media does not serve the public's best interest—because it does not advocate—it should not be considered journalism.

How, then, are journalists of the twenty-first century to engage properly in advocacy journalism? Through an analysis of the life and work of Ida B. Wells-Barnett, a methodology becomes clear. The first and most vital element remains the same as traditional journalism would recommend—use facts and details to support the story and captivate the reader. Wells' detailed descriptions of lynchings horrified men and women across the country and in Europe, working in tandem with the raw data of lynchings to prove the evil and prevalence of the crime. She did the same with her work for woman's suffrage, supporting Black women's enfranchisement by publishing the verbatim attacks of her character from those who opposed her and her mission. In the cases of individual Black men accused of crimes, she continued to rely heavily on the use of facts, disseminating them to prove their innocence and in several instances, save their lives. Advocacy journalists in the twenty-first century should take note, proposing arguments based first and foremost on facts. It is as much a facet of advocacy journalism as it is a requirement of any journalism.

The second method Wells-Barnett used was diversifying her audience. It is most clearly demonstrated by her anti-lynching crusade. The former schoolteacher from Memphis managed to reach audiences in Europe, and the color line did not stop her from publishing in the Black *and* white presses. Her anti-lynching campaign depended, in large part, upon the variety of her readers. She used the same tactics of breaking the press' color barrier in her fight for Black woman's suffrage and for the rights of the Black accused. Key to all three causes was her willingness to print and publish her own pamphlets, distributing them around the regions in which she wrote.

Proposing a solution represents the third aspect to Wells-Barnett's advocacy journalism. Throughout her life—whether advocating against lynching, for Black enfranchisement, or on behalf of the accused—she never neglected the goal of her writing. She always proposed solutions to the atrocities she covered. Often, these solutions were calls for funding activists, like herself, who battled injustice. She also suggested boycotts, setting a precedent for the successful practices of the Civil Rights Era. And in a neat full-circle of her methodology, she frequently called on her readers to spread the facts and details of injustice, duplicating her own effect at an exponential rate. This third method, if applied to online journalism, adds legitimacy to the author—as it did to Wells-Barnett.

Together, the three aspects of Wells-Barnett's methodology contributed to the end of lynching, the beginning of woman's suffrage, and the justice of the Black accused. In so doing, she established a blueprint for others to follow. As "objective" journalism becomes more subjective and opinionated, today's journalists can follow her example to produce ethical advocacy journalism.

NOTES

1. Linda O. McMurry, *To Keep the Waters Troubled: The Life of Ida B. Wells* (New York: Oxford University Press, 1998), 26.

2. Piyali Dalal, "Ida B. Wells," *University of Minnesota English Department,* 2001, http://voices.cla.umn.edu/artistpages/wellsIda.php.

3. Matt Carlson, *Journalistic Authority: Legitimating News in the Digital Era* (New York: Columbia University Press, 2017), 1–199.

4. Matthew Reavy, "Objectivity and Advocacy in Journalism," *Media Ethics Magazine,* 2013, http://www.mediaethicsmagazine.com/index.php/browse-back-issues/179-fall-2013-vol-25-no-1/3999003-objectivity-and-advocacy-in-journalism.

5. Richard Dorment, "How to Fix Congress Now," *Esquire,* November 2014, 143.

6. Rhett Butler, "About," *Mongabay,* 2017. http://data.mongabay.com/about.html.

7. Ibid.

8. Paula Giddings, *Ida: A Sword among Lions* (New York: HarperCollins, 2008), 193.

9. Wells, "Southern Horrors," section 3.

10. McMurry, *To Keep the Waters Troubled,* 148.

11. Ida Wells, as quoted in McMurry, *To Keep the Waters Troubled,* 193.

12. *Birmingham Daily Post,* "Lynch Law in the United States," Birmingham, England, May 17, 1894, from University of Chicago Library, *Ida B. Wells Papers 1884–1976.*http://pi.lib.uchicago.edu/1001/scrc/md/ibwells-0008-010-05.

13. McMurry, *To Keep the Waters Troubled,* 222.

14. Ibid., 216.

15. Sims, *Ethical Complications,* 47.

16. Ida B. Wells, "A Red Record: Tabulated Statistics and Alleged Causes of Lynching in the United States, 1892–1893–1894. Respectfully Submitted to the Nineteenth Century Civilization in 'the Land of the Free and the Home of the Brave'," Pamphlet, Illinois During the Gilded Age, Northern Illinois University Libraries, section 23, http://gildedage.lib.niu.edu/islandora/object/niu-gildedage%3A23615.

17. Ibid., section 24.

18. Ibid., section 70.

19. Jinx Coleman Broussard, *Giving a Voice to the Voiceless: Four Pioneering Black Women Journalists* (New York: Routledge, 2003), 41.

20. Wells, "A Red Record," section 107.

21. Ibid., section 111.

22. Wells, as quoted in McMurry, *To Keep the Waters Troubled*, 280.

23. Lillian Jiminez, "Lynchings, by Year and Race, 1882–1968," *The Charles Chesnutt Digital Archive*, 2008, http://www.chesnuttarchive.org/classroom/lynching_table_year.html.

24. McMurry, *To Keep the Waters Troubled*, 340.

25. Monee Fields-White, "How Racism Tainted Women's Fight to Vote," theroot.com, 2011, http://www.theroot.com/articles/politics/2011/03/womens_suffrage_and_racism_ida_b_wells_vs_frances_e_willard.2.html.

26. Ibid., 2.

27. McMurry, *To Keep the Waters Troubled*, 212.

28. Ibid.

29. Fields-White, "How Racism Tainted," 6.

30. McMurry, *To Keep the Waters Troubled*, 247.

31. Ida B. Wells, as quoted in Giddings, *Ida*, 312.

32. McMurry, *To Keep the Waters Troubled*, 312.

33. Ibid., 305.

34. "Marches in Parade Despite Protests," *Chicago Defender*, March 8, 1913, 1.

35. Wells, as quoted in McMurry, *To Keep the Waters Troubled*, 310.

36. Broussard, *Giving a Voice to the* Voiceless, 31.

37. Rutherford, para. 16.

38. Ibid., 549.

39. "Chicken Joe Innocent, Negro Lawyer Says," *Chicago Defender*, July 14, 1915, 7.

40. "The . . . of the 'Solitary' Mrs. Barnett Protests Against It," *Chicago Defender*, June 26, 1915, 4.

41. "Chicken Joe Campbell Trial On: Great Interest throughout the State," *Chicago Defender*, November 6, 1915, 3.

42. McMurry, *To Keep the Waters Troubled*, 299.

43. Ibid., 316.

44. Giddings, *Ida*, 563.

45. McMurry, *To Keep the Waters Troubled*, 315.

46. Ibid., 298.

47. "The Negro Fellowship League," *Chicago Defender*, February 19, 1916, 4.

48. Patricia A. Schechter, *Ida B. Wells-Barnett and American Reform, 1880-1930* (Chapel Hill: The University of North Carolina Press, 2001), 195.

49. Giddings, *Ida*, 495.

50. "Steve Green Liberated," *Chicago Defender*, September 24, 1910, 1.

51. Thomas Carlyle, "Lecture V: The Hero as Man of Letters. Johnson, Rousseau, Burns," *On Heroes, Hero-Worship, and the Heroic in History*, section 392, Project Gutenberg, 2007, http://www.gutenberg.org/files/20585/20585-h/20585-h.htm#lecturev.

52. Danny Crichton, Ben Christel, Aaditya Shidham, Alex Valderrama, Jeremy Karmel, "Journalism in the Digital Age," Introduction, 2011, http://cs.stanford.edu/people/eroberts/cs201/projects/2010-11/Journalism/index7f0d.html?page_id=16.

53. Jeff Jarvis, "Journalist as Organizer, Advocate, and Educator," *Geeks Bearing Gifts*, 2014, https://medium.com/geeks-bearing-gifts/journalist-as-organizer-advocate-and-educator-7aa720b8bed6.

54. Michael Brenner, "Thanks Social Media—Our Average Attention Span Is Now Shorter Than a Goldfish," *B2b Marketing Insider,* 2014, http://www.b2bmarketinginsider.com/content-marketing/thanks-social-media-average-attention-span-now-shorter-goldfish.

BIBLIOGRAPHY

Brenner, Michael. "Thanks Social Media—Our Average Attention Span Is Now Shorter Than a Goldfish," *B2b Marketing Insider,* 2014. http://www.b2bmarketinginsider.com/content-marketing/thanks-social-media-average-attention-span-now-shorter-goldfish.

Broussard, Jinx Coleman. *Giving a Voice to the Voiceless: Four Pioneering Black Women Journalists.* New York: Routledge, 2003.

Butler, Rhett. "About," *Mongabay,* 2017. http://data.mongabay.com/about.html.

Campbell, W. Joseph. "About That Hearst Quote on Public's Fondness for Entertainment," *Media Myth Alert,* August 2015. https://mediamythalert.wordpress.com/tag/new-york-journal/.

———. "FAQs about *The Year That Defined American Journalism* and the author's replies," *The Year That Defined American Journalism,* 2006. http://academic2.american.edu/~wjc/1897/faq.html.

Carlyle, Thomas. "Lecture V: The Hero as Man of Letters. Johnson, Rousseau, Burns," *On Heroes, Hero-Worship, and the Heroic in History,* section 392, Project Gutenberg, 2007. http://www.gutenberg.org/files/20585/20585-h/20585-h.htm#lecturev.

Crichton, Danny, Christel, Ben, Shidham, Aaditya, Valderrama, Alex, and Karmel, Jeremy. "Journalism in the Digital Age," Introduction, 2011. http://cs.stanford.edu/people/eroberts/cs201/projects/2010-11/Journalism/index7f0d.html?page_id=16.

Dalal, Piyali. "Ida B. Wells," *University of Minnesota English Department,* 2001, http://voices.cla.umn.edu/artistpages/wellsIda.php.

Dorment, Richard. "How to Fix Congress Now," *Esquire,* November 2014, 143.

Fields-White, Monee. "How Racism Tainted Women's Fight to Vote," theroot.com, 2011. http://www.theroot.com/articles/politics/2011/03/womens_suffrage_and_racism_ida_b_wells_vs_frances_e_willard.2.html.

Giddings, Paula. *Ida: A Sword among Lions, Ida B. Wells and the Campaign against Lynching.* New York: HarperCollings, 2008.

Jarvis, Jeff. "Journalist as Organizer, Advocate, and Educator," *Geeks Bearing Gifts,* 2014. https://medium.com/geeks-bearing-gifts/journalist-as-organizer-advocate-and-educator-7aa720b8bed6.

Jiminez, Lillian. "Lynchings, by Year and Race, 1882-1968," *The Charles Chesnutt Digital Archive,* 2008. http://www.chesnuttarchive.org/classroom/lynching_table_year.html.

McMurry, Linda O. *To Keep the Waters Troubled: The Life of Ida B. Wells.* New York: Oxford University Press, 1998.

Reavy, Matthew. "Objectivity and Advocacy in Journalism," *Media Ethics Magazine,* 2013. http://www.mediaethicsmagazine.com/index.php/browse-back-issues/179-fall-2013-vol-25-no-1/3999003-objectivity-and-advocacy-in-journalism.

Rutherford, Karen. "Ida B. Wells-Barnett," *The Mississippi Writer's Page*, January 2004, http://mwp.olemiss.edu//dir/wells-barnett_ida/.

Schechter, Patricia A. *Ida B. Wells-Barnett and American Reform, 1880-1930*. Chapel Hill: University of North Carolina Press, 2001.

Sims, Angela. *Ethical Complications of Lynching*. New York: Palgrave Macmillan, 2010.

Wells, Ida B. *Crusade for Justice: The Autobiography of Ida B. Wells*, edited by Alfreda M. Duster. Chicago: The University of Chicago Press, 1970.

———. "The Red Record: Tabulated Statistics and Alleged Causes of Lynching in the United States, 1892–1893–1894. Respectfully Submitted to the Nineteenth Century Civilization in 'the Land of the Free and the Home of the Brave'," Pamphlet, *Illinois During the Gilded Age*, Northern Illinois University Libraries, section 23, http://gildedage.lib.niu.edu/islandora/object/niu-gildedage%3A23615.

9

What Would Ida Do?

Considering the Relevancy of Ida B. Wells-Barnett's Legacy to Journalism Students at an HBCU

Chandra D. Snell Clark

She would blog. She would tweet. She would take to the streets.

Such were the researcher's speculations while following the recent shooting deaths of Trayvon Martin, Jordan Davis, Oscar Grant, Sean Bell, Michael Brown, Eric Garner, Tamir Rice, and other unarmed African-American males over the past several years. Scholarly interest in Wells-Barnett has grown in recent decades.[1] To the researcher, an Ida B. Wells performer, associate professor of speech, and then-adjunct assistant professor of journalism at a public Historically Black College and University (HBCU) in the South, the parallels between lynchings, hangings, and other means of violence toward African Americans—primarily men—and the more recent shootings of African-American men are obvious; however, she pondered over what the students in this JOU 1005: Language Skills for Media Professionals, composed overwhelmingly of African Americans, and all students of color, thought.

Attempting to find out, students in this gatekeeper, entry-level course were assigned the following research question in a 500-word paper: "What, if any, is the relevancy of Ida B. Wells-Barnett's "crusade for justice"[2] to the Trayvon Martin, Jordan Davis, or Michael Brown cases? What are the implications of Wells-Barnett's crusade, if any, for today's journalists?"[3] The purpose of this project was to identify, through a discourse analysis of their responses; specifically: 1. How these students framed their arguments relating to their perceived relevancy, if any, of Wells-Barnett's activist legacy to the recent shooting deaths of African-American males by whites; and 2. How they framed their arguments relating to their perceptions of Wells-Barnett's relevancy, if any, to today's journalists. Results suggested that students perceived a connection between events in Wells-Barnett's time and today, and that they are now beginning to discover that journalism, more than being merely a glamorous career, also can be a noble calling. Insights from this project are not only relevant to those teaching journalism at HBCUs, but also to all media historians, communication professors, and other educators, who seek to help their students discover the connections among the past, the present, and their professional and personal futures.[4]

Over the past four decades, media historians largely have taken up the charge put forth by James Carey and David Sloan to enrich and expand journalism history by incorporating multiple cultures, voices, and perspectives.[5] In revisiting the state of media history scholarship, John Nerone reminded, "History is not about the past but about the relationship between the past and the present."[6] Further, he contended, "There are two roles for journalism history to play. One is to deconstruct the familiar object of study. The other is to expand the range of objects of study."[7] This last assertion may be of even greater importance to HBCUs, which produce about eighty percent of working African-American journalists.[8] An August 2013 teaching panel, co-sponsored by the Association for Education in Journalism and Mass Communication (AEJMC) History Division and Council of Affiliates "universally emphasized that history remains relevant to the mass communication curriculum, [that] connections are necessary between historical and current concepts, and [that] historical topics can and should be incorporated into non-history classes."[9] Media historian Andie Tucher noted, "Journalism history matters because we can't use journalism to know about history—or to know about the present either—without knowing how journalism worked *in* history."[10]

Students of color in the United States, because of the country's racist past and as yet unrealized ideal of full racial equality and harmony, need a full historical context within which to situate themselves, their future field, and their career aspirations. To this end, of the nine ACEJMC-accredited journalism and mass communication programs at HBCUs, more than half offer some type of media history course stressing the contributions of African Americans and/or other People of Color. This institution, despite being one of the first accredited HBCU journalism programs, is not one of them; however, professors in the journalism school, including the researcher, try to incorporate African-American media history into their existing courses. This current project and this analysis of it is an outcome of that effort. This chapter considers whether these students perceived Ida B. Wells-Barnett's life and work to be relevant to contemporary journalism and society.

RECENT SHOOTING DEATHS OF AFRICAN-AMERICAN MALES AS OF FALL 2014

Although they were not the only victims of such incidents during the period, the shooting deaths by whites of unarmed African-American teens Trayvon Martin, Jordan Davis, and Michael Brown have garnered the most media attention during the past several years. Martin, seventeen, was killed by neighborhood watchman George Zimmerman in Sanford, Florida, on February 26, 2012.[11] Zimmerman's acquittal of second-degree murder and manslaughter charges on July 13, 2013, sparked a wave of activism against perceived racism in the criminal justice system, racial profiling, and "stand your ground" laws, defined by the Black Clergy Women of the United Methodist Church's 2014 "Resolution Against Stand Your Ground Laws" as "a type of self-defense law that gives individuals the right to use deadly force . . . without any requirement to evade or retreat from a dangerous situation."[12] Philip Agnew, executive director of Dream Defenders, a nonprofit human rights group formed after the Zimmerman verdict, told *USA Today*, "After that [verdict], it was really, really clear that we are prisoners of war. Our communities are occupied by a police force that kills, that profiles and is deputizing citizens and allowing them to treat poor people and people of color the same way."[13] In an address to the nation following the verdict, President Barack Obama acknowledged, "Trayvon Martin could have been me thirty-five years ago," gaining even more media attention for the case.[14]

Only months later, Jordan Davis, also seventeen, was shot and killed by Michael Dunn on November 23, 2012, in Jacksonville, Florida, over an alleged incident involving loud music.[15] *Jet* editor-in-chief Mitzi Miller stated in the magazine's January 14, 2013 issue:

> The first time I read about the shooting that claimed Jordan Davis' life, I lost my breath. I read the article twice because I was so confused: A middle-aged adult instigated an argument with a group of teenagers (children) over the volume of the music playing inside their car. And then, because the kids refused to adhere to this stranger's demand to turn down the radio, he pulled out a gun and fired at their vehicle . . . eight or nine times? For real?

> Unfortunately, no one can bring back Jordan, Trayvon, or any of the other victims of the flawed Stand Your Ground law, But together, we can make a difference by keeping his story alive and actively working toward societal change. Now.[16]

Unlike the Zimmerman case, however, Davis' killer was found guilty of first-degree murder[17] and sentenced to life in prison.[18]

Ironically, just days after the Black Clergy Women of the United Methodist Church presented its "Resolution Against Stand Your Ground Laws" at its annual meeting in Orlando, Florida, Michael Brown, eighteen, was shot to death by Officer Darren Wilson on August 9, 2014, in Ferguson, Missouri.[19] Brown's death, and a grand jury's subsequent decision not to indict Wilson, sparked riots and looting, as well as thousands of protests and demonstrations nationwide.

The protest slogans "I Can't Breathe," "Hands Up, Don't shoot," "Black Lives Matter," "I Am Trayvon (or Michael Brown, etc.)," and "No Justice, No Peace," particularly gained momentum and popularity among protesters. "'I Can't Breathe': After Indictment Decision, Eric Garner's Final Words Become a Symbol of Anger, Frustration," declared a headline in the December 3, 2014, edition of the *Washington Post*.[20] According to Bowerman, protest slogans can be traced back to the civil rights era with "I am a man," "We shall overcome" (which has its roots in a Negro spiritual of the nineteenth century, according to Kyle and Roberts of the March 15, 2015 *New York Times*[21]), and "I'm Black and I'm proud" during the 1960s[22]; more recent descendants include "Fight the power," made famous by the rap group Public Enemy during the late 1980s. *USA Today* credits Alicia Garza and Patrisse Cullors with origi-nating "Black Lives Matter."[23] "*No justice, no peace* has been around since the 1970s," declares Wordsworth in the January 18, 2014, edition of *The Spectator,* although "No one knows the originator of the slogan."[24] According to Zimmer, "'No justice, no peace' is a more traditional statement of anger over institutionalized racism. Dating to the New York protests in the 1980s and revived after the shooting death of Trayvon Martin, it sets up a dire promise: without racial justice, we will not have peace."[25]

THE INSTITUTION

According to its website, Florida A&M University is one of the top-ranked public HBCUs in the US, enrolling more than 10,000 full-time students from through-out the country, as well as more than seventy countries, including "representatives from all ethnic, socioeconomic, and religious backgrounds."[26] The great majority of students at this land grant, comprehensive/doctoral university identify as Black and are in-state residents.[27] Rich in tradition, the institution is a pivotal part of the local community, as well as a major incubator of African-American professionals through-out the state and nation. Events, such as its annual homecoming and football games, bring out scores of alumni and students, who appear to wear the university's signa-ture colors with pride.

The website identifies journalism as one of its top programs.[28] The journalism school offers majors in journalism, public relations, and graphic design, and its students regularly win national awards; its more than seven hundred students have the opportunity to gain experience at its television and radio stations, magazine, and online newspaper.[29] Its mission statement reads, in part: "We endeavor to help shape our students into ethically and socially responsible leaders in a global society by help-ing students understand the importance of respecting the dignity of individuals and others from different ethnic backgrounds."[30]

Offered for many years, JOU 1005 was initially named "Language Skills for Journalists," but was recently renamed "Language Skills for Media Professionals" (although the former name is still listed in the university catalogue). The course is open to all majors; most take it with hopes of majoring in the program; others take it as an elective. Its catalog description reads: "Practice in the application of basic gram-mar principles needed to practice effective journalistic writing."[31] Students must have passed basic English courses before enrolling in the class.[32] They learn grammar principles through a variety of means, such as grammar exercises and quizzes, but mainly through writing. Students must earn at least a C before further progressing in the journalism program.

In fall 2014, the instructor/researcher was assigned the course; the Brown shoot-ing had occurred about two months prior. Thirty-nine students were enrolled; twenty-nine of these were journalism school or pre-journalism school majors; the rest included students classified as pre-business, pre-health care, theater, Access Sum-mer Bridge program (consisting of undeclared majors), pre-architecture, criminal justice, and undecided.[33] Most students were classified as freshmen or sophomores.[34]

The instructor/researcher's impression of the class was that students were, over-all, eager to improve their grammatical skills, and were particularly curious about AP style; they appeared to understand the course's practicality—the relevancy of having strong writing skills to future employment prospects. The instructor/researcher wondered, though, whether they were aware of the rich legacy of African-American journalists, such as Wells-Barnett, or if they were instead operating mainly in an historical vacuum. Also curious in light of the recent Brown case, the instructor/researcher asked the class about six weeks into the term whether they had heard of Ida B. Wells-Barnett. This question earned blank stares from most, tentative head nodding from several, and more confident nodding from a couple. One responded, "She was a journalist, right?" One said he had heard the name, but that was the extent of his knowledge. The instructor/researcher decided that there was work to be done.

Shortly thereafter, the instructor/researcher showed the class the documentary *Ida B. Wells: A Passion for Justice*.[35] Immediately following the viewing, the instructor/researcher assigned the aforementioned 500-word research paper addressing the following questions: "What, if any, is the relevancy of Ida B. Wells-Barnett's 'crusade for justice' to the Trayvon Martin, Jordan Davis, or Michael Brown cases? What are the implications of her crusade, if any, for today's journalists?"[36] The Martin, Davis, and Brown cases were chosen because they had generated the most publicity. Students were directed to use a minimum of five primary sources and were given about two months to complete the assignment. After discussing source credibility and the differences between primary and secondary sources, the instructor/researcher directed the students to submit a preliminary list of sources about a month before the research paper's final due date.

METHODOLOGY

Of thirty-six assignments submitted, three were eliminated due to the failure to follow instructions, and one was eliminated for extensive grammatical errors. Although most responses addressed both research questions, of the remaining thirty-two, the papers were then divided into those that more clearly answered the first research question (initially twenty-two) and those that more clearly answered the second (initially ten). From these, the most articulate responses then were chosen for analysis—these most clearly written responses totaled twelve papers for the first RQ and six for the second (N=18). Commonalities among students' responses, such as structure, discourse fragments, cultural references, and linguistic and rhetorical features, were identified.

WHAT WOULD IDA DO?

Structurally, ten of the remaining eighteen papers began with biographical background information about Wells-Barnett. Thirteen papers then responded to the first research question by comparing and contrasting Wells-Barnett's anti-lynching writings and the racial situation of her time with the recent shooting deaths and the current racial climate. Half of the papers addressed the research questions in the order in which they were presented when the assignment was given. Students were instructed to chose the Martin, Davis, or Brown cases to focus on—five papers picked Martin, three Davis, seven Brown, one all three, and two other. Specific references to Martin, Davis, and/ or Brown occurred at different points throughout the texts—some near the beginning, others in the middle, some at the end, and some scattered throughout.

RESEARCH QUESTION 1

All eighteen responses suggested that students found Wells-Barnett's "crusade for justice"[37] relevant to the recent shooting deaths; however, of the twelve that most clearly addressed this question, one particularly struck me for its originality in including the student's personal response:

> This is a hard paper to write! Reading the *Red Record, The Memphis Diary* and *On Lynch-ings* made me sick in the stomach for a while, and I still don't get it—What?
>
> You ask me if there is any relevancy of Sister Ida Wells' "crusade for justice" to the Michael Brown case, and, are there any implications for today's journalist—What?
>
> So we take this little excursion on the time machine and arrive at the conclusion that post-Reconstruction has lingered on into 2014, and with that, comes another calling for another "crusade for justice." Blacks as well as whites knows [*sic*] all of this all ready [*sic*]—What?[38]

Most students, however, were more straightforward in their responses. The twelve papers all included discourse fragments such as the words "relevant" (four), "rel-evancy" (three), "still" (two), "legacy" (two), and/or "similar" (one). In an example using "relevant," a student wrote: "Jordan Davis was killed unjustly. . . . This case is relevant to Ida B. Wells' 'crusade for justice' because she stated that no matter how many rights African Americans attained, white Americans always reserved the right to inflict bodily harm when threatened by blackness (Wells, 2002)."[39] In a paper using "still," another student wrote: "Much like in the time . . . of Wells, Black men are still being killed at the hands of whites, who oftentimes face little to no punish-ment for these crimes."[40] The one respondent employing "similar" wrote: "A Black man's name [in Wells-Barnett's time] would be defiled with accusations of rape to justify his death at the hands of people who weren't even policemen; these . . . are not the same in . . . Brown's case, but they are similar in how they try to give a Black person a reason to 'deserve' death instead of justice."[41] Another response including "relevancy" (in addition to Student Response #1) read:

> Ida B. Wells-Barnett's "crusade for justice" has relevancy to all three cases involving the death[s] of African-American teens Trayvon Martin, Jordan Davis and Michael Brown. . . . The year is 2014, and although we seldom hear about African Americans being hung from trees . . . we have a new modern day type of lynching . . . police brutal-ity and the laws set before us.[42]

The other response employing "still" read: "Ida B. Wells fought for the equality of African-American men, and in today's society, we are still fighting for the same justice."[43]

"NO JUSTICE, NO PEACE"

Contrary to Wordsworth's assertion that the origin of the currently popular protest slogan "No Justice, No Peace" is unknown,[44] three students out of four employing this cultural reference or a derivative ("No Justice and Peace") in their papers identified Wells-Barnett as its originator in assessing her relevancy to recent shooting deaths. Two of the four included the slogan or a derivative ("No Justice as Peace") as the title of their papers. Quoting from Wells' *Memphis Diary*,[45] one respondent wrote, "I have firmly believed all along that the law was on our side and would, when we appealed to it, give us justice. I feel shorn of that belief and utterly discouraged, and just now if it were possible, would gather my race in my arms and fly away with them. O God, is there no redress, *no peace, no justice* in this land for us?" (emphasis added).[46] The student continued, "In my opinion, God heard her plea. He would . . . grant Ida the talents of speech and writing to use as weapons against those who would lynch and perpetrate injustices against African Americans."[47] Wells had written the lament employing "No Peace, No Justice" in her diary following an April 1887 court decision that reversed an earlier ruling in her favor, after she had filed suit against a railroad line over being forcibly removed from a train after refusing to sit in the Black section.[48] Another paper, after quoting this same passage from Wells' diary, read: "It sounds as if it had just been written last week."[49] Another response crediting Wells with originating the slogan read: "The killer of Trayvon Martin was found not guilty, which started a nationwide "No Justice, No Peace" protest. In coincidence, Ida B. Wells created the same slogan in her crusade for justice.[50]

LINGUISTIC AND RHETORICAL FEATURES

Student responses employed language choices that suggested they perceived a connection between the lynchings of African-American males that Wells-Barnett fought against and recent shooting deaths of African-American males by whites. For example, of the papers most clearly responding to the first research question, five responses out of twelve contained the words "lynch," "lynched," or "lynching" when referring to current shootings; four used the terms "racial profiling" or "racially profiled"; three used the terms "killed wrongfully," "wrongfully killed," or "unjustly killed"; two employed "victim" or "victimized," as well as "murdered" and "racial injustice," and one paper each contained "gunned down," "shot dead," "stereotyped," "innocent," "injustice," "police brutality," "persecution," "racially motivated," "tragedy," or "racial murder." Notably, one response, through the use of

example, compared the Martin shooting to the murder of Emmett Till, as the sixti-
eth anniversary of his death approached:

> Her [Wells-Barnett's] findings still resonate in present day America. The tragic ending of
> Emmett Till in 1955 wasn't the last we would see of that type of lawlessness. In 2013,
> the shooting death of Trayvon Martin would ignite a fire in the African-American com-
> munity that hadn't been seen since the days of Emmett Till. Soon after Martin's case,
> we would find many more Black men being killed by the hands of law enforcement and
> other white men.[51]

Grammatically, all twelve responses mainly employed the third-person perspective, although eight of the twelve papers also used the first person plural ("we,"
"us," and/or "our" in referring to African Americans). First-person plural pronouns
appeared to function to establish African Americans as protagonists, and a distinct,
frequently wronged group, as opposed to the antagonists—identified by the use of
the third person "they" or "them" in several papers (whites, "racist people, whether
they are police officers, prosecutors, judges or juries"[52] or the US government),
thereby attempting to foster and/or strengthen group solidarity. For example,
one respondent wrote: "They will continue to murder *our* people, using violence
against *us* because *they* know *they* will get away with it. . . . It's clear that Stand
Your Ground is a prime example of the traditional belief in the right to do anything *they* want . . . to Blacks" (emphasis added).[53] Furthermore, another student
wrote, "*We* have been oppressed in this country for over the past 400 years, all *our*
leaders get killed and *they* set up false leaders to keep *us* blind" (emphasis added).[54]
Second-person perspective ("you," "your," and/or "yourself") was found in only a
couple of papers.

Responses included a variety of rhetorical and/or literary features, including repetition: "*The so-called Black person in America* all feel [*sic*] that the law is against us.
The so-called Black person in America today feels as if there is no justice in this land"
(emphasis added).[55] Also:

> *It is relevant* [Wells-Barnett's anti-lynching work] in that lynch law and lynchings trans-
> lates [*sic*] in today's language as police brutality, racial profiling, and the white survival
> of the fittest complex. . . . *It is relevant* in that every time a lynching/police brutality and
> injustice happens, the people should put up a very strong protest. . . . *It is relevant* in that
> we should always be fighting for "equality before the law" and for just and evenhanded
> law enforcement. (emphasis added)[56]

Figurative language included the use of "in cold blood,"[57] "passed on the torch,"
"stood in the gap,"[58] and "drugged [*sic*] through the mud."[59] Somewhat surprisingly,
only one paper among the twelve contained a rhetorical question: "Wells stood up
to protect the Black community . . . who's going to come in [*sic*] the defense of . . .
teens like Michael Brown?"[60]

Direct speech included the frequent use of Wells-Barnett's quotes. As noted
earlier, "no peace, no justice" was found in several responses; additionally, students

included a variety of other direct Wells-Barnett quotes in their responses as evidenced in arguing for their perceived connections between violence used against African Americans then and now.[61] As well, a third of the papers referenced, by either direct quotes or paraphrasing, the 1892 lynching of Wells' friends Thomas Moss, Calvin McDowell, and William Stewart.[62] In paraphrasing the incident, one respondent wrote, "On March 9, 1892, Thomas Moss, Calvin McDowell, and Henry Stewart, close friends of Wells, were unjustifiably shot and hanged by a white mob. . . . Although the lynchers were identified, they were never brought to justice. The killing of innocent Black men by whites in the 19th century is unfortunately similar to many cases in the 21st century."[63] Another responded:

> It was in Memphis, Tennessee, where Wells began her fight for racial equality and justice. A tragic incident occurred in 1892 when three of her close friends were lynched, and nothing was done about it. . . . In comparison, 17-year-old Trayvon Martin was gunned down by George Zimmerman for "looking suspicious" . . . In both cases, Black men were brutally murdered . . . and in neither stories [*sic*] did the victims commit a crime.[64]

Five of the twelve papers included modalities. One respondent's call to action read: "The people *should* put up a very strong protest . . . we *should* always be fighting . . . all churches and Christians and moral forces *should* already be in unison on the issue . . . government on all levels *ought* to intervene" (emphasis added).[65] Another noted: "African Americans *have to* continue to unify and support each other to be successful in their fight to end racial injustice in America" (emphasis added).[66] An additional response asserted: "We *can* change the world, one pen at a time" (emphasis added).[67]

Few papers included evidentialities, but those doing so attempted to back their truth claims with facts. One read:

> [On] November 24, 2014, the decision by the grand jury . . . was aired. During the period between the death of Brown and the verdict, Officer Wilson was a free man that went untouched by the law. *The facts in this case further the ideology that Black lives don't matter.* Just as Ida B. Wells says [*sic*] that many Negro men died without due process of law in 1895, we are seeing the same pattern in 2014. (emphasis added)[68]

Another respondent said, "*It is obvious* that Wells-Barnett's social activism *would* make her the quintessential 'community other mother' for the Black community [today]" (emphasis added).[69]

RESEARCH QUESTION 2

Of the six responses that more clearly addressed students' perceptions of the relevancy, if any, of Wells-Barnett's anti-lynching work to today's journalists, all suggested that students found implications for today's work. Students employed a variety of discourse fragments when referring to Wells-Barnett, such as "crusader"[70]; "committed"; "fearless"[71]; "not afraid"[72]; "an example"[73]; "advocate [sic] journalist"[74]; and "an advocate."[75] These descriptions suggest that the students all perceived these traits as desirable in a journalist, including those of today. One student wrote:

> She [Wells-Barnett] was *committed* to getting the information out to the public, and that's the mentality that all journalists should have today. . . . Additionally, Wells was *fearless*. . . . What today's journalists can receive from Wells' life-threatening experience is that not everyone is going to agree with what you write. . . . However, you can't allow this to stop you in your crusade for whatever you believe in. (emphasis added)[76]

Another responded, "Wells was *not afraid* to write how she felt about . . . injustices, and we need someone like her during these present times. . . . There is a need for Black journalists who can speak out against these injustices done to young Black men such as Mike Brown. Hopefully, the current generation will have the courage to step up and report" (emphasis added).[77] Another asserted, "We as a society need more people willing to raise their voice when injustice is brought among us. Without a voice, the killings will continue."[78]

"THE SOCIAL MEDIA OF HER TIME"

Four of the six responses more clearly addressing the second research question suggested a perceived connection between Wells-Barnett and the cultural reference of modern-day social media. Three of these four appeared to perceive this connection independently, while one credited another writer with Wells-Barnett's relation to social media. Of the three seeming to independently discern a relationship, one noted: "While social media hasn't brought the shooting[s] to a halt, it has opened the eyes of the uneducated. Ida B. Wells was the social media of her time, informing the community of . . . wrongdoings and asking that her readers become aware."[79] Another stated, "There were thousands of posts on Twitter and Instagram fighting for justice for Mike Brown. This started a rally for a 'crusade for justice' just as Wells . . . during her time."[80] The third respondent seeming to independently perceive a connection stated, "Journalists [today] are doing the work that Ida B. Wells did during the 1800s. She wrote books about what was happening. . . . Protestors are . . . using the different forms of media to get attention and influence others to make a change. For example, when we write on social networks about how we feel to get a situation trending, it then gets notice[d]."[81] The final paper asserting a connection between Wells-Barnett and today's social media credited Sarah Seltzer with making this connection first, quoting from Flavorwire[82]: "Wells' technique of work is similar to today's social media activists. Tweets, live streams, and blogs attempting to piece the true stories together followed the death of Trayvon Martin all the way through the Zimmerman trial. Having said that, we can respectfully call Ida B. Wells the pioneer of online journalism."[83]

LINGUISTIC AND RHETORICAL FEATURES

Grammatically, as with the twelve papers more clearly addressing the first research question, those six responses better answering the question regarding the implications, if any, of Wells-Barnett's legacy for today's journalists primarily used the third-person perspective, although most also employed the first- or second-person perspective. An example using first-person plural pronouns read: "Today *we* have killings of people like Trayvon Martin, Michael Brown, and Eric Garner. . . . Police . . . are now being looked at as crooked . . . and this has caused *our* society to go into an uproar" (emphasis added).[84] Another stated, "The way Ida B. Wells fought for something she believed in, resembles how *we* fought for what *we* believed in when the Trayvon Martin incident occurred" (emphasis added).[85]

Unlike the use of the first-person plural in the earlier examples, however, the use of first-person plural in the student responses that more clearly addressed the second research question did not seem to delineate so distinctly a clear group of protagonists and antagonists. Instead, their use of first-person plural appeared to function in these students' arguments, when they more explicitly addressed the second research question, to mainly refer to society in general, and thus appeared less antagonistic. A respondent using the second person point of view, also seeming to be more general, versus more antagonistic, wrote: "If *you* passionately believe in something, then *you* should not be afraid to report it . . . not everyone is going to agree with what *you* write. There are going to be some people that oppose what *you* believe, and even challenge what *you* write. However, *you* can't allow this to stop *you* in *your* crusade for whatever you believe in" (emphasis added).[86]

Three of the six papers also included literary and/or rhetorical devices. For example, two respondents began their papers with definitions—one defining "crusader"[87] and the other "lynch."[88] Another employed parallelism: "She wrote. . . . She traveled. . . . She continued to write."[89]

Three of the six responses also used direct and/or indirect speech, with two of these directly quoting Wells-Barnett herself and/or quotes relating to Wells-Barnett, and two also directly quoting other sources, such as Seltzer.[90] "Should" was the most popular modality, occurring three times in two papers (once in one paper and twice in the other), as in the following example: "She [Wells-Barnett] was committed to getting the information out to the public, and that's the mentality that all journalists *should* have today" (emphasis added).[91] As in the case with the texts more clearly addressing the first research question, these modalities seemed to function in student responses as a call to action for today's journalists.

A third of the papers included evidentialities, such as: "The lynchings that happened in the South during that time *can easily be compared* to the shootings of Black men by white officers" (emphasis added).[92] Furthermore, "Given her [Wells-Barnett's] strong desire for equal treatment, *it's not hard to imagine* how she might react to the recent cases of Trayvon Martin, Jordan Davis, Michael Brown, and others . . . *it's safe to assume* that she would've approached the case with some form of outrage to be sure" (emphasis added).[93] Rather than presenting these evidentialities as mere common sense, however, each of these students includes facts as evidence in attempting to buttress their claims—in each case by referencing Wells-Barnett's anti-lynching writings and/or other activism.

DISCUSSION

Of the twelve responses more clearly addressing the question of Wells-Barnett's relevancy, if any, to the recent shooting deaths of Martin, Davis, and/or Brown, discourse analysis results suggest that all twelve students perceived a connection between Wells-Barnett's work and these current events. Regarding how students framed their arguments addressing RQ 1, discourse fragments such as "lynched" and "racial profiling" (etc.), suggest students perceived a connection. Grammatical features such as the use of "they" and "we" suggested that students employed them to establish clear dichotomies between African Americans and those committing the recent shootings, as well as the power structures supporting them. Several students credited Wells-Barnett with originating the protest slogan "no justice, no peace." Although responses mainly employed the third-person point of view, other perspectives also were used on occasion; particularly the first-person plural. Student papers also included a variety of linguistic and rhetorical features. Direct speech primarily consisted of direct Wells-Barnett quotes. Half of the responses used modalities such as "should" in making their cases. Evidentialities were seldom used, but students attempted to back up their claims with facts, when they did employ evidentialities.

Of the six student papers that more clearly addressed the question of Wells-Barnett's relevancy, if any, to today's journalists, all six responses, through their use of discourse fragments such as "crusader" and "advocate" (etc.), suggest that students found Wells-Barnett relevant to today's journalists. Respondents' inclusion of grammatical features such as "they" and "we" did not appear to function in the same way as in the previous responses; here, the use of these features appeared to function in the opposite manner—as a way of fostering unity. Students also appeared to connect Wells-Barnett with the role of social media in advocating causes, thus, adding substance to the researcher's initial speculation ("She would blog. She would tweet. She would take to the streets"). As in the case of the student responses more clearly addressing the first question, these students used a variety of linguistic and rhetorical devices in buttressing their claims. Again, the third-person point of view predominated, although other perspectives also were used on occasion, such as the first-person plural. Half of the responses included modalities, and half used evidentialities; responses, as before, used facts as evidence to support their claims when evidentialities were used.

CONCLUSION

These results all suggest that students perceived a connection between Wells-Barnett's anti-lynching activism and writings and recent police shooting deaths of

African Americans. Michael Brown's August 2014 death, subsequent police actions in Ferguson, Missouri, and the resulting public outcry led to widespread calls for increased police accountability, according to the July 7, 2016, *Washington Post*.[94] The protest movement Black Lives Matter, according to its website, was formed after the 2012 shooting death of seventeen-year-old Trayvon Martin and the subsequent acquittal of shooter George Zimmerman.[95] Since this project began in the fall of 2014, other high-profile police shooting deaths of African Americans such as Freddie Gray, Philando Castile, Alton Sterling, and Walter Scott, among others, have increased perceptions among African-American college students, in particular, that they are part of a people under siege; these perceptions have become anecdotally evident to the researcher based upon personal conversations, as well as these students' frequent choice of police brutality and "what to do if stopped by a police officer" as subject matter for presentation topics in speech communication courses.

As media historian Earnest Perry states:

> We, as media historians, have an obligation to use this critical moment to change the way we teach history, especially as it relates to civil rights. . . . In the age of Black Lives Matter and the fight for social justice, journalists need to know more. Our students need to know more. We need to provide history lessons whenever and wherever they are possible.[96]

This study's results also suggest that, although journalism, history, political science, and other educators may need to be quite intentional in introducing students to the lives and work of historical figures such as Ida B. Wells-Barnett, the potential for all students to discern a connection between such figures and the implications for their own lives exists. If students are directed to and encouraged to engage with primary sources on significant historical figures and/or movements, most can then readily perceive the continuum between past, present, and future. Class projects such as this one have the potential to free history from its relegation to the distant past, allowing it to then become part of the larger, ever-needful, dynamic now.

NOTES

1. See, for example, Paula J. Giddings, *Ida: A Sword among Lions* (New York: Amistad, 2008); Mia Bay, *To Tell the Truth Freely: The Life of Ida B. Wells* (New York: Hill and Wang, 2009); School of Journalism & Electronic Media, "The Ida Initiative," *University of Tennessee Knoxville*, 2013, https://theidainitiative.wordpress.com.

2. Ida B. Wells-Barnett, *Crusade for Justice: The Autobiography of Ida B. Wells*, ed. Alfreda M. Duster (Chicago: University of Chicago Press, 1970).

3. Chandra D. Clark, "Ida B. Wells and Beyond Project" (Language Skills for Media Professionals class project, Florida A&M University, 2014).

4. Amber Roessner, Rick Popp, Brian Creech, and Fred Blevens, "A Measure of Theory?": Considering the Role of Theory in Media History," *American Journalism* 30.2 (2013): 260–78.

5. James W. Carey, "The Problem of Journalism History," *Journalism History* 1.1 (1974): 1–7; David Sloan, *Perspectives on Mass Media History* (Hillsdale, NJ: Lawrence Erlbaum Associates, Inc., 1991).

6. John Nerone, "Does Journalism History Matter?" *American Journalism* 28.4 (2011): 7.

7. Ibid., 18.

8. "Journalism Professor Explores Unique Challenges of Historically Black Colleges," *U.S. Fed. News Service, Including U.S. State News* (2013). ProQuest (Document ID 1283787651).

9. Erika Pribanic-Smith, "AEJMC Teaching Panel Emphasizes Connections Between Past and Present," *AJHA Intelligencer* 30.4 (2016): 10.

10. Andie Tucher, "Why Journalism History Matters: The Gaffe, the 'Stuff,' and the Historical Imagination," *American Journalism* 31.4 (2013): 444.

11. Yamiche Alcindor, "Fighting for Change: George Zimmerman Verdict, One Year Later," *USA Today*, July 13, 2014, 1B.

12. Vanessa Stephens Lee and Tara Sutton, "Resolution Against Stand Your Ground Laws" (Black Clergy Women of the United Methodist Church, 2014), paragraph 1.

13. Alcindor, "Fighting for Change," 2B.

14. "Trayvon Martin Could Have Been Me 35 Years Ago," *CNN*, July 19, 2013, www.cnn.com.

15. Denene Millner, "Standing Our Ground," *Jet*, January 14, 2013, 19.

16. Mitzi Miller, "Moments," *Jet*, January 14, 2013, 3.

17. Simon McCormack, "Michael Dunn Found Guilty of First-Degree Murder in Killing of Jordan Davis," *Huffington Post*, October 1, 2014, www.huffingtonpost.com.

18. "Michael Dunn Sentenced to Life in Prison for 'Loud Music' Killing of Jordan Davis," *Huffington Post*, October 17, 2014, www.huffingtonpost.com/2014/10/17/michael-dunn-sentenced_n_6003868.html.

19. Rachel Clarke and Christopher Lett, "What Happened When Michael Brown Met Officer Darren Wilson," *CNN*, November 11, 2014, www.cnn.com/interactive/2014/08/us/ferguson-brown-timeline/.

20. Philip Bump, Peter Holley, and Wesley Lowery, "'I Can't Breathe': After Indictment Decision, Eric Garner's Final Words Become a Symbol of Anger, Frustration," *Washington Post*, December 3, 2014, www.washingtonpost.com/news/post-nation/wp/2014/12/03/I-cant-breathe-after-indic....

21. Ethan J. Kytle and Blain Roberts, "Birth of a Freedom Anthem," *New York Times*, March 15, 2015, 5SR.

22. Mary Bowerman, "'I Am a Man' to 'I Am Michael Brown': A Closer Look at Protest Slogans," *USA Today Network*, December 9, 2014, http://usat.ly/1D3IKzU.

23. Jessica Guynn, "3 Women, 3 Words, a New Movement: Take a Facebook Post that 'Black Lives Matter,' Add a Hashtag, and Watch the Change," *USA Today*, March 8, 2015, 6B.

24. Dot Wordsworth, "Where Did 'No Justice, No Peace' Come From? Mark Duggan's Supporters Are Using a Slogan with a Surprisingly Long History among the Chanting Classes," *Spectator*, http://spectator.co.uk/life/mind-your-language/9116721/dot-wordsworth-where-did-no-justice-no-peace-come-from/.

25. Carl Zimmer, "The Linguistic Power of the Protest Phrase 'I Can't Breathe,'" *WIRED*, December 10, 2014, www.wired.com/2014/12/ben-zimmer-on-i-cant-breathe/.

26. "About Florida Agricultural and Mechanical University: Academic Excellence, Affordability, Diversity," Florida A&M University, paragraph 2, www.famu.edu/index.cfm?AboutFAMU.

27. "Overview," Florida A&M University, www.famu.edu/index.cfm?AboutFAMU& Overview.

28. FAMU School of Journalism and Graphic Communication," Florida A&M University, paragraph 1, sjgc.famu.edu/index.cfm/linkservd/0C3AA456-BDF0-1C46-10D3CDDD 1D49A624/showMeta/0.

29. Ibid., paragraphs 2 and 3.

30. "Mission," Florida A&M University School of Journalism and Graphic Communication," paragraph 2, sjgc.famu.edu/m/index.cfm/about-us/mission.

31. 2014/2015 General Catalog," Florida A&M University, catalog.famu.edu/content. php?filter%5B27%5D=JOU&filter%5B29%5D=1005&filter%5Bcourse_type%5D=1&filte r%5Bkeyword%5D=&filter%5B32%5D=1&filter.

32. Ibid.

33. "JOU 1005 Section 001," Language Skills for Media Professionals, Florida A&M University School of Journalism and Graphic Communication, September 2014.

34. Ibid.

35. William Greaves, *Ida B. Wells: A Passion for Justice*, DVD, Directed by William Greaves (San Francisco: California Newsreel, 1989), VHS.

36. Clark, "Ida B. Wells and Beyond Project," 2014.

37. Wells, *Crusade for Justice.*

38. Student Response #1 (Ida B. Wells and Beyond Class Project, JOU 1005, School of Journalism and Graphic Communication, Florida A&M University, Tallahassee, Florida, 2014), 2.

39. Student Response #2 (Ida B. Wells and Beyond Class Project, JOU 1005, School of Journalism and Graphic Communication, Florida A&M University, Tallahassee, Florida, 2014), 1.

40. Student Response #3 (Ida B. Wells and Beyond Class Project, JOU 1005, School of Journalism and Graphic Communication, Florida A&M University, Tallahassee, Florida, 2014), 1.

41. Student Response #4 (Ida B. Wells and Beyond Class Project, JOU 1005, School of Journalism and Graphic Communication, Florida A&M University, Tallahassee, Florida, 2014), 1.

42. Student Response #5 (Ida B. Wells and Beyond Class Project, JOU 1005, School of Journalism and Graphic Communication, Florida A&M University, Tallahassee, Florida, 2014), 1.

43. Student Response #6 (Ida B. Wells and Beyond Class Project, JOU 1005, School of Journalism and Graphic Communication, Florida A&M University, Tallahassee, Florida, 2014), 1.

44. Wordsworth, *Where Did "No Justice, No Peace" Come From?*

45. Ida B. Wells, *The Memphis Diary of Ida B. Wells*, ed. Miriam Decosta-Willis (Boston: Beacon Press, 1995), 141.

46. Student Response #7 (Ida B. Wells and Beyond Class Project, JOU 1005, School of Journalism and Graphic Communication, Florida A&M University, Tallahassee, Florida, 2014), 2.

47. Ibid.

48. Patricia A. Schechter, *Ida B. Wells-Barnett and American Reform, 1880–1930* (Chapel Hill: The University of North Carolina Press, 2001).

49. Student Response #8, 1.

50. Student Response #9, 1.

51. Student Response #10 (Ida B. Wells and Beyond Class Project, JOU 1005, School of Journalism and Graphic Communication, Florida A&M University, Tallahassee, Florida, 2014), 2.

52. Student Response #2, 2.

53. Ibid.

54. Student Response #8 (Ida B. Wells and Beyond Class Project, JOU 1005, School of Journalism and Graphic Communication, Florida A&M University, Tallahassee, Florida, 2014), 2.

55. Ibid.

56. Student Response #1, 4.

57. Student Response #10 (Ida B. Wells and Beyond Class Project, JOU 1005, School of Journalism and Graphic Communication, Florida A&M University, Tallahassee, Florida, 2014), 1.

58. Student Response #11 (Ida B. Wells and Beyond Class Project, JOU 1005, School of Journalism and Graphic Communication, Florida A&M University, Tallahassee, Florida, 2014), 2.

59. Student Response #4, 4.

60. Student Response #11, 2.

61. Wells-Barnett, *The Memphis Diary*.

62. Schechter, *Ida B. Wells-Barnett and American Reform*.

63. Student Response #3, 1.

64. Student Response #9, 2.

65. Student Response #1, 4.

66. Student Response #12 (Ida B. Wells and Beyond Class Project, JOU 1005, School of Journalism and Graphic Communication, Florida A&M University, Tallahassee, Florida, 2014), 2.

67. Student Response #11, 2.

68. Student Response #10, 2.

69. Student Response #8, 1.

70. Student Response #13 (Ida B. Wells and Beyond Class Project, JOU 1005, School of Journalism and Graphic Communication, Florida A&M University, Tallahassee, Florida, 2014), 1.

71. Student Response #14 (Ida B. Wells and Beyond Class Project, JOU 1005, School of Journalism and Graphic Communication, Florida A&M University, Tallahassee, Florida, 2014), 1.

72. Student Response #15 (Ida B. Wells and Beyond Class Project, JOU 1005, School of Journalism and Graphic Communication, Florida A&M University, Tallahassee, Florida, 2014), 1.

73. Student Response #16 (Ida B. Wells and Beyond Class Project, JOU 1005, School of Journalism and Graphic Communication, Florida A&M University, Tallahassee, Florida, 2014), 1.

74. Student Response #18 (Ida B. Wells and Beyond Class Project, JOU 1005, School of Journalism and Graphic Communication, Florida A&M University, Tallahassee, Florida, 2014), 1.

75. Student Response #17 (Ida B. Wells and Beyond Class Project, JOU 1005, School of Journalism and Graphic Communication, Florida A&M University, Tallahassee, Florida, 2014), 2.

76. Student Response #14, 1.

77. Student Response #15, 1.
78. Student Response #16, 3.
79. Ibid.
80. Student Response #15, 2.
81. Student Response #13, 1.
82. Sarah Seltzer, "Ida B. Wells, Anti-Lynching Crusader, Was the Godmother of the Social Justice Internet," *Flavorwire*, November 2014, 2014, http://flavorwire.com/489781/ida-b-wells-anti-lynching-crusader-was-the-godmother-of-the-social-justice-internet.
83. Student Response #18, 2.
84. Student Response #16, 2.
85. Student Response #13, 1.
86. Student Response #14, 2.
87. Student Response # 13, 1.
88. Student Response #16, 1.
89. Student Response #15, 1.
90. Seltzer, "Ida B. Wells. "
91. Student Response #15, 1.
92. Student Response #15, 1.
93. Student Response #17, 1.
94. Julie Tate, Jennifer Jenkins, Steven Rich, John Muyskens, Kennedy Elliott, Ted Mellnik, and Aaron Williams, "How the Washington Post Is Examining Police Shootings in the United States," *Washington Post*, July 7, 2016, http://wshingtonpost.com/national/how-the-waashington-post-is-exam.
95. "About the Black Lives Matter Network," Black Lives Matter, accessed January 13, 2017, www.blacklivesmatter.com/about/.
96. Earnest L. Perry, Jr., "Professional Notes: Teaching History in the Age of Black Lives Matter: Embracing the Narratives of the Long Struggle for Civil Rights," *American Journalism* 33.4 (2016): 468.

BIBLIOGRAPHY

Alcindor, Yamiche. "Fighting for Change: George Zimmerman Verdict, One Year Later." *USA Today*, July 13, 2014.

Bay, Mia. *To Tell the Truth Freely: The Life of Ida B. Wells*. New York: Hill and Wang, 2009.

Bowerman, Mary. "'I am a Man' to 'I am Michael Brown': A Closer look at Protest Slogans." *USA Today Network*. December 9, 2014. http://usat.ly/1D3IKzU.

Bump, Philip, Holley, Peter, and Lowery, Wesley. "'I Can't Breathe': After Indictment Decision, Eric Garner's Final Words Become a Symbol of Anger, Frustration." *The Washington Post*. December 3, 2014. http://www.washingtonpost.com/news/post-nation/wp/2014/12/03/I-cant-breathe-after-indi.

Carey, James W. "The Problem of Journalism History." *Journalism History* 1.1 (1974): 1–7.

Clark, Chandra. "'Ida B. Wells and Beyond' Project." School of Journalism & Graphic Communication, Florida A&M University, 2014.

Clarke, Rachel, and Lett, Christopher. "What Happened When Michael Brown Met Officer Darren Wilson." CNN. November 11, 2014. www.cnn.com/interactive/2014/08/us/ferguson-brown-timeline/.

Giddings, Paula J. *Ida: A Sword among Lions*. New York: Amistad, 2008.

Guynn, Jessica. "Three Women, Three Words, A New Movement: Take a Facebook Post That 'Black Lives Matter,' Add a Hashtag, and Watch the Change." *USA Today*. March 8, 2015.

Ida B. Wells: A Passion for Justice. Directed by William Greaves. San Francisco, California: California Newsreel, 2004. DVD, 120 minutes.

"Ida B. Wells Initiative." *University of Tennessee Knoxville School of Journalism & Electronic Media*. http://theidiainitiative.wordpress.com.

"Journalism Professor Explores Unique Challenges of Historically Black Colleges." *U.S. Federal News Service, Including U.S. State News*, 2013. ProQuest (1283787651).

Kytle, Ethan J., and Roberts, Blain. "Birth of a Freedom Anthem." *New York Times,* March 14, 2015.

Lee, Vanessa Stephens, and Tara Sutton. "Resolution against Stand Your Ground Laws." Black Clergy Women of the United Methodist Church, 2014.

McCormack, Simon. "Michael Dunn Found Guilty of First-Degree Murder in Killing of Jordan Davis." *Huffington Post*, October 1, 2014. www.huffingtonpost.com.

"Michael Dunn Sentenced to Life in Prison for "Loud Music" Killing of Jordan Davis." *Huffington Post*, October 17, 2014. www.huffingtonpost.com/2014/10/17/michael-dunn-sentenced_n_6003868.html.

Miller, Mitzi. "Moments." *Jet* 122.1 (January 14, 2013): 3.

Millner, Genene. "Standing Our Ground." *Jet* 122.1 (January 14, 2013): 16–23.

Nerone, John. "Why Journalism History Matters to Journalism Studies," *American Journalism* 30.1 (2013): 15–28.

Nerone, John. "Does Journalism History Matter?" *American Journalism* 28.4 (2011): 7–27.

Perry, Earnest L. "Professional Notes: Teaching History in the Age of Black Lives Matter: Embracing the Narratives of the Long Struggle for Civil Rights." *American Journalism* 33.4 (2016): 465–70.

Powell, Azizi. "The History and Meaning of the Chant 'No Justice, No Peace,'" August 20, 2014. http://pancocojams.blogspot.com/2014/08/the-history-and-meaning-of-chant-no.html.

Pribanic-Smith, Erika. "AEJMC Teaching Panel Emphasizes Connections between Past and Present." *AJHA Intelligencer* 30.4 (2016): 10–11.

Schechter, Patricia A. *Ida B. Wells-Barnett and American Reform, 1880–1930*. Chapel Hill: University of North Carolina Press, 2001.

Sloan, David. *Perspectives on Mass Communication History*. Hillsdale, NJ: Lawrence Erlbaum Associates, Inc., 1991.

Tate, Julie, Jenkins, Jennifer, Rich, Steven, Muyskens, John, Elliott, Kennedy, Mellnik, Ted, and Williams, Aaron. "How the Washington Post Is Examining Police Shootings in the United States." July 7, 2016. http://washingtonpost.com/national/how-the-washington-post-is-exam.

"Trayvon Martin Could Have Been Me 35 Years Ago." *CNN*. July 19, 2013. www.cnn.com/2013/07/19/politics/obama-zimmerman.

Tucher, Andie. "Why Journalism History Matters: The Gaffe, the 'Stuff,' and the Historical Imagination," *American Journalism* 31.4 (2014): 432–44.

Wells, Ida B. *Crusade for Justice: The Autobiography of Ida B. Wells*, edited by Alfreda M. Duster. Chicago: University of Chicago Press, 1970.

Wells, Ida B. *The Memphis Diary of Ida B. Wells*, edited by Miriam Decosta-Willis. Boston: Beacon, 1995.

Wordsworth, Dot. "Where Did 'No Justice, No Peace' Come From? Mark Duggan's Supporters Are Using a Slogan with a Surprisingly Long History among the Chanting Classes." *The Spectator*, January 18, 2014, http://spectator.co.uk/life/mind-your-language/9116721/dot-wordsworth-where-did-no-justice-no-peace-come-from/.

Zimmer, Carl. "The Linguistic Power of the Protest Phrase 'I Can't Breathe.'" *WIRED*, December 10, 2014. http://www.wired.com/2014/12/ben-zimmer-on-i-cant-breathe/.

Afterword

Ida B. Wells-Barnett and the "Racist Cover-Up"

Kathy Roberts Forde

When Ida B. Wells returned in 1893 from her British-speaking tour on lynching, she turned her attention to the World's Columbian Exposition in Chicago. She was outraged. Organizers of the world's fair refused to allow any Black individuals to help with the planning, despite repeated protests. They also refused to include any representation of African-American experience and accomplishment in the fair exhibit halls. Their intransigence made perverse sense, given the story they designed the sparkling White City to tell: a triumphal narrative of white Western civilization and its many achievements, with America leading the way. The bloody reality of centuries of white supremacist oppression of Black Americans through slavery, lynching, and convict leasing simply did not suit.[1]

Before the tour, Wells had initiated an effort to expose this reality to travelers from around the world who would attend the fair: a pamphlet to be distributed titled *The Reason Why the Colored American Is Not in the World's Columbian Exposition*. When she learned from Frederick Douglass upon her return that fundraising efforts for the pamphlet had failed, she took charge. She persuaded Douglass, Garland Penn, and Ferdinand L. Barnett (whom she later married) to contribute chapters, wrote her own chapter on lynching, and raised just enough money to print 10,000 copies. In addition to telling the story of remarkable Black gains and achievements in the years since emancipation, *The Reason Why* told the history of slavery and exposed "the twin infamies" of convict leasing and lynching, brutal systems of oppression Black Americans had suffered since the end of the Civil War—including the six months fair-goers enjoyed the delights of the White City.[2]

The attempted exclusion of African-American achievement and experience in the American historical narrative presented at the World's Columbian Exposition in 1893 was hardly the first or the last such whitewashing of American history. Neither was it the first or last time Black Americans would fiercely resist and challenge such exclusion through the power of print culture. As the chapters in this volume demonstrate, Wells-Barnett used an inventive range of communication strategies across her life to advocate for racial and gender equality and to expose unjust systems of oppression. Her work laid the path not only for the future inclusion of the African-American experience in American historical narratives, but also for a future reckoning with the vexing and enduring American problem of white supremacy and racial terror.

Subsequent activists and scholars have used Wells-Barnett's extensive documentary record of lynching—compiled through her stunningly courageous investigations—in their own efforts to combat racial terror and to illuminate the sources of racial inequality and violence in the United States today. Across the first half of the twentieth century, for example, the NAACP investigated and documented lynchings and lobbied for anti-lynching legislation. While no legislation was ever passed, the NAACP campaign managed to persuade some Southern newspapers to oppose lynching in the interest of attracting potential Northern investors and likely played a role in its decreasing incidence in the years before World War II.[3] Recently, the Equal Justice Initiative, under the leadership of Bryan Stevenson, documented 4,075 "racial terror lynchings" of Black Americans between 1877 and 1950 in the South, finding at least 800 more instances than were previously known.[4] Like *Southern Horrors* and *A Red Record*, the Initiative's public report, *Lynching in America*, argues that lynching was a form of racial terror meant to subordinate and control Black people. It was hardly ever, as its justifiers argued at the time, a response to Black men raping white women. "We cannot heal the deep wounds inflicted during the era of racial terrorism until we tell the truth about it," Stevenson has said. "Only then can we meaningfully address the contemporary problems that are lynching's legacy."[5]

Those contemporary problems include racially unjust systems of criminal justice and mass incarceration, which can be traced to the "twin infamies" of convict leasing and lynching in the late nineteenth and early twentieth centuries. Wells and Douglass targeted both for exposure in *The Reason Why*, but their efforts, along with those of many other Black activists, journalists, and intellectuals of their era, did little to change these systems of racial control. In *Southern Horrors*, Wells drew a straight line from lynching to the New South ideology of Henry W. Grady, the white managing editor of the *Atlanta Constitution* who had died prematurely just a few years earlier. As the celebrated spokesman of the New South movement, Grady preached industrial growth as the solution for the South's economic problems, enticing Northern industrialists with assurances that relations between the races were settled and amicable and that labor was cheap and plentiful. While his first proposition was at best delusional and at worst deceitful, his second was true enough.[6]

After the Civil War, the state of Georgia leased its convicts to private concerns in railroading, coal mining, and farming—and the majority were Black. Various state laws known as Black codes targeted African Americans and allowed their arrest for minor infractions, the most popular being vagrancy. Southern authorities used the vagrancy law as a pretext for the wanton arrest and conviction of Black men (and sometimes women and children) to provide unpaid labor for private industry through the convict lease. In 1886, the year Grady gave the New South speech that brought him national acclaim at Delmonico's Restaurant in New York City, Georgia had a mostly Black convict population of 1,527, each leased for a pittance of five cents per day. At Dade Coal mines, convicts worked on the capricious task system: They either produced a prescribed daily quota of coal or received corporal punishment. Punishment was brutal and inventive. In fact, the word *torture* is more apt than punishment. In addition to whippings with broad leather straps often dragged wet through sand to take off the skin, prisoners were subjected to the water cure, sweat box, and blind mule, in which a prisoner's wrists were tied with a rope hoisted by a pulley until the toes were barely touching the ground. A Black teenage girl named Carrie Massie endured this last torture for six hours.[7]

In 1886, prisoners in one of the six stockades at Dade Coal Company rebelled, barricading their stockade and refusing to work unless improvements were made to the punishing work schedule, inadequate food, and brutal punishments. As one prisoner said, they were "ready to die, and would as soon be dead as to live in torture." At some point before the rebellion, Grady had visited the mines and reported to readers that convicts were chained together at night through ankle shackles that ran from bunk to bunk. When he learned of the uprising, he sent a reporter to cover it for the *Atlanta Constitution*. The governor ordered the convicts starved into submission; when they surrendered, they were brutally whipped. Grady's reporter, apparently amused, called the scene a "special matinee" in his report for the *Constitution*.[8]

The owner of the mines was Joseph E. Brown, a US senator that Grady had helped elect. Grady had long been the mastermind of the Atlanta ring of Democratic politicians who rotated through the governorship and federal senate seats for nearly two decades, and the *Atlanta Constitution* became his mouthpiece in the effort.[9] Alfred H. Colquitt, the second senator from Georgia and a member of the ring, invested in Brown's coal company, and James Warren English, ring member and chairman of Atlanta's Board of Police Commissioners, worked convicts in his Chattahoochee Brick Company, run by a notorious whipping boss.[10] Reverend William J. White, editor of the *Georgia Baptist*, described the situation well: "[T]he fortunes of many a prominent white Georgia family [are] red with the blood and sweat of Black men justly and unjustly held to labor in Georgia prison camps."[11] By 1880, Brown was a millionaire.[12] The *Constitution*, noting he had made nearly $100,000 just the previous year, told its readers, "It is a good thing to turn a coal mine into a gold mine."[13]

Such was the ugly underbelly of the New South promise of cheap and plentiful labor. And such was the delusion or deceit of Grady's assurances at Delmonico's that "relations of the southern people with the negro are close and cordial" and "[f]aith has been kept with him in spite of calumnious assertions to the contrary."[14] With his trademark irony, historian C. Vann Woodward described Grady's New South doctrine as "a cheerful gospel of progress, prosperity, industry, and nationalism with a sugary icing of reconciliation of all classes, sections, and races—all of course under proper white supremacy."[15]

Nearly a century earlier, in *Southern Horrors*, Wells felt much the same, but she put her opprobrium in more personal and pointed terms:

Henry W. Grady in his well-remembered speeches in New England and New York pictured the Afro-American as incapable of self-government. Through him and other leading men the cry of the South to the country has been "Hands off! Leave us to solve our problem." To the Afro-American the South says, "the white man must and will rule." There is little difference between the Antebellum South and the New South.[16]

Invoking Grady's name in a pamphlet excoriating the White South for tolerating lynching took courage. In 1892, when *Southern Horrors* was first published, Grady had been dead for only three years and elevated to near sainthood among Southern journalists and New South followers. As Grady's first biographer wrote in besotted prose more than half a century later, "With this movement [the New South] his name was to be as inseparable as is Webster's with Union, Davis's with Secession, or Lincoln's with Emancipation."[17]

Wells had read the famous 1885 exchange between Grady and novelist George W. Cable in *Century Magazine*.[18] Cable, a white Southerner, penned a forceful defense of Black civil rights and a critique of white supremacy and racial segregation in the South titled "The Freedman's Case in Equity." Southern newspapers attacked him, and white Southerners attacked the *Century* with outraged letters. When the magazine's editor asked Grady to respond, Grady cemented his claim as the preeminent spokesman of the New South with his article "In Plain Black and White: A Reply to Mr. Cable." Segregation in the South was natural, Grady claimed. "The assortment of races is wise and proper, and stands on the platform of equal accommodations for each race but separate." Without the "race instinct" for separation, there would be "a breaking down of all lines of division and a thorough intermingling of whites and [B]lacks." The resulting "disorganization of society" would produce "internecine war," he threatened. "The whites, at any cost and at any hazard, would maintain the clear integrity and dominance of the Anglo-Saxon blood." While Grady refrained from explicitly invoking the popular New South trope of the Black man as rapist of white women, and the threat of lynching, he invoked them just the same. Wells-Barnett understood his meaning—and she spent the greater part of her life challenging the trope and trying to eradicate the threat.[19] As Ibram X. Kendi trenchantly observed in his award-winning book *Stamped from the Beginning: The Definitive History of Racist Ideas in America*, in his reply to Cable, Grady birthed "the racist idea of 'separate but equal,' when he knew southern communities were hardly separate or equal."[20]

What did Grady have to say explicitly about lynching? "Editorially, the *Constitution* was mostly silent," Grady biographer Harold E. Davis has written. But coverage in the newspaper demonstrated "the relative frequency of lynchings, and the news copy, especially the headlines, seems frivolous. Many of the latter make light of, acquiesce in, suggest, or condone the practice." Examples included "The Triple Trapeze: Three Negroes Hung to a Limb of a Tree" and "Two Minutes to Pray Before a Rope Dislocated Their Vertebrae."[21] Several years before Grady became managing editor and part owner of the *Constitution*, the Chancellor of the University of Georgia wrote to chastise him for his "apparent want of reverence, and the marked levity of your style, even when writing about the most serious matters." He pointed to an article about the legal hanging of three Black men in South Carolina headlined "The Swing in Carolina" and another hanging for a notorious murder headlined "Terrible Twist."[22] He neglected to mention a headline from a month earlier: "Nicked in the Neck."[23] If past is prologue, Grady helped lay the path for one of the most shameful episodes in the *Constitution*'s history.

Ten years after Grady's unexpected death in 1889, the *Atlanta Constitution* breathlessly covered a lynch mob chasing Sam Hose, a Black man who killed his white employer in self-defense. The *Constitution*'s day-by-day reports stirred passions through exaggerated and invented descriptions of the crime, including the claim that Hose had raped the employer's wife. The newspaper offered a five-hundred-dollar reward for the capture of Hose and published, as Philip Dray wrote, "eleven days of hysterical, incendiary newspaper articles."[24] The result was an especially brutal lynch murder, mutilation, and burning alive of Hose in front of a celebratory crowd of four thousand whites, many having arrived by train from Atlanta. Some left carrying bones and other remains as souvenirs.

The day after the lynching, W.E.B. Du Bois was walking to the offices of the *Atlanta Constitution* to introduce himself to editor Joel Chandler Harris, Grady's old friend, and to present his social scientific work in hopes of beginning an anti-lynching movement. Along the way, he learned of the barbarity of Hose's murder and was told his charred knuckles were for sale in a grocery store window several blocks away. Shaken to the core, Du Bois turned around, giving up on his mission. He later observed, "[O]ne could not be a calm, cool, and detached scientist while Negroes were lynched, murdered and starved." This moment marked a break in the trajectory of Du Bois' life. He began to turn away from academia and toward activism, helping to found the Niagara Movement in 1905 and the NAACP in 1909.[25]

Wells-Barnett was known and despised by whites in the deep South, and it was deemed too dangerous for her to make the trip to Atlanta to investigate the Hose lynching. She hired a private white investigator to go in her stead, and he received a thorough education in white supremacy during his visit, ultimately condemning the *Atlanta Constitution* for its role in the affair. "I made my way home," he wrote in his report on the lynching, "thoroughly convinced that a Negro's life is a very cheap thing in Georgia."[26] In June of that same year, Wells-Barnett published "Lynch Law in Georgia," a report documenting the lynchings of twelve Black men in Georgia during six weeks in March and April. With acid irony, she subtitled the report to reveal that much of her source material was gathered from the white press itself: "A Six-weeks' Record in the Center of Southern Civilization, as Faithfully Chronicled by the 'Atlanta Journal' and the 'Atlanta Constitution.'"[27]

Ida B. Wells-Barnett spent her life advocating for African-American civil rights and equality—which also meant fighting against the racial violence of white supremacy, and her work contributed to the efforts of latter-day freedom struggle activists. The authors in this volume have recovered her pioneering use of the communication network of her day to do this work. At various points and for various purposes, she documented African-American life and argued for its dignity and worth in the pages of the Black press and pamphlets; through the techniques of public relations and public campaigns; and with her strong voice. This volume furthers the project of expanding the historiography on Wells-Barnett—and the Black press, Black print culture, and the Black freedom struggle. It takes inspiration from Wells-Barnett's insistence that the African-American experience is central to the story of America.

As we continue to expand our historical knowledge about African-American print culture, we also must document more fully the role the white press played in building, nurturing, and protecting the white supremacist systems of racial domination and violence that Black journalists and activists so often dedicated themselves to resisting. In this afterword I've briefly documented the role the *Atlanta Constitution*'s editor and New South prophet Henry W. Grady played in building a white supremacist political machine in Georgia that enriched the so-called best men of the state through the brutal and criminal exploitation of Black convict labor. What's more, as Kendi has demonstrated persuasively, Grady's New South doctrine, trumpeted in the pages of the *Constitution* during his lifetime and for decades thereafter, introduced the "racist idea" of separate but equal as the justification for segregation (and a cover for profound racial injustice and violence) that became enshrined in *Plessy v. Ferguson*.[28] Finally, the *Constitution* did little to resist and much to provoke the racial terror of lynching for decades.

Journalism historiography is almost completely silent on the constitutive role the white press played in creating, supporting, and enforcing white supremacist public policies and practices in the South from post-Reconstruction through World War II. Grady and the *Constitution* were hardly aberrations. In 1898 in North Carolina, for example, *Raleigh News & Observer* editor Josephus Daniels used his newspaper to spread racist propaganda falsely claiming a scourge of Black men raping white women. He was helping to orchestrate the Democratic Party's election-year campaign strategy to drive a wedge through the bi-racial Fusion Party then in power in state government. It was a devious plan—and it was wildly successful. The propaganda campaign whipped up white supremacist furor across the state, and, with the additional tool of racial violence, the Democrats wrested power of state government from the Fusionists. With that feat accomplished, an organized white "mob" overthrew the bi-racial municipal government of Wilmington, massacred Black citizens, and burned the Black press whose editor had deigned to challenge their racist propaganda.[29]

In *Southern Horrors*, Wells-Barnett demonstrated how the white press in Memphis organized "the leading citizens" to destroy her press and threaten her with lynching. Her offense? She published an editorial in the *Free Speech* that documented the brutal lynching of three of her friends and exposed the rape justification as an "old thread-bare lie." She blew the cover of what Kendi has called "the racist cover-up," and she was exiled from Memphis and the South forever.[30] Her many reports on lynching document, again and again, how the white press aided and abetted lynching by spreading the lie of rape.[31]

To understand the role of the Black press and print culture in resisting white supremacy, we must also understand the role of the white press in constituting it. We have a leader to follow in this important work, and her name is Ida B. Wells-Barnett.

NOTES

1. Patricia A. Schechter, *Ida B. Wells-Barnett & American Reform, 1880–1930* (Chapel Hill: University of North Carolina Press, 2001), 94–96; Linda O. McMurry, *To Keep the Waters Troubled: The Life of Ida B. Wells* (New York: Oxford University Press, 1998), 199–205; Gail Bederman, "'Civilization,' the Decline of Middle-Class Manliness, and Ida B. Wells's Antilynching Campaign (1892–1894)," in *"We Specialize in the Wholly Impossible": A Reader in Black Women's History*, ed. Darlene Clark Hine, Wilma King, and Linda Reed (Brooklyn: Carlson Publishing, 1995), 407–13.

2. Ida B. Wells, ed. *The Reason Why the Colored American Is Not in the World's Columbian Exposition* (Chicago, 1893), http://digital.library.upenn.edu/women/wells/exposition/exposition.html.

3. Equal Justice Initiative, *Lynching in America: Confronting the Legacy of Racial Terror,* third edition, https://lynchinginamerica.eji.org/report/.

4. Ibid.

5. "Lynching in America: Confronting the Legacy of Racial Terror," Equal Justice Initiative, https://eji.org/reports/lynching-in-america.

6. James C. Cobb, *Industrialization and Southern Society 1877–1984* (Lexington: University Press of Kentucky, 1984), 12–13.

7. Matthew J. Mancini, *One Dies, Get Another: Convict Leasing in the American South, 1866-1928* (Columbia: University of South Carolina Press, 1996), 90; Alex Lichtenstein, *Twice the Work of Free Labor: The Political Economy of Convict Labor in the New South* (Verso: 1996), 129; Talitha L. LeFlouria, *Chained in Silence: Black Women and Convict Labor in the New South* (Chapel Hill: University of North Carolina Press, 2015), 74–77.

8. Derrell Roberts, "Joseph E. Brown and the Convict Lease System," *Georgia Historical Society* 44.4 (1960): 403; Harold E. Davis, *Henry Grady's New South: Atlanta, a Brave and Beautiful City* (Tuscaloosa: University of Alabama Press, 1990), 146–47.

9. Harold E. Davis, "Henry W. Grady, Master of the Atlanta Ring—1880–1886," *Georgia Historical Quarterly* 69.1 (1985).

10. Roberts, "Joseph E. Brown"; Allison Dorsey, *To Build Our Lives Together: Community Formation in Black Atlanta, 1875-1906* (Athens: University of Georgia Press, 2004), 148.

11. Jay Winston Driskell, Jr., *Schooling Jim Crow: The Fight for Atlanta's Booker T. Washington High School and the Roots of Black Protest Politics* (Charlottesville: University of Virginia Press, 2014), 49.

12. David M. Oshinsky, *"Worse Than Slavery": Parchman Farm and the Ordeal of Jim Crow Justice* (New York: Free Press, 1996), 64.

13. "We Are Told," *Atlanta Constitution,* June 4, 1880, 4.

14. Henry W. Grady, "The New South," in Raymond B. Nixon, *Henry W. Grady: Spokesman of the New South* (New York: Russell & Russell, 1943), 340–450.

15. C. Vann Woodward, *The Future of the Past* (New York: Oxford University Press, 1989), 281.

16. Ida B. Wells-Barnett, *Southern Horrors: Lynch Law in All Its Phases,* 1892, https://www.gutenberg.org/files/14975/14975-h/14975-h.htm#THE_OFFENSE.

17. Nixon, *Henry W. Grady,* 332.

18. Ida B. Wells, *The Light of Truth: Writings of an Anti-Lynching Crusader* (New York: Penguin, 2014). The exchange consisted of three articles, including Cable's initial statement about the injustice of Southern segregation of the races, Grady's reply, and Cable's final

response: George W. Cable, "The Freedman's Case in Equity," *Century* 29 (January 1885): 409–18; Henry W. Grady, "In Plain Black and White: A Reply to Mr. Cable," *Century* 29 (April 1885): 909–17; George W. Cable, "The Silent South," *Century* 30 (September 1885): 674–91.

19. Paul Gaston, *The New South Creed: A Study in Southern Mythmaking* (Montgomery, Ala.: NewSouth Books, 2002, originally published 1970), 139–52; Fred Hobson, *Tell About the South: The Southern Rage to Explain* (Baton Rouge: Louisiana State University Press, 1983), 115–17.

20. Ibram X. Kendi, *Stamped from the Beginning: The Definitive History of Racist Ideas in America* (New York: Nation Books, 2017), 9, 265.

21. Davis, *Henry Grady's New South*, 151.

22. William Rutherford, Chancellor, University of Georgia, to Henry W. Grady, May 9, 1877, Henry Woodfin Grady Papers, Rose Library, Emory University.

23. "Nicked in the Neck," *Atlanta Constitution*, April 28, 1877, 1.

24. Philip Dray, *At the Hands of Persons Unknown: The Lynching of Black America* (New York: Random House, 2007), 3–16.

25. David Levering Lewis, *W.E.B. Du Bois: A Biography* (New York: Henry Holt and Company, 2009).

26. Dray, *At the Hands of Persons Unknown*, 3–16; "Circle of Vengeance Slowly Closing on Fleeing Sam Hose," *Atlanta Constitution*, April 18, 1899, 1; "Sam Hose Still Eagerly Pursued: There Is No Thought of Giving up the Chase," *Atlanta Constitution*, April 19, 1899, 3; "Sam Holt, Murderer and Assailant, Burned at the Stake at Newnan," *Atlanta Constitution*, April 24, 1899, 1.

27. Ida B. Wells-Barnett, *Lynch Law in Georgia*, June 20, 1899, http://memory.loc.gov/cgi-bin/query/r?ammem/murray:@field(DOCID+@lit(lcrbmrpt1612div1)).

28. Kendi, *Stamped from the Beginning*, 278–79.

29. Timothy B. Tyson, *The Ghosts of 1898*, special insert, *Raleigh News & Observer*, November 17, 2006.

30. Ibram X. Kendi, "Trump Sounds Ignorant of History. But Racist Ideas Often Masquerade as Ignorance," *Washington Post*, November 13, 2017, https://www.washingtonpost.com/news/posteverything/wp/2017/11/13/trump-sounds-ignorant-of-history-but-racist-ideas-often-masquerade-as-ignorance/?utm_term=.b59eca0057e0.

31. McMurry, *To Keep the Waters Troubled*, 160.

BIBLIOGRAPHY

Bederman, Gail. "'Civilization,' the Decline of Middle-Class Manliness, and Ida B. Wells's Antilynching Campaign (1892–1894)," In Darlene Clark Hine, Wilma King, and Linda Reed, eds., *"We Specialize in the Wholly Impossible": A Reader in Black Women's History*, 407–13. Brooklyn: Carlson Publishing, 1995.

Cobb, James C. *Industrialization and Southern Society 1877–1984*. Lexington: University Press of Kentucky, 1984.

Davis, Harold E. "Henry W. Grady, Master of the Atlanta Ring—1880–1886," *Georgia Historical Quarterly* 69.1 (1985).

———. *Henry Grady's New South: Atlanta, a Brave and Beautiful City*. Tuscaloosa: University of Alabama Press, 1990.

Dorsey, Allison. *To Build Our Lives Together: Community Formation in Black Atlanta, 1875–1906*. Athens: University of Georgia Press, 2004.

Dray, Philip. *At the Hands of Persons Unknown: The Lynching of Black America*. New York: Random House, 2007.

Driskell, Jr., Jay Winston. *Schooling Jim Crow: The Fight for Atlanta's Booker T. Washington High School and the Roots of Black Protest Politics*. Charlottesville: University of Virginia Press, 2014.

Gaston, Paul. *The New South Creed: A Study in Southern Mythmaking*. Montgomery, AL: NewSouth Books, 2002, 1970.

Hobson, Fred. *Tell about the South: The Southern Rage to Explain*. Baton Rouge: Louisiana State University Press, 1983.

Kendi, Ibram X. *Stamped from the Beginning: The Definitive History of Racist Ideas in America*. New York: Nation Books, 2017.

LeFlouria, Talitha L. *Chained in Silence: Black Women and Convict Labor in the New South*. Chapel Hill: University of North Carolina Press, 2015.

Lewis, David Levering. *W.E.B. Du Bois: A Biography*. New York: Henry Holt and Company, 2009.

Lichtenstein, Alex. *Twice the Work of Free Labor: The Political Economy of Convict Labor in the New South*. Verso: 1996.

McMurry, Linda O. *To Keep the Waters Troubled: The Life of Ida B. Wells*. New York: Oxford University Press, 1998.

Mancini, Matthew J. *One Dies, Get Another: Convict Leasing in the American South, 1866–1928*. Columbia: University of South Carolina Press, 1996.

Oshinsky, David M. *"Worse Than Slavery": Parchman Farm and the Ordeal of Jim Crow Justice*. New York: Free Press, 1996.

Roberts, Derrell. "Joseph E. Brown and the Convict Lease System," *Georgia Historical Society* 44.4 (1960): 403.

Schechter, Patricia A. *Ida B. Wells-Barnett and American Reform, 1880–1930*. Chapel Hill: University of North Carolina Press, 2001.

Wells, Ida B. *The Light of Truth: Writings of an Anti-Lynching Crusader*. New York: Penguin, 2014.

Woodward, C. Vann. *The Future of the Past*. New York: Oxford University Press, 1989.

Appendix: Writing against the Bias

Integrating the Curriculum with Ida B. Wells-Barnett's Texts and Testament

Norma Fay Green

In the 1980s, I began teaching the History of Journalism course at Columbia College Chicago, an arts and media school just four miles from where Ida B. Wells lived. By then, her nearly century-old newspaper and pamphlet work was all but forgotten. Even some of my first students, who lived in the Ida B. Wells Homes, a Chicago Housing Authority Project, said they knew nothing of her journalism. I tried to remedy that by referring to her as a consummate example of courageous investigative reporting. I was on a crusade for the crusading journalist.

Journalism history textbooks of the time gave her a paragraph at most in several-hundred-page tomes. I was heartened to learn that the tide seemed to be turning by the 1990s with the announcement of a new textbook approach to journalism history that was more inclusive and diverse, reflecting my student body and including the voices of more women and People of Color. Alas, when the first edition debuted, I was disappointed to find no mention of Ida. Fortunately, that was soon remedied in subsequent editions.

In the late twentieth and early twenty-first century, I was heartened by the burgeoning scholarship across various disciplines that examined Wells' writing. And, of course, there was the living legacy encouraged through the personal efforts of her descendants, notably her daughter Alfreda Duster who edited her mother's autobiography, as well as the work of grandson sociologist Troy Duster and great granddaughter writer Michelle Duster. I felt confident that the writing of Ida B. Wells would not be unknown but perhaps still underappreciated and unread in college courses.

The main purpose of my presentation is to provoke you, the teachers and scholars, to continue to consider Wells' contribution and find new creative ways to expose your students to her remarkable expressions of courage under fire. And to inspire them to consider the question, "What Would Ida Do Today?"[1]

HISTORY OF JOURNALISM /
INTRODUCTION TO JOURNALISM COURSES

A History of Journalism or even Introduction to Journalism course is a natural launching pad to discuss the journalistic contributions of Ida B. Wells, especially her three most famous writings: *Southern Horrors: Lynch Law in All Its Phases*; *A Red Record*; and *Mob Rule in New Orleans*. Often her work has been compartmentalized in journalism history textbooks under the general category of ethnic, immigrant, and reform press, and that is the topic area where it is typically covered in a survey course. However, I would argue it could be introduced at other junctures of those survey courses as well—to demonstrate the power of the press.

Southern Horrors: Lynch Law in All Its Phases was part of a larger pamphlet titled *The Reason Why the Colored American Is Not in the World's Columbian Exposition* distributed at the 1893 World's Fair held in Chicago.[2] Organizers of the fair, which was designed to showcase the progress and innovation of the United States, deliberately and systematically kept African Americans from participating in the preparation and exhibitions. Their exclusion from the so-called and ironically dubbed "White City" (so-labeled because of its complex of white neo-classical buildings) sparked a protest and the publication of the illustrated pamphlet about racial injustices containing the writings of Ida B. Wells, along with those of Frederic Douglass, Irving Garland Penn, and Ferdinand L. Barnett. (Mr. Barnett was a Chicago lawyer, assistant state's attorney, and editor of the *Chicago Conservator*, Chicago's first Black newspaper founded in 1878. He also was the president of the Ida B. Wells Club when he and Ida met. They married in 1895.) The pamphlet, distributed to some twenty-thousand fairgoers, embarrassed the exposition staff, who hastily organized a "Colored American Day," which Wells, in turn, boycotted.

Her pamphlet chapter, titled "Lynch Law," anticipates the curiosity and possible skepticism of a large general audience. She starts with a historical overview dating from the eighteenth century and explains how and where the term "lynch law" came to be known as the summary infliction of punishment by private and unauthorized citizens. She then proceeds to chronicle and quantify—in tabular form—the number of people tortured and killed by lynching based on categories of criminal charges and by state. She also quotes excerpts about specific lynching incidents from the leading mainstream newspapers of the day in both the South and the North including the *Memphis Commercial, Memphis Public Ledger, Chicago Tribune*, and *Chicago Inter-Ocean*. She was savvy enough to know that references to mainstream newspapers might carry more weight and credibility with potential readers, than just her recounting of the evidence. Modern-day students, with their shortened attention spans, typically find the brief piece accessible with its straightforward language and a powerful example of persuasive writing.

Prior to having students actually read her pieces, it is helpful to contextualize her writing, and I often have done that by showing excerpts from documentaries. These include: *The Rise & Fall of Jim Crow*, a documentary about the era she grew up in especially as it relates to the pent-up hunger for literacy among former slaves and their children in the heady time just after emancipation; *Soldiers without Swords*, an excellent documentary about the Black press; and the PBS biographical documentary "A Passion for Justice" from *The American Experience* PBS series.[3] You also might want to quiz students, to encourage active viewing, by asking them:

- How and why did Wells get started in journalism and what kept her involved?
- What barriers did she face in her pursuit of journalism?
- What do you see as her main frustration in journalism?
- What would you say is Wells' greatest accomplishment?

HISTORY OF JOURNALISM / INVESTIGATIVE REPORTING COURSES

A longer piece, *The Red Record: Tabulated Statistics and Alleged Causes of Lynchings in the United States, 1892–1894,* is a good example of investigative journalism techniques.[4] Speaking truth to power, Wells not only laid out the factual information with statistical analysis—what today we would call Big Data aggregation, but she also included a plan of civic action:

- To disseminate the facts of lynchings to the public via the media and all religious and civic organizations;
- To bring economic pressure by boycott or blocking investment in states where segregation, codified in law, thwarts economic advancement of Afro-Americans and fosters lynching;
- To press Congress for resolutions and for legislation guaranteeing all Americans their full rights of citizenship.

In the book, *Civic Passions: Seven Who Launched Progressive America (And What They Teach Us),* author Cecelia Tichi, who is an English professor at Vanderbilt University, notes that Wells was armed for a battle: "Her weapons of choice were the pen and the printing press." Tichi said, "[s]weet, sentimental terms had their place, but she must marshal facts and couch them in biting irony and scathing indictment. The social critic inside her—the spitfire—claimed primacy."[5] In Wells' pamphlet from 1900, titled *Mob Rule in New Orleans: Robert Charles and His Fight to the Death,* she once again quotes reports of the leading newspapers, in this case, the *New Orleans Times-Democrat* and *New Orleans Picayune.*[6] As scholars who have analyzed her writing style indicate, her use of mainstream sources helps to legitimize and authenticate her own reporting. In the introduction to *Mob Rule,* she declares:

> The publisher hereof does not attempt to moralize over the deplorable condition of affairs shown in this publication, but simply presents the facts in a plain, unvarnished, connected way, so that he who runs may read. We do not believe that the American people who have encouraged such scenes by their indifference will read unmoved these

accounts of brutality, injustice and oppression. We do not believe that the moral conscience of the nation—that which is the highest and best among us—will always remain silent in face of such outrages, for God is not dead, and His Spirit is not entirely driven from men's hearts.[7]

Wow! There is much for students to chew on just in that one small deceptively plainspoken paragraph. Yet, it is not enough to do her work justice.

MEDIA ETHICS COURSE

Lynch Law might be a good starting point to discuss media ethics and how writers choose to address social issues. In *Lynch Law*, Wells condemned the hypocrisy and systematic racism of the US media organizations, stating: "They belong to the race which holds Negro life cheap, which owns the telegraph wires, newspapers, and all other communication with the outside world."[8] Scholar Melba Joyce Boyd noted that Wells observed the media's complicity with the lynchers.[9] Angela Sims, an ethics and Black church studies professor at St. Paul School of Theology in Kansas City, Missouri, examined Wells' interrogation of American terror in her book titled, *Ethical Complications of Lynching*. Sims posits that Wells' approach might be a "viable option to address systemic forms of oppression."[10] Specifically, Sims observed:

> Wells presented both an analysis of atrocities of lynch law and a guide to understand the pervasiveness of mob rule and its associated propaganda and tactics. Her arguments suggest that failure to think critically and to raise pertinent concerns may result in diminished liberties that quickly become accepted procedure. . . . It is important to remember that a response to an encounter with injustice can become a catalyst to promote justice.[11]

OPINION AND EDITORIAL WRITING COURSE

Regrettably no extant copies of the *Memphis Free Speech and Headlight*, the newspaper Wells owned and operated, have been unearthed. Her fiery editorials fanned the flames of Black empowerment as she advocated boycotts and Oklahoma homesteading among Black Memphis residents. Those same editorials angered white citizens and led to the destruction of the newspaper office, continued death threats against her, and her eventual exile from the South for several decades.

IDA B. WELLS / WOMEN AND THE MEDIA COURSES

After years of assigning bite-size pieces of Wells' writing within the context of a survey course, I decided to be bold. (I got that from studying Ida.) I branched out and decided to propose a whole buffet of her writings—both public and private. I created a free-standing one-credit, two-week elective during one of our college intersessions between fall and spring semesters.

Besides an intense reading and rhetorical analysis of her most famous writings, I also assigned articles she wrote for the *Chicago Inter-Ocean* while on a speaking tour in England, Scotland, and Wales in 1894, as well as articles she wrote from 1885 to 1888 for *The Living Way, New York Freeman,* and *Fisk Herald.* The news stories in the Chicago newspaper, particularly, were a way to discuss her international impact and the power of written words and speech to influence and change.

In addition, I asked students to read aloud in class excerpts from the Memphis Diary of 1885–1887 and the brief entries from her Chicago Diary of 1930.[12] The 2010 compilation, titled *Ida from Abroad,* published by Ida B. Wells' great granddaughter Michelle Duster also contains fascinating contextual correspondence between Ida and Frederick Douglass in 1894 as well as a heartfelt and compelling first-person account of Ida's impact on her descendent, Michelle, which is titled: "Ida and I: Blazing My Own Trail, Gaining Global Perspective, from Intimidation to Inspiration, Feeling Free." Michelle Duster is a writer, speaker, project manager, and artist who, following in the footsteps of her great-grandmother, went to college. Duster earned a bachelor's degree in psychology from Dartmouth and a master's degree in communication from the New School of Social Research in New York. I was privileged to have her come and speak to my class on one frigid January day after a blizzard when we had to nix a planned walking tour of the nearby Bronzeville neighborhood and a visit to one of the houses where she and her family lived that is now a National Historic Landmark.

ENTREPRENEURSHIP COURSE

We often concentrate on the positive points of Ida's life but what about incorporating some of the difficult lessons she learned as part of say, a new all-college course, on risk-taking. Entrepreneurship is a new term in journalism courses this century, and Wells definitely was an entrepreneur, despite racism and sexism. I've been reading *Being Wrong: Adventures in the Margin of Error,* by journalist Kathryn Schultz title, and thinking about some of the failures in Ida's life.[13] How did she cope with setbacks, and would her strategies be a good lessons for today's students often unaccustomed to failure?

- She was orphaned as a teenager and left college to support her younger siblings with a teaching job, one of the few respectable positions outside the home for women.
- She lost her teaching job when she wrote about the shoddy working conditions.
- She initially won a discrimination lawsuit against the Chesapeake, Ohio & Southwestern Railroad, lost in the state court of appeals, yet won in the court of public opinion when she wrote about her experience and launched her journalism career.

- She became owner of the Memphis *Free Press & Headlight* newspaper but was unable to continue after death threats and the destruction of her printing offices. She was in exile from the South for over thirty years.
- She wrote for *New York Age* and eventually came to Chicago.
- She operated *The Chicago Conservator* newspaper, founded by her husband.
- She was one of two women cofounders of the NAACP, yet her anti-lynching campaign was subsumed, and scholars have noted her original research was appropriated.
- She was criticized professionally and personally for her decisions including marriage and children.
- She even had unsuccessful run for the Illinois state senate office.

What could we and our students learn from her setbacks and compromises? She seemed often to be redeemed by writing—either privately in her diary or publically in newspapers.

She did not dwell on tragedies and disappointments, but they were part of her experience that made her who she was.

Near the end of her life, she started her autobiography, *Crusade for Justice*, eventually completed by her daughter, Alfreda. In the book, Ida B. Wells-Barnett said she wrote it "for the young people who have so little of our race's history recorded that I am for the first time in my life writing about myself."[14] Today, in order to reach the young people, would she have a website and be blogging and tweeting about human rights and social justice issues? It would be an interesting speculative assignment for your students to imagine.

Since I started teaching my journalism history course in the 1980s, Ida B. Wells has been resurrected—up from the footnote[15]—and into the spotlight. Dozens of journal articles and books have been written about various aspects of her life. There is an effort afoot to have a statue of her erected in Chicago on the site of the former housing project named after her. But I challenge you to continue to devise creative ways to incorporate her writings into various journalism courses, assignments, and special projects so that we, as professors and professionals, can engage young people to keep her work in our collective consciousness.

NOTES

1. A version of this appendix was presented as an invited panel presentation for a special Ida Initiative session, "Ida B. and Beyond: The Life, Work, and Legacy of Ida B. Wells-Barnett," hosted by the University of Tennessee-Knoxville School of Journalism & Electronic Media in conjunction with the twenty-first Symposium on Nineteenth Century Press, The Civil War, and Free Expression sponsored by the West Chair of Excellence, the University of Tennessee at Chattanooga communication and history departments, the Walter and Leona Schmitt Family Foundation Research Fund and the Hazel Dicken-Garcia Fund for the Symposium.

2. Ida B. Wells, *Southern Horrors and Other Writings: The Anti-Lynching Campaign of Ida B. Wells, 1892–1900,* Edited by Jacqueline Jones Royster (New York: MacMillan, 2016).

3. Richard Wormser, *The Rise and Fall of Jim Crow*, Thirteen, 2002, https://www. thirteen.org/wnet/jimcrow/index.html; Stanley Nelson, Jr., *Soldiers without Swords*, California Newsreels, 1999, www.pbs.org/blackpress/; William Greaves, "Ida B. Wells: A Passion for Justice," *California Newsreels*, 1989, http://newsreel.org/video/ida-b-wells.

4. Wells, *Southern Horrors and Other Writings*.

5. Cecelia Tichi, *Civic Passions: Seven Who Launched Progressive America (And What They Teach Us)* (Chapel Hill: University of North Carolina Press, 2009), 261.

6. Ida B. Wells, *Mob Rule in New Orleans* (Chicago: Self, 1900).

7. Ibid., 5.

8. Wells, *Southern Horrors and Other Writings*.

9. Quoted in Angela D. Sims, *Ethical Complications of Lynching: Ida B. Wells's Interrogation of American Terror* (New York: Palgrave Macmillan, 2010), 113.

10. Ibid., 133.

11. Ibid., 111.

12. Miriam DeCosta-Willis, ed., *The Memphis Diary of Ida B. Wells* (Boston: Beacon Press, 1995).

13. Kathryn Schultz, *Being Wrong: Adventures in the Margin of Error* (New York: Harper Collins, 2011).

14. As quoted in Ida B. Wells, *Crusade for Justice: The Autobiography of Ida B. Wells*, edited by Alfreda M. Duster (Chicago: University of Chicago Press, 1970), 4.

15. Marion Marzolf, *Up from the Footnote: A History of Women Journalists* (New York: Hasting House, 1977).

BIBLIOGRAPHY

Athey, Stephanie. *Race in Feminism: Critiques of Bodily Self-Determination in Ida B. Wells-Barnett and Anna Julia Cooper*. Boston: William Monroe Trotter Institute, University of Massachusetts at Boston, 1996.

Bay, Mia. *To Tell the Truth Freely: The Life of Ida B. Wells*. New York: Hill and Wang, 2010.

Boyd, Melba J. "Canon Configuration for Ida B. Wells-Barnett." *Black Scholar* 24.1 (1994): 8–13.

Braxton, Joanne M. "Crusader for Justice: Ida B. Wells." In *Black Women Writing Autobiography: A Tradition Within a Tradition*, by Joanne M. Braxton, 102–38. Philadelphia: Temple University Press, 1989.

Broussard, Jinx Coleman. *Giving a Voice to the Voiceless: Four Pioneering Black Women Journalists*. New York: Routledge, 2004.

Campbell, Karlyn Kohrs. "Style and Content in the Rhetoric of Early Afro-American Feminists," *Quarterly Journal of Speech* 72.3 (1986): 434–45.

Carby, Hazel V. "On the Threshold of the Woman's Era': Lynching, Empire, and Sexuality in Black Feminist Theory." *Critical Inquiry* 12.3 (1985): 262–77.

Carnes, Mark, ed. *Invisible Giants: Fifty Americans Who Shaped the Nation but Missed the History Books*. New York: Oxford University Press, 2002.

Foreman, P. Gabrielle. "Review of The Memphis Diary of Ida B. Wells by Ida B. Wells-Barnett." *African American Review* 31.2 (1997): 363–65.

Fradin, Dennis. *Ida B. Wells: Mother of the Civil Rights Movement*. New York: Clarion Books, 2000.

Giddings, Paula. *A Sword among Lions: Ida B. Wells and the Campaign against Lynching*. New York: HarperCollins, 2009.

Hutton, Mary. *The Rhetoric of Ida B. Wells: The Genesis of the Anti-Lynching Movement*. Ann Arbor, MI: University Microfilm International, 1975.

Klots, Steve. *Ida Wells-Barnett: Civil Rights Leader*. Pennsylvania: Chelsea House Publishers, 1994.

Lisandrelli, Elaine. *Ida B. Wells-Barnett: Crusader against Lynching*. Springfield, NJ: Enslow, 1998.

Logan, Shirley W. "Rhetorical Strategies in Ida B. Wells' Southern Horrors: Lynch Law in All Its Phases," *Sage* 8.1 (1991).

Lunsford, Andrea A., ed. *Reclaiming Rhetorica: Women in Rhetorical Tradition*. Pittsburgh: University of Pittsburgh Press, 1995.

McMurry, Linda O. *To Keep the Waters Troubled: The Life of Ida B. Wells*. New York: Oxford University Press, 1998.

McKissack, Pat and Frederick. *Ida B. Wells-Barnett: A Voice Against Violence*. New York: Enslow Publishers, Inc., 1991.

Miller, Ericka. "The Other Reconstruction: Where Violence and Womanhood Meet in the Writings of Ida B. Wells-Barnett," Angelina Weld Grimke and Nella Larsen. Dissertation Abstracts International: 1995.

Schechter, Patricia A. *Ida B. Wells-Barnett and American Reform, 1880–1930*. Chapel Hill: University of North Carolina Press, 2001.

Schiff, Karenna G. *Lighting the Way: Nine Women Who Changed Modern America*. New York: Hyperion, 2005

Shelf-Medearis, Angela. *Princess of the Press: The Story of Ida B. Wells-Barnett*. New York: Lodestar Books, 1997.

Sims, Angela D. *Ethical Complications of Lynching: Ida B. Wells's Interrogation of American Terror*. New York: Palgrave Macmillan, 2010.

Sterling, Dorothy. *Black Foremothers: Three Lives*. Old Westbury, NY: Feminist Press, 1979.

Thompson, Mildred. *Ida B. Wells-Barnett: An Exploratory Study of an American Black Woman, 1892–1930*. Brooklyn: Carlson Publishing Inc., 1990, based on 1979 thesis.

Tichi, Cecelia. *Civic Passions: Seven Who Launched Progressive American (And What They Teach Us)*. Chapel Hill: University of North Carolina Press, 2009.

Townes, Emilie Maureen. "Ida B. Wells-Barnett: Her Social and Moral Perspectives." In *Womanist Justice, Womanist Hope*, Emilie Maureen Townes, 107–30. Atlanta, GA: Scholars Press, 1998.

Welch, C. *Ida B. Wells-Barnett: Powerhouse with a Pen*. Minneapolis, MN: Carolrhoda Books, 1999.

Wilkinson, Brenda. *African American Women Writers (Black Stars)*. Hoboken, NJ: John Wiley & Sons, Inc., 2000.

Index

193

About the Contributors

ABOUT THE EDITORS

Lori Amber Roessner is associate professor at the University of Tennessee's School of Journalism and Electronic Media. In fall 2012, Roessner launched the Ida Initiative, a public history initiative designed to promote the study of the life, work, and legacy of Ida B. Wells-Barnett through experiential learning projects at the undergraduate level and through research initiatives in the academy. The public history initiative contributed to the organization of Ida B. & Beyond, a one-day conference held at the University of Tennessee on March 26, 2015, featuring research on the life, work, and legacy of Ida B. Wells-Barnett and other like-minded social justice crusaders; many of the chapters in this volume were presented in earlier form at that conference. Roessner's cultural histories on the role of American media in the production of mass icons have appeared in *Journalism & Mass Communication Quarterly*, *Journalism History*, and *American Journalism*, among others, and contributed to her earning the distinction of *American Journalism*'s Inaugural Rising Scholar in 2014. She also is the author of *Inventing Baseball Heroes: Ty Cobb, Christy Mathewson, and the Sporting Press in America* (2014) and a forthcoming history on presidential politicians and the press in the 1970s.

Jodi L. Rightler-McDaniels is Senior General Studies Department chair and associate professor of communication at South College in Knoxville, Tennessee. She holds a PhD from the University of Tennessee's College of Communication and Information and a graduate certificate in Cultural Studies of Educational Foundations. Her critical/cultural research on race relations and gender "norms" in American media have appeared in *Mass Communication and Society*, *Social Semiotics*, *Journal of Magazine & New Media Research*, and *Sport in Society*. As a scholar of race, gender, and the unique intersection of the two, Rightler-McDaniels has worked on numerous Ida B. Wells-Barnett studies alongside Roessner.

ABOUT THE CONTRIBUTORS

Jinx Coleman Broussard is full professor and the Bart R. Swanson Endowed Memorial Professor in the Manship School of Mass Communication at Louisiana State University. Broussard is the author of the national award-winning book titled *African-American Foreign Correspondents: A History* as well as *Giving a Voice to the Voiceless: Four Pioneering Black Women Journalists*. Broussard is recognized as an expert on the history of the Black press. She also spent three decades as a public relations professional.

Chandra D. Snell Clark is associate professor of speech at Florida A&M University. She has performed her original one-woman dramatic monologue, "Through Voice and Pen: Ida B. Wells-Barnett and the First Amendment," at colleges, conferences, and festivals throughout the country.

Kris DuRocher is professor of history at Morehead State University. She is the author of *Ida B. Wells: Social Reformer and Activist* (2016) and *Raising Racists: The Socialization of White Children in the Jim Crow South* (2011). Her research interests include the intersections of gender, race, violence, and culture.

Kathy Roberts Forde is associate professor in the Department of Journalism at the University of Massachusetts-Amherst. Her book, *Literary Journalism on Trial: Masson v. New Yorker and the First Amendment* (2008), received the Frank Luther Mott-KTA book award and the AEJMC History Division book award. She is writing a publication and reading history of James Baldwin's *The Fire Next Time*, a book project that examines the role of black cultural expression in shaping US social thought and public policy.

Norma Fay Green, professor emerita at Columbia College Chicago, began teaching journalism history courses in the 1980s at the urban campus just four miles from where Ida B. Wells lived and died. By then, Wells' nearly century-old newspaper and pamphlet work was all but forgotten. While leading journalism history textbooks of the time gave her a paragraph, if that, Green was determined to resurrect her and inspire students by her courageous investigative reporting despite racial, gender, age, and economic obstacles. What started out as a one-session discussion of Wells eventually morphed into a free-standing elective course where students from all over the college read, analyzed, and learned from Wells' writings. Green holds a PhD in mass media and a BA in journalism from Michigan State University, as well as an MSJ from Northwestern University. She spent twenty-five years in newspaper, magazine, and book publishing before committing to a full-time academic career. The Wells course is among eleven creations of twenty-three courses she taught at Columbia. Green has been published in ten scholarly books and four academic journals and received AEJMC (Multicultural Curriculum first-place), Lilly Endowment, Ethics & Excellence in Journalism Foundation, Poynter Institute, Ford

Foundation, National Endowment for Humanities, National Federation of Press Women, and Women in Communications awards, as well as Fulbright Scholar and Fulbright-Hays grants.

Joe Hayden is a scholar of media history and politics and a professor of journalism at the University of Memphis. A former television news writer, reporter, and producer, he is the author of two books on presidential-press relations, a third on American journalists at the end of World War I (*Negotiating in the Press*), and a fourth on Southern editors during the Civil War (*Journalism in the Fallen Confederacy*). His interests include writing and foreign languages. He has taught writing for over twenty years and published two books on the subject—*The Little Grammar Book* (2012) and *The Little Style Book* (2015). In 2008, he received the Thomas W. Briggs Award for Excellence in Teaching. In 2015, he received a Faudree Professorship. He also has taught in Mainz, Germany, and in Cairo, Egypt.

Patricia A. Schechter has taught women's history at Portland State University since 1995. Her first book, *Ida B. Wells and American Reform, 1880–1930* (2001) won the Sierra Book Prize from the Western Association of Women Historians. Her second book, *Remembering the Power of Words: The Life of an Oregon Activist, Legislator, and Community Leader* (2011), co-authored with Avel Louise Gordly, was a library *Choice* noted title. She recently completed a podcast—*Fanny and Sam: A New York Love Story*—based on her grandparents' love letters from the 1920s, which is available online at PDXscholar. Her current research is a women's labor history of a French mining village in southern Spain during the interwar period.

R. J. Vogt is a reporter. He currently covers legal news at Law360.com based in Los Angeles, writing about Supreme Court decisions and other litigation. Previously, he worked as a reporter and editor at the *Myanmar Times* in Yangon, Myanmar. His work has been published in *Esquire* magazine, *VICE Sports*, *McSweeney's Quarterly* and *Atlas Obscura*, among others. He earned his undergraduate degree in literary journalism from the University of Tennessee, Knoxville, where he wrote his senior thesis on the advocacy journalism of Ida B. Wells-Barnett.

CPSIA information can be obtained
at www.ICGtesting.com
Printed in the USA
LVHW110854030123
736294LV00001B/12

9 781498 530347